A YOUTHFUL ABSURDITY

A YOUTHFUL ABSURDITY

by

Frederick E. Smith

Dales Large Print Books
Long Preston, North Yorkshire,
BD23 4ND, England.

British Library Cataloguing in Publication Data.

Smith, Frederick E.
A youthful absurdity.

A catalogue record of this book is
available from the British Library

ISBN 978-1-84262-857-7 pbk

First published in Great Britain 2010 by Emissary Publishing

Cover illustration by arrangement with Frederick E. Smith

Published in Large Print 2011 by arrangement with
Frederick E. Smith

Dales Large Print is an imprint of Library Magna Books Ltd.

Printed and bound in Great Britain by
T.J. (International) Ltd., Cornwall, PL28 8RW

SOURCES OF INFORMATION

My mother's autobiography
My father's notes
My own diaries

To my beloved Shelagh
Who brought light and love
into a chaotic and uncertain world.

FOREWORD

There comes a time when a man feels the need to pay tribute to those who have nurtured, guided, and supported him throughout his life. My debt to them is immeasurable and I can only hope this autobiography and the one that follows it does them justice.

However, events have a way of shaping a man's life too, and in chronicling them I have the hope, forlorn though it may be, that I might be better understood and even forgiven by those whose patience I must have tried so often.

Because this book covers my earlier years and because my age fated me to serve throughout the second world war, this means some of these events took place during that conflict.

But take heart those who are sated with war stories. It is not the intention of this book to dwell on the brutal aspects of war, which have been detailed often enough by those who saw more of it than I. Apart from isolated incidents that had their effect on me, it covers in the main the painful, the bizarre, and the often downright absurd events that plagued me from birth up to my twenty-sixth year. It is hoped they will provide more interesting reading than my few and doubtless ineffectual tilts against the common enemy.

ONE

I was standing in a deep trench with my feet covered in water. Ahead of me were rotting bags with sand running from them. In my hands was a strange instrument with a sharp knife attached to one end. Vague figures, out of focus, stood on either side of me. I was frightened, the fear that makes the breathing shallow and knots the stomach. I knew something terrible was about to happen but had no idea what it was.

Then a shrill whistle sounded and along with the others I climbed up to a wooden ledge. The fear became terror as the whistle sounded again and forced me to climb over the wet bags. I could see nothing ahead but a grey mist but some power greater than mine made me run into it.

I could hear staccato tapping sounds now, followed by cries and screams. I wanted to turn back and run away but my body would not obey my fear. I stumbled over something that hurt my leg, then fell into a pool of icy water.

I climbed out and ran on for a few more yards. Then something hit me in the chest. I fought for breath but the pain was too much and I fell to the ground. I tried to cry out as I lay there but my heart was dying. A moment later the mist turned black and closed all around me.

Such was the nightmare that, according to my parents, I must have suffered from the early days of my birth. My tiny hands would screw up, my body sweat profusely, and fear distort my face. There was no way I could communicate my dream because I had no name for a rifle or sandbags or firing steps and I had no conception of an enemy whose task was to kill me. I was simply a child born a year after the bloodiest war in human history and it was not until years later when I saw a photograph of a wartime trench and the British soldiers manning it that I was able to describe the substance of my dream.

What it means I shall not attempt to explain. All I can do is record it and say that for the first twenty years of my life it was a regular if unwelcome visitor.

According to my mother, life began for me, Frederick Escreet Smith, on the 4th April, 1919, during an early morning spring thunderstorm, an event that does not surprise me in the least. In view of all that was to happen later, my only surprise is that I was not born three days earlier.

I was also born with a caul over my face,

which carried the belief in those days that a child was born with a charmed life and would never drown. Indeed local fisherman would pay handsomely for the dried piece of membrane in the belief it would give them the same immunity. No parent in those days would dream of making such a sale, however, and many years later my mother was to present it to me with instructions to carry it always as it might well save my life. In view of the happenings to follow, who am I to dispute her claim?

My place of birth was No. 579, Anlaby Road, Kingston upon Hull, Yorkshire, a house that was to become a victim of another world war less than two decades later. In my childhood memories it was an enormous place with huge rooms, dormers that almost reached up to heaven and a back garden with a spacious lawn and huge flowerbeds. In truth it was a five bedroomed house with a somewhat pretentious hall and upper landing, and ornated by bow and dormer windows: the kind of dwelling that northern middle-class families felt obliged to occupy in those days.

Not that my mother, oddly christened Elma Constance Escreet, could any longer regard herself as middle-class. Prior to the war, she had received the kind of education reserved for respectable young ladies and had learned to play both the piano and the mandolin. She had played the latter instrument in a band and performed on the piano so well that I was told she once accompanied the violinist Albert Sandler for a time while his regular accompanist was unwell.

But then she committed the mortal sin in her mother's eyes of marrying Harry Sydney Smith, the son of a deceased railway worker and a gentle Chapel-going woman who, on a pittance of a wage, had somehow brought up three sons and two daughters before wearing herself out and dying in her early forties.

William Escreet, who had two daughters, my mother and Lena Beatrice, appears to have shared most people's liking of the young man and made a friend of him from the outset. My maternal grandmother, however, who bore the gentle name of Alice, never accepted him. In the whole of my life I never remember her saying one good word about him and, after the premature death of William, began to punish both him and my mother for their transgression. As Alice was to live until she was ninety-two and my parents were to hold together through thick and thin, there was a long, long time to go.

As Harry, or Sydney as he was generally known, was one of the gentlest and most lovable men I have ever known, one must assume this dislike was born of his background. Not only was he working class but he came from chapel folk and Alice was strictly High Church of England. Add to that the proletariat name that he inflicted on Alice's elder daughter, and some of her dislike might be explained.

Not that Alice's own cupboard was free of skeletons. Although she would have died rather than make the admission, it seemed that one of her aunts had been committed to a mental home after giving birth to a deformed child. So hush hush were such misfortunes in those days that even my mother only saw fit to tell it to me on my fiftieth birthday!

For that matter William, her husband, had suffered his ups and downs too. At some period either before or after his marriage, William had had a massive quarrel with his father, a wholesale chemist and druggist, and been ordered to go his way and never to darken his family doorstep again. As in those sunlit days pride had great stamina, this is precisely what happened. With William's family consisting of seven sisters and six brothers, this schism meant that my mother and her sister were effectively alienated for the rest of their lives from all their aunts, their uncles, and their subsequent progeny.

To make matters worse, William, previously trained by his father to follow in his footsteps, had the audacity to open out as a 'Wholesale Chemist and Dry Salter' in direct opposition to his family. If such a move had not been unforgivable in itself, William compounded it by being successful. Thus by the time World War 1 had started, the polarisation of the Escreet family was complete.

A few words on the name Escreet (which I carry as my second forename) would not perhaps be amiss. Until recently I had ascribed it to a French ancestor. This suited me admirably with its French connotation with literature. However, a cousin has recently produced a genealogical chart, and as the middle of the sixteenth century was as far back as he could research, his chart shows a very English Sir Rolland Eskricke topping the family tree. From then onwards, as the name mutated to Escreet, all the family lived in Yorkshire and, until the late 19th Century, all appeared to have been respectable land owners and farmers. I find this very disappointing. I had hoped for at least one bar sinister and a highwaymen or two to break the monotonous symmetry of our family tree.

To understand better what is to follow, the family house, No. 579, stood on one of the main arterial roads that runs into Hull. The druggist warehouse over which my grandfather presided lay behind these solid front road houses and was approached by a lane that ran behind and parallel to them.

My arrival at 579 was due to William. Before the First World War began, Elma had married Sydney and Lena had met her future husband, a Hull man named Harold Wilson. Sydney had been a fireman on the LNER Railways, a job he liked, but William, no doubt seeing in the bright young man someone who could run his beloved business after his death, had asked my father to come and work for him and Sydney had agreed. At this point the young couple rented their own home.

Then the war had begun and, with Sydney called up and sent to France, William suggested that Elma should share 579 with himself, Alice, and Lena until the war ended. Elma and Sydney agreed and their furniture was stored in one of the warehouse rooms. Although after William's death this move was to prove a disaster, no one could know this at the time. With my mother pregnant with her first born (my brother Raymond), and with the Zeppelin raids starting, it must have been a comfort to my father to know his wife would be well looked after.

And looked after she was, at first. She had always been William's favourite – indeed at her wedding he had somewhat tactlessly put his arms round her shoulders and declared that he was losing his right-hand man! The reference had been to my mother's business sense, which Alice totally lacked, and which had led William to prefer using my mother in his office instead of Alice.

To her death my mother believed Alice had never forgotten this slight and been jealous of her thereafter, for there was no doubt Alice was greatly in love with William. A bluff man with the Yorkshireman's contempt of pomposity; generous to a fault; and with a mischievous sense of humour, six feet four inches in his socks, William was a big man in every sense of the word, and when he died at the age of forty-five in 1917, the public trams slowed down as they passed 579.

Indeed, it has always been my regret I was born too late to know him. Yet despite his Edwardian insistence that he was the master of his household and the fact that he was the one man that Alice obeyed, there must have been some part of him that was intimidated by Alice's haughty ways. Some days after his death an old tramp came knocking at the door of 579, asking what had happened to 'the master'. In the interrogation that followed, it came out that for years the tramp had visited the warehouse every Monday lunchtime and, unknown to Alice or the children, had been given William's packed lunch. As there was no financial need that could account for the gesture, one has to assume that even the forthright William quailed at telling Alice he shared a weekly lunch hour with a tramp.

From everything my mother told me, William's premature death was a massive shock to Alice, who wore black for years afterwards. There would seem no doubt that she was devoted to him, worked hard for him, and, while he was alive, behaved in a reasonable and motherly way towards her daughters. His early death, however, seemed to create a bitterness in her towards a world that had wounded her so cruelly, and from that day she changed her behaviour to all around her.

Although the family decided to continue running the business after William's death, the Drugs Act demanded they must have another qualified chemist to replace him. At first this proved difficult because most of the local men had been called into the Forces. Finally they made arrangements with a chemist in York to work with them.

My father returned home in 1918. He had had a bloody war, having served on the Somme, then at Ypres, and finally in the region of Hamm and Villers Bretneaux when the Germans had launched their fearsome, all or nothing 1918 offensive. Along with one other man, he was the only survivor in his platoon from a gas attack and for the rest of his life he suffered skin trouble as a consequence. In later years, during one of the rare times he spoke about the war, he likened the swarms of Germans attacking them in the March 1918 offensive to a football crowd pouring out rampant into the streets. Another vivid memory was how the bolt of his rifle had become red hot from overuse.

But none of this affected him as much as an incident involving a friend. He had joined up with a lad who lived next door and whom he had known for many years. The boy, only sixteen years and three months at the time, had lied about his age as so many youngsters did at that time, and he had been in the same platoon as my father right up to the Battle of the Somme.

There it had happened. The boy, still under eighteen, had lost his nerve during the slaughter and run blindly away before my father could stop him. He had been caught by the Battle Police, court-martialled, and sentenced to be shot. To my father's horror, he was one of the men ordered into the firing squad that was to carry out the execution.

My father refused point blank to take part. At once he was arrested for insubordination and for a day or two it seemed he might meet the same fate as his friend. Then someone somewhere recognised the inhumanity of the order and he was released but given the task of burying his friend after the execution.

He spoke only once to me about this murder. He made no comment on his feelings when he picked up the still warm body of his friend because, sensitive man though he was, he was still a Yorkshireman and Yorkshiremen find it hard if not impossible to express their deeper feelings. But I have never escaped the belief that on the day he saw his best friend shot by his own comrades, the religion that his gentle mother had so painstakingly taught him had blighted and died.

In fact, my father emerged from one war only to enter another. With William gone and with helpless captives in her house, Alice allowed her bitterness to splash on everyone around her. By this time Lena had married Harold, who came back from Salonika in poor health, and Alice told the newly-married couple they could stay in 579. At the same time she offered to buy a house nearby in which Elma and Sydney could live as paying tenants.

There was one critical proviso, however. They must leave Raymond behind. She could not bear it if her only grandchild were to be taken from her.

There is no doubt that she thought the world of Raymond. Since his birth she had embraced him as if he were her own child and given him toys and clothes without stint.

Because of her feelings towards my father, it seems somewhat odd she should idolise his child in this way. One can only assume it was because the baby had entered the world when her beloved William was alive and the two were associated in her mind. No other explanation makes any sense because when

I made my entry, I was virtually ignored: indeed my mother stated in her autobiography that days passed before Alice entered the room to take a look at me. But that was to happen later. At this point in time there was only Raymond, and Alice wanted him and intended to have him.

Alice's first ploy was to point out that on my parents' wages, Raymond would lose all the benefits he enjoyed at the moment. When this had no effect, she turned to emotional blackmail. William had died young and Raymond was her only comfort. Would Elma, to whom she had given shelter during the war years, reward her by being so hard-hearted as to take the child from her? How would she, or Sydney for that matter, be able to live with themselves if she, Alice, found the loss too much to bear?

I think it was this unspoken threat of suicide that won her the day. Both of my parents were painfully aware by this time of her emotional condition and both were tender-hearted people. Today the rule book would say that for the child's sake, Alice's cards should have been called. But my parents were young and naive and child psychology was in its infancy. Neither of them had the slightest idea what might happen to Raymond in later years if he were left with his granny who so patently adored him.

All they knew at that time were the tearful

pleas of my brother to stay with her. He had known only her good side, the presents she bought him and her unquestioned devotion, and there is no doubt that his desire to stay with her was a major factor in their decision.

To be realistic, there might have been another factor, although I never heard it voiced by my parents. If her plea had been ignored, Alice might well have taken her revenge by selling the business and throwing my father and Harold on to the massive unemployment pile that existed at that time.

So Raymond was left while my parents moved into their new home, which was only two streets away. The agreement was that he should pay them frequent visits but, I am told, he seldom came. Whether this was of his choosing or Alice's, I have no way of knowing, but it was a sad arrangement, and although in itself it did not last long, it set a precedent that was to have profound effects on our family in the years to come.

TWO

This new situation, with Lena and Harold now facing Alice's storms and tantrums alone, lasted only a few months. One day there was a knock on my parents' door and

Elma found a tearful Lena standing there. Their mother, she sobbed, was making them miserable and destroying their marriage. Wouldn't Elma and Sydney help them by returning to 579 and allowing her and Harold to move into their house?

Remarkably, my parents agreed. Their desire to live with Raymond again was undoubtedly the compelling factor, although a secondary one was probably my mother's concern for Lena. As the elder sister, she had been protective towards Lena all her life and would certainly have been distressed to hear her marriage was imperilled.

Whatever the reasons, my parents made the fatal mistake of moving back. With Alice outraged at Lena's behaviour, they took the full brunt of the storm. Her children were ungrateful wretches, Alice raged. She had worked her flesh to the bone for them and how did they repay her? If William had lived he would have been horrified by their ingratitude. And so on and so on.

There seemed no way of keeping peace with her. Afraid of anything that might cause more trouble, my mother was weeks before she dared tell her she was carrying me.

Another storm broke immediately. Had Elma no sense of responsibility? How did she think she was going to manage the business with another child on the way? Why was she not content with the one dear little child that she already had? According to my mother she went on and on until Elma felt she was committing a felony.

Like most children of that time I was born at home but Alice didn't let that soften her resentment. It seems even the nurse, Nurse Collinson, who looked after my mother for six weeks, was shocked by her behaviour and remonstrated with her but to no avail. My brother could do no wrong and she would give him expensive toys, clothes, almost anything he wanted. I was never more than tolerated.

Of course this favouritism had no effect on me. I was far too young at this time to know the difference between an expensive and a cheap toy, and even as I grew older, what small boy cares about the clothes he wears? At the same time, her blatant favouritism must have distressed my parents, although there was nothing they could do to prevent it.

Memories are inevitably scarce during the first of those early years but my nightmares, which puzzled and disturbed my parents because they could not determine their cause, are vivid in my mind. I also have a memory involving the last flight of the airship R.38 when she broke up in flames over the river Humber. It seems I had been taken out that day in my pram by a girl engaged to look after me when my mother was employed in the warehouse. The girl had taken me to the riverside pier and, while we were there, the R.38 had passed overhead and then burst into flames.

This information came to my mother via the girl who was highly distressed when she brought me home and so might have coloured the incident. Yet I have a single vivid recollection of lying in a small rectangular vehicle with canvas sides rising above me and seeing a great burst of flame in the sky above. And at the same time hearing a woman's scream. That and nothing more.

In the years that followed, while my mother managed the office, father spent his days looking for orders to restore the business to its former health. He had only a bicycle to make these rounds and, although I would be no more than four at the time, I can clearly remember the sight of him arriving home on winter evenings, exhausted, cold, and often wet through. Still suffering the effects of the war, he would drop exhausted in front of the coal fire after changing his clothes, only for my grandmother to hurry out and return with a brush and shovel.

It is true she had a fetish for cleanliness but there is no doubt that her real reason for this behaviour was to give my father no mental or physical rest. She would approach his chair and her stare would demand his withdrawal from the fire while she busied herself sweeping up imaginary specks of mud from the carpet around it.

Many men, I among them, would have borne it for so long and then exploded. But I never remember my father, whose war record had earned him the choice of a commission or a Military Medal, do more than sigh and draw back. His tolerance, of course, was for my mother's sake, but in my young mind it seemed to me the stuff of which saints are made.

Nevertheless this behaviour was only the tip of the iceberg. I was too young to know the cause of the quarrels between Alice and my mother that seemed to happen almost every day, but the sound of Alice's voice rising into a scream of fury is something that haunted my dreams for many years. Even to this day, if I hear a woman screaming in temper I have to walk away. The scars on one's psyche are not easily erased.

Of course at this time I was too young to be consciously unhappy. Nor as yet were my brother and I estranged. We would play in the garden or go for walks in the fields that in those days lay opposite 579. As I was still small enough for the uncut grass in the fields to reach up to my waist, my memories are fragmentary but very poignant.

There were the weekly sounds of the coalman, a stentorian voice that one felt could awaken the dead. There was the cry of the mussel-man, from whom one bought the shellfish in pint portions. There was the sight from the front bedroom window of the steam train bringing its daily ration of coal along the Hull and Barnsley railway that ran on an embankment round the fields opposite. There were the fogs that descended suddenly, blanketing out vision and sound and giving one the eerie sensation of being detached from one's lower body.

There were the visits in the winter to see Alice's old mother, resident in Lees' homes. (Winters always seemed to have snow in those days and I can remember the feel of it on my bare legs as we trudged to the old ladies' homes). And there were the Front Rooms. No memories of a Yorkshireman could ever be complete without mention of that remarkable institution. Every house worthy of the name had one and 579 was no exception.

Front Rooms were sanctum sanctori. Whatever improprieties might occur in the rest of the house, they were never allowed to happen in Front Rooms. Their contents varied according to the owner's social status but in every case they contained his or her most valued possessions. Alice's contained an organ and a piano, a suite of furniture that looked as if it had never been defiled by human contact, antimacassars, a stuffed falcon in a glass case, and a huge pair of bronze gladiators. They stood on either side of the hearth like Horatius and Lars Porsena, ready to defend to the death its black-leaded grate against the pollution of a fire.

One was not allowed to pollute anything in Front Rooms. At 579, Raymond and I were only allowed inside the room on Sundays and even then only if accompanied by Alice or our parents. Nevertheless, we still found ourselves walking on tiptoe. We were acutely conscious the room was a shrine and we must respect it by talking in whispers.

Front Rooms, I am trying to infer, were a Northern way of life. Many years later I heard about a nervous, highly-strung girl from overseas who had married a Yorkshire boy and was forced to live with his parents for a while until they could afford their own home. She had not been with the family long before she noticed her mother-in-law furtively unlocking the Front Room door and tip-toeing inside with a broom and dust cloth.

She was too shy and diffident to ask her husband about this strange behaviour but as weeks went by she began to fret. Every time she passed the locked door of the sanctum, she would find herself holding her breath and listening. The strain grew until her husband noticed her state of nerves and asked its cause. The girl held out for a few more days then broke down and confessed all.

What was the secret of the Front Room? Was someone dying and was it so awful that she must not see the sufferer? Or was it worse? Was it a skeleton in the family cupboard? That was it, wasn't it? Someone of the family was mad and kept locked in that dreadful room. But why couldn't they trust her? She wouldn't tell: she wanted to help. But, oh, tell her. Please, please tell her.

The young man told his mother, who had a conference with his father, and after lengthy deliberations the sanctum was opened to the girl's inspection. Although her fears were quelled, she was heard to state later that she could never walk past a Front Room without holding her breath, and to spend an hour in one was to leave her indisposed for a week.

I know her feelings exactly. They were mine on the Sundays we were allowed into Alice's sanctum. There is one thing, however, that can be said for Front Rooms. Hermetically sealed as they were, sterile of dust and exhibiting one's finest possessions, they were clearly kept for a purpose. As I doubt that even Northerners believed that one day God would suddenly appear all bright and shiny on the spotless sofa, there can be only one other interpretation. Deep down in his psyche, every Northerner believed that one day Royalty would pay him a visit and The Room would ready and waiting. In other words Front Rooms knock the hell out of the belief that the North suffers a deep-rooted inferiority complex.

Front Rooms or not, as a child I hated those Sundays. To me they were days of infinite melancholy that would begin with Alice playing the organ in the front room, continue with Sunday School and a teacher whose lugubrious face was only matched by his threadbare broadcloth suit, and end with a trip to an aunt whose name eludes me but whose sanctimonious aspect and ways would have made a saint change his allegiance. Aware that to speak would be the ultimate blasphemy, my brother and I would sit with knees pressed together on a hard couch, listen to conversation that we could not understand, and wait an interminable time until we were given two small wedges of stale bread and dry cucumber. After that we had the long walk home through rain and deserted streets.

To me it always rained on Sundays. Not fierce exciting rain but a steady depressing drizzle that sank remorselessly into the soul. Nor did I ever see a happy face on Sundays. Women seemed to come off the best because churchgoing gave them an excuse to wear their best hats and finery, although any pleasure they felt was sternly hidden by demureness and piety.

But for the men there were no such compensations. Hating their best suits as all Northerners did, they would sit in their pews and later walk the wet streets home with their shiny faces expressing an agony of discomfort and embarrassment.

I cannot imagine a greater destroyer of religion than those Northern Sundays. The message that Christ had come on earth to save us sinners and we should all sing Hallelujah and be joyful went right over my puzzled head. The organ music, the Sunday School, the rows of suffering faces in Church, the rain and the incessant warnings about hellfire and damnation, made me think that the God to whom we were committed had only one intent: to make us so miserable on earth that we should long, nay pray, for its ending so we could join him in Heaven (although what gloom awaited us there made the mind boggle).

Nor did the bleeding figure on the cross dispel my childhood fantasies. To me everything about Christianity seemed about doom and gloom and the fact that my grandmother was one of its strongest adherents hardly strengthened my religious fervour.

But, thank God, there were other days than Sundays. To a child, one of the few benefits of our association with Alice was the warehouse yard which we could use when work there had ceased. My parents told me that Raymond seldom used it but I went there often. By this time a horse named Prinny and a cart had been added to our primitive transport system and I can remember sitting proudly alongside my father when he made a delivery in place of the 'rullyman' that we now employed. I can also remember climbing up and sliding down the pile of oats in the horse's bin, which meant I must have been very small indeed at that time.

A task I enjoyed as I grew older was helping my mother to prepare orders in her office on the first floor, a room surrounded by shelves lined with coloured bottles of all shapes and sizes. I would sit opposite her at a table on which there were piles of tiny pill boxes and a bowl of pills. A requisite number of the pills would be put into each box which would then be sealed. Her autobiography gives their content and prices. Aspirin tablets were 16 for three pence. Shampoo powders a penny each. Temple powders for neuralgia: ten for a penny. And so on. Afterwards I would be allowed to play with a large wooden train that made a hollow rumbling sound as its wheels ran over the bare wooden boards of the rooms that made up the first floor of the warehouse.

It was during these early days that I broke my left arm. I had been climbing over the shafts of the horse-drawn lorry and fell to the ground. Although I had to wander about in a splint for a few weeks, the flexible bone soon healed and gave me no trouble later in life.

Another memory of the warehouse was its huge vats of pickled onions and red cabbage that stood on the ground floor. I can't remember whether I was officially allowed into these rooms or not but with the help of an overturned box I could just reach the top of these vats to gain handfuls of delicious red cabbage. I've never found out what red cabbage does to a boy's stomach but if it does anything, it must have done it to mine.

During these years Alice's behaviour worsened, if such a thing were possible, and the day came when my parents decided they must move out whatever the consequences. Badly paid as they were and needing to live near the warehouse, they chose one of the tiny terraced houses in a street that ran off Anlaby Road only a stone's throw from 579. As Stirling Street was a somewhat mean street in those days, it was definitely a move down-market but the best my parents could afford.

The new house stood down one of the terraces that ran off the street, each containing eight houses apiece. With a front garden hardly bigger than a postage stamp, it stood cheek to jowl with three others at one side of a narrow path and faced four others of similar shape and size opposite. As our house number was 4, this meant it was at the end of the terrace, with only a wall separating its minute back garden from the warehouse yard. Thus, with a ladder placed on either side, my father and mother had only to clamber over the wall to be at work.

But they were not to escape from Alice's clutches as easily as that. Apart from still owning the business, Alice had no more intention of losing her influence over Raymond than she had before. Moreover she had stronger claims now. With Lena and Harold gone, she would be entirely alone if Raymond were taken away. Knowing my parents better than they knew themselves, I've no doubt she made the greatest possible use of this weapon.

So the painful decision was made. Raymond would once again be allowed to stay with Alice until such time as she got used to being alone in the house. It was a fudged decision and in retrospect a foolish one but had much to do with the make-up of my parents who had an extraordinary capacity to forgive. It was not the first time in this imperfect world, nor will it be the last, when the better qualities of men have brought them nothing but grief and sorrow. The expression that 'no good deed ever goes unpunished' might have been made for my parents.

So Raymond was left in the large house with Alice while I and my parents went to live in the tiny 'shamfour' house in Stirling Street. In distance we cannot have been a quarter of a mile apart. In consanguinity a crevasse now divided the ground between us and it was to grow wider by the year.

THREE

Although we were relatively poor, my memories of our days in Stirling Terrace are not unhappy ones. I did perhaps miss the long garden of 579 with its lawn and flower-beds but children are infinitely adaptive and although the tiny plot of cement that made the back garden of No. 4 was little use for anything but sedentary games, there was always Stirling Street itself and the ware-house yard to play in.

The new house was certainly very tiny, with only two main rooms above and below, but my mother's autobiography tells this mattered little beside her relief at getting away from Alice again.

But she did have one regret. Her father had owned a beautiful mahogany sideboard which she had always admired. I vaguely remember it, a massive, beautifully carved piece of furniture of highly-polished ma-hogany, with bevelled mirrors everywhere.

Some idea of its quality can be gained from the £50 William had paid for it when a member of the landed gentry had been compelled to auction off his home.

Knowing my mother's love of the piece, William had left it to her in his will, much to Alice's annoyance who argued (with some justification) that it needed a large house to do it justice. It had been back with her ever since my parents returned to 579 and with 4 Stirling Villas being such a tiny house, my mother had been forced to leave it behind on the understanding she could collect it if and when she could afford a larger home.

It is an odd fact that until we moved down this street, I can't ever remember playing in it even although it was so near to 579 and the other main road houses. The demarcation lines of class and privilege must have been as well defined geographically as they were in other aspects of society, even although as children we were never conscious of them. On Anlaby Road, Raymond, two middle-class friends of mine, Jackie Stonehouse and Leslie Miller, and I had played hide and seek in the garden or rigged up makeshift tents with old blankets and imagined ourselves Hiawatha or pioneer explorers.

In Stirling Street, so close by, the games were very different and more energetic. Here one raced about with wooden hoops which were kept rolling by striking them with a stick, risking one's life every time they ran across the road. Or whipping wooden tops with bootlaces tied to a stick and running for cover when the homemade whip clung too long to the top and flung it through a nearby window.

Other games sprang from the environment. Where the terraced houses stood back to back, with only an alley to give access to their backyards, there was a narrow ravine that led up to their smoking chimneys. Bracing our feet and hands against the bricks on both sides we'd edge our way upward. It was the equivalent of the modern game of chicken: the higher you went the braver you were.

The problem was not in going up, it was in coming down when one's hands and feet lost their purchase. More than one boy broke a leg or an ankle through miscalculation and more than one boy suffered a hiding from his father if seen playing the game. Yet in the way of boys, the double threat only added to the game's attraction.

These games I shared with my newly-found friends in Stirling Street, while still seeing my other friends, Jackie and Leslie. However, I saw little of my brother after our move. He became very aloof and seldom came round to visit us, which caused my parents much distress.

I suspect my popularity with the urchins of Stirling Street was due to my having the warehouse yard to play in. Fortunately my grandmother seldom visited the warehouse or she would almost certainly have banned my new proletariat friends from using it. But as my parents had no objection, there were sometimes as many as eight or nine boys playing in the yard when the day's work was over.

By this time I had been at school for well over a year. This schooling was the only aspect of my life that differed from my new friends. Whether it was due to my father's sparse education and his wish I should have a better one, or whether my mother's middle-class upbringing was the reason, I never knew, but I had been sent to a tiny private school standing at the corner of Melrose Street, only a couple of blocks away. Private schools were everywhere in Hull during those times and this one, Eversleigh High School, was run by two eminently respectable spinsters, Miss Knowles and Miss Smith, the former being the proprietor and headmistress.

An interesting fact (at least to me when my interest in flying developed) was that Amy Johnson, Hull's illustrious pioneer flyer of the Thirties, had attended this same school eleven years earlier.

From memory, girls outnumbered boys by four to one, which ten years later would have made the establishment a paradise but to a boy of six was only an embarrassment. At the same time no upbringing could have been more conservative or more loyalistic. On entering the tiny hall one was confronted by a huge map of the world with one quarter of it proudly coloured in red and bearing the legend: 'The Empire on which the Sun Never Sets'. We would have morning prayers, led with great gusto and fervour by Miss Knowles, and then get down to a curriculum that was heavily weighted with the three Rs. Geography and History took fourth and fifth place and of course allowed the Empire theme to return.

As for national heroes, there was no debunking them at Miss Knowles' seat of learning. They were brought out almost daily from their niche in history, exhibited with pride, then dusted carefully until their next exhumation. The patriotic theme of England's glory was continued in the songs we sang or the poems we recited. There was Rule Britannia, Hearts of Oak, Land of Hope and Glory, and Jerusalem. And there was Mother Of Mine, whose words I shall never forget. They ran:

'I see the Mighty Dead pass in line,
Each with undaunted heart,
Playing his gallant part,
Making thee what thou art, Mother of
Mine.'

I often wonder what it all did to us and whether it hindered or aided us in the perilous years to come. I also wonder what Miss Knowles would have thought had she survived until today, to find her beloved Britain shorn of her great Empire and seemingly populated by a race fiercely critical of its imperial past and cynically indifferent of its future.

Dear Miss Knowles. How you loved your England. You were wrong in your xenophobia, of course you were. But were you totally wrong? Is a belief in something worse than a belief in nothing? I don't know the answer. I only ask the question.

I think I was a reasonable student. Somehow or other I had learned to read before I went to school and so had a head start if not a whole length's start on my classmates. Certainly I seemed to win many prizes both for academic work and for sport although looking back I doubt if the competition was very exacting. Nevertheless at this time – I stress this time because of what was to come later – I must have been quite a strong, wiry, self-possessed child because I could more than hold my own among the urchins with whom I was now playing.

In fact one looks back almost with horror at the dangerous games we used to play. Apart from the wall game, Cowboys and Indians was one of the most popular and to be a good Red Indian one had to learn to shoot with a bow and arrow. Somehow we obtained these weapons – possibly we made them – and the skills we developed were remarkable. I can clearly remember standing an apple on the head of one of my friends and putting an arrow through it at a distance of perhaps ten yards. Equally, my friends must have done the same to me. Although the arrows were probably not steel-tipped, it still seems a miracle that none of us were scarred or blinded. I need hardly say that these games were played without the knowledge of our parents.

The General Strike of 1926 broke out during our stay in Stirling Villas. I don't think it affected the warehouse staff but I can still see the trams passing by at the end of Stirling Street. As I learned later, they were mostly manned by university students and professional men. As they passed by, groups of cloth-capped men on the pavements would hurl catcalls, jeers, and yells of scab after them.

I can also remember our first forays to a cinema down Anlaby Road. It used to have matinees on Saturday afternoons for children and the staple fare was silent movies with cliffhanger endings to tempt us back the following week. We would jeer at the villains, shout 'watch out, mister' to the heroes, and invariably come back with a flea or two for our pains.

Another pastime was stamp collecting and I can well remember picking up German stamps worth half a million marks at a ha'penny apiece. How little we knew at the time what these things meant and how they would affect our lives in the years to come.

I think I must have been an odd little creature. Although I played frequently enough with the other boys in the street, there was also a part of me that needed to be alone. As this was difficult in the small house, in the spring and summer evenings I would sometimes take a book, climb over the intervening wall, and sit down in one of the doorways of the locked warehouse. There I would read until the sun began to dip over the rows of terraced houses opposite. Then I would lower the book and sit watching the smoking chimneys silhouetted against the sunset.

I have no idea why I found this sight beautiful but I did. On windless evenings the smoke would rise gently into the scarlet sky and with little traffic about at that time, the only sounds would be the occasional whinny of the horse in its stable or the eventide song of the birds in the trees at the far end of the yard.

I used to find those moments both peaceful and evocative. I would sit watching the sky turn from red into orange and then purple and my young mind would fill with imaginings. In some way I cannot explain, the magic of the world into which I was growing came to me on those soft, sunlit evenings.

There is no doubt I was an imaginative child. Because of the books I read, I fought the Alamo with Davy Crockett, sailed the Pacific Islands with Cook, went with Scott to the South Pole, and found the source of the Nile with Livingstone.

Today television has replaced reading for many children and I find that sad. The wonder of a child lies in its imagination and for this to flourish it must be stimulated and challenged.

The written word does this superbly. The skilled writer does not give away too much but calls on the reader's intellect and imagination to play its part. The result is like the scattering of seeds on fertile soil. In the symbiosis that follows, the child's mind becomes a garden of glorious colour.

It is no surprise to me to learn that children who are encouraged to read early in life are twenty-five percent more advanced than those who are left by their parents to stare at television. There is no challenge in moving pictures. Too much is provided: too little is left to stretch the imagination.

The same applies to the elaborate and expensive toys that are given to so many children today. There is little call to create with them. When we children were given a hammer, a packet of nails, and an old wooden box to break up and reassemble, we loved the weird things we created. The funny little boat that would have sunk straight to the bottom of the first pond we pushed it into (had we been so foolish) became the Santa Maria when we sat inside it on the concrete apron that was the back garden. It was our ship, built with our own hands, and we treasured it a hundred times more than any of the expensive toys that in her ignorance Alice bought my brother. The child and the man value most the things into which they invest their labour and intellect.

I consider myself extraordinarily lucky for the circumstances that allowed my parents to buy me only the simplest of toys. Nor did my luck stop there. I was allowed to read whatever I could obtain and so much of my time was spent swapping comics and books with my friends.

Nevertheless, while poverty aided my self-reliance and imaginative development, I was fortunate in having had a relatively wealthy grandfather. He had been able to buy books and magazines that my own parents could never have afforded, and as my grandmother seemed to have little liking for reading, they were passed on to me. Most of the classics were there along with magazines such as the

Strand, which published the Sherlock Holmes mysteries, and the National Geographical Magazines whose articles opened up an exciting world to a young and eager mind.

All these works I devoured avidly while at the same time putting all my pocket money into more reading matter. Reading was a passion with me and I liked nothing better than to be left alone with my latest book or comic. At this time, unable to afford to travel further afield, my parents would take their one week a year holiday at either Bridlington or Withernsea, two resorts on the East Yorkshire coast.

The boarding house they took at Withernsea was at the corner of Arthur Street. It was sited almost opposite the lighthouse and the room we occupied on the first floor faced the huge white tower. The room had a large bay window with a seat running round it and my parents would leave me there with a book while they went out for a couple of hours in the evenings.

It was no hardship for me. With a book I was happy and would read until the twilight came. Then I would watch the lighthouse flashing its warning and my mind would fill with imaginings, often related to the book I had been reading.

Thus at a very young age I was reading both classics and pulp fiction with equal fervour. It was, I feel, a most fortunate background for the novelist that in future years I was to become. Classical literature is excellent for the study of character creation, but with such a highly developed skill their writers often find no need for a strong plot and so sometimes neglect the art. In contrast the lesser writer has to make up his deficiencies by good plot construction and so often becomes a master in this field. As two skills are better than one (and in my view produce a better balanced novel) it seems a pity that more education authorities do not hold the same opinion.

During this time two odd things happened, both difficult, if not impossible, to explain. The first came about when a woman who claimed to be a phrenologist paid us a visit. Why she came I've no idea although I would guess my father had encountered her while on his rounds, and she had offered to read our futures from the 'bumps' of our heads. For this purpose my brother was also present.

As we were a fairly typical Northern family in our scepticism of such claims, I'm certain we all privately treated the readings as something of a joke. And yet this is what the woman read from the head shapes of my brother and myself. He had a love of the theatre and one day would go on the stage to make it his career. And I had a great love of books and one day would make my living from writing them. All this from a woman we had never seen before, and long before these ambitions had surfaced in either of us.

The second event was, to me as a child, quite terrifying. For three weeks our next-door neighbours had guests, a man and wife who claimed to be spiritualists. Finding them interesting, our neighbours asked if we would like a demonstration of their powers. I don't think my parents were that eager but my grandmother heard of the offer and persuaded them to agree.

So an evening arrived when my parents, my grandmother, and my uncle and aunt were all crowded into our small living room along with the spiritualists whose names I have long forgotten. For some reason Raymond was not present. Until then everyone had believed the spiritualists would hold a conventional séance but instead they brought with them a huge sheet of white paper which they lay over the kitchen table. On this they placed a planchette and invited all the adults present to lay two fingers on it.

For those who have never seen a planchette, it is a shield shaped piece of wood with two wheels on universal joints affixed to its two corners and a pencil attached to its pointed end. This configuration allows it to move in any direction, and as it slides over the paper its pencil traces out the path it has taken. Its purpose, of course, is to write out any message that supposedly comes from the spirit that is presiding at the time.

For a good five minutes it seemed no spirit was presiding over our table because, although my grandmother had requested that William be asked to speak, the planchette doggedly refused to move. However, after the two visitors asked for silence and made some muttered entreaties, the piece of wood began to move, albeit very slowly, and we all leaned forward in anticipation.

For a few seconds the pencil did little more than trace a few wriggly lines and I believed it was being pushed around by our two guests. Then it moved forward with a spurt, taking everyone's hands with it, and as it traced a couple of words on the paper, my grandmother gave a gasp of shock, saying the lettering bore a distinct resemblance to William's bold and distinctive handwriting.

At this point the words were barely more than squiggles, and I'm sure my parents believed it was Alice's morbid imagination at work. Nevertheless, everyone was attentive now and when the two spiritualists invited Alice to ask questions and the correct answers appeared on the paper, respect began to take the place of scepticism. When it was suggested that Alice asked questions in her mind and these were also answered correctly, everyone looked impressed and not a little apprehensive.

Somewhat naturally, Alice wanted to continue but the spiritualists said the spirits found the exercise a strain and William had signified he had done enough for the moment. Had anyone else questions they would like to ask a dear one from the other side?

At this my Uncle Harold spoke up. He had lost his only brother in Salonika in the 1st World War and the War Office had never been able to provide the cause of his death or locate his grave. Would it be possible to speak to his dead brother and ask these questions?

The couple changed the paper on the table, and after a few minutes the planchette began to move again. To everyone's amazement the style of handwriting was now quite different. Looking pale, my uncle began asking his questions and they were answered in writing that, although frail, was positive in its replies. Yet when my uncle asked the location of the grave, the planchette paused and then wrote something that at first seemed illegible. (It was only days afterwards that Harold discovered the word was written in the Greek alphabet and was a place name in Salonika).

Unable to make out the word at that moment, my uncle went on asking questions. As the minutes passed, the planchette moved slower and slower as if the spirit behind it were reluctant or tired. When my uncle asked once more where the grave was, the planchette gave a sudden jerk and then, to my frightened young eyes, seemed to tear itself away from everyone's fingers and scrawled across the paper in huge letters: FOR GOD'S SAKE LET ME REST!

My uncle went ashen and walked from the room. The rest of the adults, even the two spiritualists, looked pale and shaken and no one, not even my grandmother, suggested the séance continue. For my part, I was scared, and to this day have never taken part in any activity that remotely claims to have dealings with the world of spirits.

I had now reached the age when I was becoming more conscious of the goings on of the adults around me. In particular, there was the behaviour of the housewives. As each tiny household had a front step, and as housewives judged one another on its cleanliness, a woman's first task of the day, summer or winter, was to kneel before it with a pail of hot water and a pumice stone and scrub away until the stone was spotless.

A couple of hours would then pass while she slaved away indoors at her daily chores, then, with the rest of her kind, she would appear again on her step but this time without her pail. An unwritten agreement seemed to exist that all housewives broke off their tasks at mid morning to discuss the latest tit-bits of gossip.

I don't think my mother ever joined this congress – indeed I know she did not – but the sight of those buxom housewives in their head scarves and pinnies, standing with folded arms and nodding or shaking their heads, is one of my most vivid memories of Stirling Villas.

It was, of course, the nearness of the houses that made this congress possible. The effect of it, which put eight families almost within earshot of one another, was in some way to create a larger family almost in the way of a Dyak longhouse. Everyone knew about the others' troubles and because to know is often to act, families would support one another in ways I have not known since.

At the same time, the situation made it a hotbed of gossip. One could always tell when some scandal was being discussed. As any explicit sexual word was taboo, at least in public, the women would substitute such words by an exaggerated movement of their lips. Because all the other women seemed to understand, one has to believe some kind of a secret code was involved.

Of course, there were times when one overheard their conversation, in which interestingly they always used their marriage titles. I was running down the terrace one day when I heard Mrs Jones at Number 7 tell Mrs Barnard in Number 6: 'So Mrs Wilson's back in hospital again, Mrs Barnard?'

'Aye, Mrs Jones. The poor lass's been flooding again.'

'Aye, it's a shame. You'd think they could do summat about flooding, wouldn't you, Mrs Barnard?'

'You would, Mrs Jones. But they don't seem to be able to, do they?'

Puzzled why a plumber couldn't be called in to make repairs, I asked my mother the question that night but in the way of those times I was left more mystified than ever why Mrs Wilson had such an aversion to plumbers that she needed hospital treatment.

Another time, when going to school, I saw the ambulance stop outside the terrace across the street and a body on a stretcher carried into it. When I returned home at lunchtime, the women were still discussing the incident. In their excitement they did not notice me passing by and I heard one say to the other: 'Yer know what it was, don't yer, Mrs Martin? He died on the job.'

'I'm not surprised, Mrs Jones,' came the reply. 'They always said he was too fond of it fer his own good. Or why would 'e be having it in the morning?'

Died on the job, I thought. What job? Repairing the roof? Painting the house? And why was he so fond of it? More and more it seemed adults did strange and unaccountable things.

This was brought home even more forcibly to me when I was sent off to spend a week's holiday with my father's sister in Withernsea. She was married to a station master, a huge good-natured man with a deep, infectious laugh. Because the couple had other relatives staying with them at the time, I was given a single bed in their room.

This caused me no problems until the third night when the loud creaking of a bed awakened me. Opening my eyes, I discovered that a candle alongside the couple's double bed had been lit. As my eyes adjusted to the light I saw to my horror that my uncle, totally nude, was lying on top of my aunt and heaving up and down as if trying to crush her. In turn she was making gasps and cries that suggested he was near to success.

I was frozen with fear. I wanted to leap out of bed and try to stop him but something held me back. Instead I closed my eyes tightly in the hope of ending the nightmare. But the struggling and the gasping only grew louder until my aunt gave a loud cry, a moan, and then went silent.

She was dead. Brutally murdered. And yet I might have saved her if I'd had the courage to interfere. Terrified, with my heart pounding wildly, I plucked up the courage to look again and to my amazement saw my aunt was not only alive but was kissing the man who had only seconds before been crushing her. A moment later the candle was snuffed out and I was left in the darkness to wonder at the nature of this mysterious ritual.

Yet I must have had some suspicion that all was not what it seemed because I did not ask my mother for an explanation when I returned home. Perhaps it was an indication that the years were passing and I was beginning to leave my childhood behind.

FOUR

During this time of innocence my grandmother had turned her house into two flats, she and my brother living in the five rooms upstairs and the lower flat being let to a paying tenant. Shortly afterwards she became friendly with a Hull business man named Harris and surprised her daughters by announcing she was going to Canada where she would marry him. A relatively wealthy man, he had two sons and a daughter living over there, and he wanted them to be present at his nuptials.

If it was a surprise to the rest of the family, it must have been a shattering blow to my brother who would now be around thirteen years old. Alice had made herself indispensable to him and now, quite suddenly, she was prepared to hand him back to his parents and go abroad for an indefinite period.

Nor could his present relations with us have made the move easier for him. Since I had made new friends he had long ceased to play with us and during his infrequent visits made no attempt to hide the fact he could not wait to return to his grandmother. While some of this behaviour could be explained by his resentment at being left with Alice, I feel certain she was the main cause. Alice was a master at subtle denigration and perhaps afraid that Raymond might one day want to return to us, I believe she had taken all steps possible to ensure it could never happen.

But now it was to happen – at Alice's own choosing – and the effect on my brother must have been catastrophic. Looking back, I think it explained the man he was to become. On the surface he could be very sociable, be excellent company, and certainly was popular with his friends. Yet every one I have questioned has admitted he never discussed his inner feelings with them. I believe, and so did my mother, that he lost his trust in people the day Alice sailed away without him.

Perhaps if she had been a normal grandmother this sudden shifting of allegiances might not have had such an effect. But Alice, with her aggressive personality and her claustrophobic religious practices, was anything but normal. There was a self-righteous, sanctimonious streak in her that was profoundly unhealthy for a growing child.

I used to feel it myself. For one thing she would speak a great deal about death. She would take Raymond to his grandfather's grave every few days to lay flowers on it. She made him promise he would attend to her grave after she had gone and always see it was kept clean and tidy. She emitted an odd mixture of cant and melancholy peculiar to her time and place. She would condemn scandalmongers and yet no one practised gossip more devastatingly. Her wordage was old-fashioned: her attitude self-pitying. Life was always doing unkind things to her which she bore with a brave little smile. After all, dear Dad was up there watching and waiting for her. She did not want to make him unhappy by giving way to her tribulations.

If this gives the picture of a weak woman, nothing could be farther from the truth. She was as tough as old boots as one discovered quickly enough if one crossed her. She was an extreme example of a special type that I have sometimes seen parodied on film and television. A publisher of mine once criticised me when I drew such a character in a novel, saying she could not believe such women existed. A copy-editor with a Northern background was quick to assure her the breed were very much in evidence in the days of her youth and no doubt survivors remain to this day.

One wonders what elements coalesced to produce such a mixture of cant, self-pity, cunning, courage, and sometimes (although not in Alice's case) extreme neighbourliness and generosity. Chapel or the Church? The climate or the geography? The subtle mixture of Scandinavian melancholy or Puritan and Northern deprivation? The education of the day or the macho Andy Capp husbands? It would make a fascinating thesis.

Apart from its more psychological aspects, Raymond's move to our tiny house must have been a difficult enough adjustment for the boy in purely physical terms. Although I am not certain about this, I don't think Alice made any provision for his needs after she left and so he suffered a huge drop in his standard of living. It goes without saying that an extra mouth to feed did nothing to improve our standard either.

Not that my parents were not glad to have him back. At first I had never seen my mother more happy. But when it was seen how miserable the move had made the boy, that happiness died and tensions began to appear in the tiny house that had not been there before.

My parents had another worry at this time.

Before Alice left for America, she sold the druggist business. No thought that William, so proud of his creation, had invited my father and Harold to leave their jobs to work for him, and no thought that my mother had held the business together all this time. It had to be sold before she left, and for an anxious month it looked as if both my parents would become unemployed.

Mercifully, this did not happen right away. The sweet manufacturer to whom Alice sold the business, a man called George Bean, decided to keep the druggist side of the business going for a while and employed my mother and her sister to run it for him while he concentrated on the production of sweets.

However, as he brought with him his own salesmen, there was no place for my father. What employment he found during the next few years I don't remember, nor does my mother make mention of it in her autobiography. But it can't have been well paid because our living standards dropped even further at this time.

But to be fair to Alice she did give both my mother and Lena £400 before her departure. 579 she let and arranged with my mother to collect the rent and to bank it. Then she and Harris sailed, leaving a mixture of emotions behind her. My mother and father were unashamedly relieved to have her off their backs. Raymond, as I have said, was more than distressed.

I was too young to share any of these emotions. In fact, for me this was a wonderful time because it brought me in touch with the greatest friend of my childhood.

We met in the warehouse yard the day after George Bean and his men moved in. He came running out of a door, our eyes met, and in some mysterious symbiosis the bond was sealed.

He was a huge, snow-white bulldog called Pride. He was George Bean's dog and his task was to guard the warehouse. In appearance he would have frightened any would-be burglar out of his wits with his flat, slavering face and huge muscular body. But if ever appearance belied a creature's character, it belied it in Pride. He loved people and in particular little people.

At first he terrified all my friends. Three days after his arrival I found half a dozen of them huddled in a circle on the pavement with Pride running round them, a sight reminiscent of a cluster of covered wagons being circled by Red Indians. Not a boy dared to move, thinking he would be devoured if he broke the circle.

In fact, all the dog wanted them to do was play with him. How that dog loved to play. His speciality was cricket and his position square leg. When my friends discovered he was harmless, we would play cricket in the warehouse yard with Pride crouched ten yards from the batsman. He would not poach if the tennis ball were struck elsewhere but if it came in his direction he would give a bark of joy, chase it with enormous gusto, snatch it up and run helter skelter to the wicket, where he would drop it at the base of the stumps. Then back to his position again to wait for the next strike.

Then there were the games he and I used to play on our own, which I liked best of all. One was throwing a ball for him in the warehouse yard. He would scamper after it on his stubby, powerful legs, drop it at my feet, and with his warm excited eyes beg me to throw it for him again.

Hide and seek was another of our favourites. I would close my eyes and he would run off and hide in one of the many empty packing cases heaped up at one end of the yard. After counting thirty I would hurry off to find him, often a difficult task because he understood the game and would creep in the most unlikely places. When discovered, we would reverse the game. He would lie down on the tarmac and solemnly cover his eyes with a paw while I searched for a hiding place. When I was ready, I would call and he would jump up and begin looking for me.

I loved that dog. He filled a gap in my life that I had not known existed. Soon George

Bean and his warehousemen recognised the bond between us, and although Pride remained in a kennel in the warehouse yard, to all intents and purposes he became my dog. I washed him, groomed him, and took him for his walks. Walking along with him on his lead, I was the proudest boy on earth.

He even saved my life. With George Bean continuing for the moment to sell drugs, he bought a trawler's cabin and stood it at the far end of the warehouse. As the purpose was to store volatile drugs, the cabin was made airtight. Playing hide and seek with Pride one day, frustrated at his ability to sniff me out so quickly, I slipped into the cabin and closed the door.

I was soon choking because of the fumes and tried to escape but there was no inner lever to open the door. As I hammered on the porthole window, I saw Pride outside, trying to scratch the door open. I shouted to him, choked and then everything went dark.

I learned the full story in hospital. When Pride could not get to me, he had run into the warehouse to alert the men. When everyone assumed he was playing and so took no notice, he had grabbed one of them by the trouser leg and literally dragged him to the cabin. When the door was opened, I was found unconscious on the floor and rushed to hospital. Afterwards doctors said I might have died if I'd been left there a few more minutes.

So he became my hero as well as my friend. Later, as his fame spread, he was occasionally borrowed to star in British Empire trade shows held in the city. His white coat would be dusted with chalk powder and then he would be sent out on the stage of the huge hall.

I can see him now on his first performance. He stalked out of the wings like Olivier playing Hamlet and with a spotlight playing on him, walked majestically to the centre of the stage. He paused there, gazed impassively at the audience, and then, with a grunt, flopped down on his bottom with his front legs braced on the stage. His disdain was magnificent. He was the veritable epitome of the British bulldog and I nearly burst with pride as the audience cheered and roared their approval.

I cannot remember how long I knew him. To a child's mind it seemed a long time but thinking back it can only have been a few years. He would be an adult dog when he came into my life and he died before we moved from Stirling Villas.

This was without question the blackest day of my young life. I had just returned from school when a workman ran into the house to tell me Pride was ill and I must come at once. I climbed over the wall into the warehouse yard and found a small crowd of people, my father among them, gathered round the dog who was lying on the ground. As George Bean gave him a sip of brandy and he showed no sign of recovery, my father pushed a tennis ball into my hand and told me to see if I could revive him.

Although unsure of what was happening, I remember being very frightened as I knelt beside him calling his name. For a moment he did not move but when I called his name again, he turned his head to look at me. 'Look what I've got, Pride,' I said, showing him the ball.

His huge brown eyes met mine and then his head slowly rose and with what seemed an enormous effort he took the ball in his mouth. I heard murmurs from the adults around me but those devoted eyes held my attention. Then he gave a small cry and he dropped back dead with the ball still gripped in his jaws.

I cried for weeks. For the first time in my life I understood what death meant. Never again. Never. The awful finality of it. If it were not the end of my childhood, it was the end of my innocence. The world was never quite the same place again.

FIVE

Alice and her new husband were in Canada for around eighteen months and then unexpectedly returned to Hull. One reason was an operation Harris needed. He was always a tight-fisted man and apparently it would have cost him much more to attend a hospital in Canada. In the event he gained little from the move because not long after he had the operation he died suddenly and Alice became a widow again.

It was not long after her bereavement that she decided to visit Canada once more. She stayed eight months this time and on her return made the remarkable promise that she would take me with her on her next trip. Why she should make me this promise after leaving Raymond behind on her first two visits I have no idea because in all other ways her behaviour towards me remained the same. I can only think that, fascinated as I already was about North America from the many books I had read, I might have listened to the stories of her adventures there with more interest than did Raymond and the rest of her family.

Whatever the reason, the promise was made. Had Pride still been alive I doubt if my desire to go would have been so obsessive but without him to play with, I turned all my childhood dreams on America.

In hindsight it becomes even more difficult to understand Alice's promise when it became known later that her first trip had been something of a family disaster. Although she seemed to have got on very well with Harris's daughter, she most certainly had not with his sons and particularly their wives. Whether they saw her as an interloper who was set to inherit Harris' wealth – he had been much older than she – or whether she had become a victim of her psychopathic gift of turning one person against the other, I don't know – but there seems no doubt Harris's sons did not want her back.

All the same she arranged to go although this time to stay with Harris's daughter with whom she appeared to have a better relationship. With her promise to take me with her this time, my excitement became intense. It was never my way as a child to do things by halves and this time I went the whole hog. Every book that I could find on North America I devoured and digested. I learned all about the Rockies, the Calgary rodeos, the Indian tribes, the Great Lakes, Niagara Falls, the American Badlands, the Plains, the cities... I filled up notebooks that my parents could not afford and drew map after map until I could draw every estuary and inlet by heart. In other words I became a virtual encyclopaedia on the North American Continent.

In one sense, what was to follow was made even worse because of my imagination and my memory. There seems little doubt that the latter was exceptional. My parents used to show it off to friends by producing packs of cigarette cards. In those days collecting cigarette cards was a popular hobby and we had over sixty complete sets of fifty cards in the house. Each set had its own particular theme, such as cricket players of the day, footballers, racing cars, aeroplanes, and so on. According to my parents, any card could be withdrawn from any set and if I were shown the picture on the front, I could recite precisely word for word the details printed on the back.

That memory was now at work on Canada and the U.S.A. For weeks and months I lived for Alice to keep her promise and talked about little else. I kept it up until my parents must have prayed for Alice to take me and drop me slap in the middle of the Great Plains.

But it was all for nothing. Alice went to Canada without me. She gave me no explanation: she just went. When in total bewilderment I asked my parents why she had broken her promise, they had no answer and could only say she must have changed her mind.

I don't think even they understood how I felt. I was completely heartbroken. I'd built my young life on the trip and it was cancelled without as much as an apology. I can't think how many nights I cried myself to sleep.

To this day I've never understood why she made me that promise and then broke it so casually. It cannot have been a problem of accommodation because Harris's daughter had a large house and had made provision for my arrival. Nor can it have been the cost, not when Alice was able to afford two more trips in the years ahead.

Whatever her reason, it was a devastating blow and for a while it gave me a mistrust of adults and their promises. However, one has only to live into manhood to realise there is usually a credit side to misfortunes. This one taught me never to break a promise and particularly never to deliberately break one to a child. Yet at the same time it taught something else. Never be too upset if occasionally you have no choice. It is the disappointments one suffers as a child that enables one to face the much bigger setbacks that will come later. (Mind you, having said this I don't think Alice had my future in mind!)

During their short time together after their return from America, Harris and Alice had left George Bean as a tenant in 579 and gone to live with Harris's other daughter who lived in Hull. After his death and after Alice sold 579, she shared herself for a time between Lena and Harold and ourselves.

We all began to dread her visits. Spreading antipathy seemed to come to her as naturally as breathing, and by moving from one household to the other she was in her element. Soon, without knowing how it happened, my mother and aunt were estranged. Although I was too young to understand the subtleties of my grandmother's behaviour, I could see how my parents dreaded her visits and could feel tension tighten like a rack the moment she entered the house.

These visits might have been one reason my parents decided to move to the other side of the town, hoping perhaps she might not like coming out there. A more substantial reason might have been financial expediency because house rents were cheaper in some of the housing estates there. Such a move would mean both my parents having much longer journeys to work but discomforts of that nature were allowed little consideration at that time.

For the Depression was now here with a vengeance and, with sales falling weekly, George Bean had cut the wages of his staff to the bone. He also told my mother that she would only be needed in the mornings, which reduced her wages even further. While as yet we were not as poor as the grey-faced men who began appearing in huddled groups on street corners, we had now reached the point where every penny had to be accounted for.

As with so many other burdens and responsibilities, this one fell upon my mother. My father would pass his wage packet over to her every Friday and, after being handed his few shillings of pocket money, would leave her the difficult task of distributing the rest towards our basic needs. Seven shillings would go to the rent, one shilling and six pence towards the gas, ten shillings towards the food, and, at the very last, threepence pocket money to Raymond and twopence to me.

My mother was only one of millions of women who had this task every pay day in the Thirties and yet no Chancellor of the Exchequer had greater responsibilities. One mistake, one tiny extravagance, and an entire family could find itself out in the street. Landlords were not known for their tolerance and kindness of heart.

There was irony in this working-class female responsibility because it ran counter to a society that never questioned the shibboleth that man was the master of his household. Nor did anyone defend it more than the women themselves. Even if a man were three feet tall and the woman built like

Goliath, she would defend his manhood to the death.

Be that as it may, my parents had one huge advantage over the families around them. They still had the £400 Alice had given them, although as far as we were concerned it might not have existed. My mother, an accountant to her fingertips, argued that this money, invested in a building society, was a contingency fund to be used only in a dire emergency. Not a penny of it was to used to subsidise our current living or to ease her life.

To my young eyes she never seemed to stop working. During the mornings she would be over in the warehouse office, in the afternoons and the evenings she would be stoning the front step, black-leading the grate, mending and washing our clothes, keeping the house spotless, and struggling to eke out the money. Even after I was tucked into bed I often heard the sounds of the dolly tub and mangle rising from the scullery below my bedroom.

What horrifies me now is the way we took everything for granted. We didn't just expect it: we never even thought about it. She was our unpaid provider cum nurse cum housewife cum servant cum general factotum. Her life was an endless round of unselfish service and drudgery that we all took for granted. In other words we were monsters of selfishness.

It is true that we were in Andy Capp country but I doubt if it were very different in any working class society in the land. The demarcation lines between a man's work and a woman's were more sharply defined that those of the most intransigent trade union. For a Northerner to be seen washing up dishes or pummelling clothes in the dolly tub, expulsion from the male union would have been the least of his penalties. He would have faced jeers from the local children and scorn or silence from his mates in the pub.

Nor would it end there. The women who stood on their doorsteps in their head scarves and pinnies, instead of cheering him to the echo and throwing flowers in his path for his trailblazing, would have added to his misery by their malicious whispers or outright jeers. To them he would be a wimp or a queer, certainly not a man. The tribal laws of the working class were rigid and God help those who broke them.

So I lived and played and expected to be fed and clothed and nurtured while my mother counted the pennies and wondered how she could keep the home together without doing the unthinkable by drawing on the contingency fund. Finally one day my brother and I were given the news. We were going to move from Stirling Villas to a house at the far side of town.

The reasons were complex. George Bean

had decided to give up the druggist side of his business and concentrate on the manufacture of confectionery. As he already had an office staff for this side of his business, he no longer needed my mother. This could have been something of a disaster for us had he not lost the services of a salesman at the same time. On good terms with my father, he offered him the job and my father accepted it gladly.

So we could move now to cheaper accommodation without my mother having long journeys added to her other chores. With empty houses everywhere, it was not long before Raymond and I were told we were moving into a council house in Downing Grove, East Hull.

Of course neither of us wanted to go. I don't think Raymond was as upset as I, however, because he had left school at fourteen, having no desire for further education, and was now working for a men's outfitters. As this shop was near the centre of the city, his daily journeys would barely be longer than they were before and so cause little disruption to his life. Also, by this time the visiting phrenologist was proving her prognosis right because he was showing a great interest in the theatre. One of his hobbies was building miniature stages with scenic backdrops, and for this pastime he needed few friends. Not that he would have found many if he had wanted them. We were a down-to-earth lot in Yorkshire in those days and anything to do with acting (and writing for that matter) was seen as the work of poofters and sissies.

I was more upset by the move because it not only meant leaving all my friends behind but also leaving the school where I was very happy. However, there was nothing either of us could do except prepare ourselves for a new chapter in our lives.

SIX

I remember this removal very clearly because of the cat we had, who bore the imaginative name of Tom. He was a huge independent creature who sported six claws on every paw and spent his time roving the district and raping every female he encountered. The fact he spent so little time at home is probably why I haven't mentioned him before but nevertheless he was devoted to my mother. I can still see him jumping on her back when she was cleaning out the fire grate and wrapping his black shape round her neck.

I'm not certain whether we chose him or he chose us but we must have had him quite a few years before our move across town. Long enough in any case for most fully grown cats in the district to also sport six claws. So, to do my mother justice, her choice of name was perhaps fitting after all.

He is associated with our removal in my mind because I chose to travel with him in the back of the furniture van among the few bits of furniture my parents possessed. It was quite dark inside and I certainly could see nothing of the route we took. Yet after we arrived at our new house and he was released, he vanished and was not seen for three days. At the end of this time an ex-neighbour in Stirling Villas managed to contact my father to tell him Tom had arrived back the following day and had been howling outside No. 4 ever since.

He was brought back and this time settled down without further fuss. But how that cat found its way back across the centre of a busy city, without sight or scent to guide him, has remained a mystery to me ever since.

The house in Downing Grove, built of 'breeze blocks' which was a new building material at that time, was one unit of a recently built estate. To me, instead of being cheaper than Number 4, it looked more expensive, probably because it had a rear garden, something I had not known since the days of 579.

My surprise and pleasure at this discovery

were soon subdued when my father took me to the secondary school he hoped I could attend. In those days, when a child reached his tenth or eleventh year, it was possible to take an examination for further education. If he failed, he remained at his elementary school until the age of fourteen when he was thrown out on to the labour market.

If he passed, however, a place might be found in a secondary or grammar school from which a clever child might progress via a scholarship to university. The one snag here was that parents had to pay for this secondary education and at two pounds fifty shillings a term, many could not afford it.

I shall always remember my first sight of Craven Street Secondary School. It stood on the corner of a street of that name, slap bang in the centre of an industrial area. Trams clanged and clattered along the main road in front of it, chimneys belched smoke and trains dragged their heavy loads behind it: the very air seemed full of the hard and brassy sounds of industry.

To me, used to the gentleness of Miss Knowles' Academy, the school resembled one of the Victorian monstrosities described in my copies of Dickens's novels. It certainly must have been built during that time because with its high turrets, barred windows, and spiky iron railings, it appeared more suited to a prison than a school.

By unfortunate chance my father and I arrived during the morning break when a couple of hundred ragamuffins were disporting themselves in the playground. To my horrified eyes the scene resembled Genghis Khan's hordes enjoying a killing. We had to pass through these barbarians, and the comments that were thrown at me, who had been spruced up for my interview, were a frightening warning of what was to come if I passed my test.

Our mission was to meet the Headmaster, a Mr. Harry Schoosmith. After seeing his flock, I expected to encounter a ten foot monster covered in a black pelt, but he turned out to be a charming middle-aged man with greying hair and a head that kept jerking sideways, an affliction said to be due to shell shock incurred during the First World War.

He must have noticed my apprehension because he spent some time assuring me I would be most happy in the school if I were to pass the examination. Happiness I doubted, to say the least, but after saying a tremulous goodbye to my father, who was to pick me up later, I was led into an empty classroom where I was given a set examination paper. Told I had an hour in which to complete it, I was left alone to brood on my future.

The examination itself posed no problem.

In spite of its xenophobic tendencies, Eversleigh High School had taught the education basics very well, for I had the paper finished within half an hour. For the rest of the time, with my bare legs huddled beneath the desk, I sat listening apprehensively to the sounds around me. Although the children were back in their classrooms by this time, the occasional yell from their keepers gave a hint of the young barbarians they were struggling to control. Listening to these sounds of the jungle, I decided that at ten years old I had lived too long.

Dead on the hour Mr Schoosmith returned and took me back to his office. When my father arrived he told him that I had passed my examination with honours. Indeed, because I was such a bright boy, he was going to let me start at the school on Monday instead of making me wait until the beginning of the next term.

My thoughts were bitter. All I'd had to do was put the wrong answers to those questions and I would have escaped from this nightmare. Instead, by showing off, I had sealed my own fate. Bright boy indeed! I was a cretin.

So I became a pupil at Craven Street School. I'll swear no soldier sent to the Western Front in France dreaded his posting more than I dreaded the following Monday morning. I tried my hardest to keep my fears from my parents but they must have shown because my father went with me that first morning. It was, of course, the very worst thing he could have done because he was seen by the barbarians and the yells of coward, pampered brat, and other names whose meaning I could only guess were being hurled at me even before he left. To my eternal shame I begged him not to leave me which must have been most painful to him. Indeed I learned afterwards that he'd needed two double whiskies before going on to work.

So began for me a period of my life that in many ways was pure misery. The real problem was the way I spoke. If it had not been for that, my bullies would probably have soon moved on to the next new boy, because at that time I was a small child and easily unnoticed.

But my voice could not go unnoticed. Without the accent of the other boys, I was a sitting duck for every little thug who felt a spot of bullying would wet his appetite for lunch. The two worst offenders' names are burned in my brain, McCloud and Scargill. McCloud was a boy twice my size, burly, untidy, with coarse, heavy features: the archetypal bully. Scargill was less burly, more the weasel type in manner and appearance.

Between them these two made my life purgatory for the next two years. They would tear my books away and throw then into pools of water. They would grab my satchel and swing me round on it until the strap broke. They would even follow me to the bus stop and pull at my clothes in the hope of tearing them, which they frequently did. This caused me particular distress because a boy did not tell his parents of such things in those days, probably because we knew they had enough problems already.

But a torn jacket or trousers was more than a problem, it was a minor disaster to parents who had to count every penny. So a boy was left with two choices, either to confess his miseries at school and give that extra worry to his parents or let them believe he didn't care a jot about their efforts to clothe and rear him.

While my father kept his job with George Bean and the £400 contingency fund remained intact, I suppose my problem was less serious than it might have been, although of course I never thought about the £400. I only knew of my mother's tears when I arrived home yet again with torn clothes and my own silent tears in my bedroom that she should think I was uncaring and irresponsible.

The effect of all this was to turn my dislike of McCloud and Scargill into hatred. How I longed to grow tall and be able to pay them back.

My behaviour with these two, and other

boys at the school for that matter, has often puzzled me. After all, I had handled boys like them in Stirling Street and invariably come out on top. As I have said, although small for my age, I was wiry and surprisingly strong.

So why was I such a ready victim for these bullies? I can only think it was the ambience of that school. All my life I've been impressionable to atmosphere and environment, and from the onset that school had seemed to depress me and haul down my spirits. It was to remain this way for the next two years.

But in spite of the bullying and the school that I hated, there were compensations. One was my growing interest in flying. It was the time of the pioneer fliers and most boys were interested in aeroplanes and airships. In my usual way, my interest became total. Soon I was reading every book on aviation that I could afford or borrow. I thrilled at the exploits of the air aces in the First World War. I learned about Allsop and Brown and their epic Atlantic crossing in 1919. I followed every pioneer flight that was taking place with bated breath. With the blotting-paper mind youngsters have, I soon knew as much about modern aircraft and their engines as was humanly possible in my circumstances.

The next step was to build model aircraft and this I did. I even built a dirigible that, filled with coal gas, would fly. I was playing with this in my bedroom, with tiny self-made models of SE5s zooming around it on the very morning when the news came over the radio that the R101 had crashed at Beauvais in France. Later I was to buy a groundsheet of the fabric of her sister ship, the R100, when she was scrapped.

Along with my new friends, I became a public nuisance, flying model aircraft around the street and into people's gardens. When I took the bus to school every day, I would run through in my mind the procedures of take-off as the bus pulled away from each stop: throttle forward, stick back to keep the tail down until my imaginary plane gathered speed, then stick gently forward, more throttle, then back with the stick until I was gloriously airborne. Then the reverse procedure as we slowed down to the next stop. Time and again I would run through this routine, all the way to school and all the way home.

Then, to get nearer real aircraft, I and a friend began walking the five or six miles to the municipal airfield at Hedon. We did this every Saturday, our mouths agape as the little Tiger Moths took off and landed. Eventually we became so well known that the pilots used to wave to us as they swept over the hedge to land. This gave us a tremendous kick, for to us those pilots were full of glamour.

This hero worship must have gone on for months until one of the pilots offered me a free flight. I had no idea how my parents would respond to this offer but equally I'd no intention of going home to ask them. Grabbing the invitation with both hands, I literally ran towards the little plane.

Many years later I tried in a novel to describe the sensations of that first flight. The tremendous noise, the shuddering of the little biplane that made it feel alive, the feeling of great speed, then the incredible moment when the ground fell away. The sight of the great white castles of cloud drifting past, with the sun plying rainbows among their spires. It was one of the great days of my young life and set a seal on my love affair with flying that was to last for many a year.

SEVEN

In spite of my problems at school, my memories of the years spent in the Downing Grove house are not unhappy ones. As children do, I soon made new friends, and although Alice would not have approved of their rugged ways, in view of what was happening to me at school, this tougher environment was no bad thing. For good or bad, my genteel Eversleigh High School days were over and the sooner I acclimatised to this new way of life the better.

Two of the boys I remember well. One, John Sellars, lived with five brothers in a house that stood at one side of a small cul-de-sac that ran behind our house. His father was a docker and as tough as they come. The other boy, Arthur Marsden, was the son of a railway clerk whose house stood at the other side of the small square. The senior Marsden was a tall, cadaverous man with a constant dry cough which my parents attributed to tuberculosis. Anyone with a cough in those days was suspected to have TB. The scourge of the time, it was feared as much as Aids or cancer today.

The two boys were almost replicas of their parents. John was thick set with a shiny red face and spiky fair hair. Arthur was an inch or two taller but painfully thin with stooping shoulders and lanky black hair. Although it was said that their fathers did not like one another, we all played together regardless.

Until one summer evening a few weeks after our move to Downing Grove, when the two boys threw punches at one another and their fathers saw them. Instead of being told to shake hands as would have happened among the middle-class families of my earlier days, both fathers insisted they settled their differences with a proper fight. So buckets were brought out on the pavement and both boys sent out into the middle of the square to settle the quarrel.

I witnessed the entire affair as did both my parents from the rear window of the house although I don't believe that Raymond was present. As neither boy wore boxing gloves it was both brutal and one-sided because Arthur Marsden was totally out-matched by the Sellars boy. Time and time again he was knocked down, to be picked up by his father, have the blood sponged from his face, and then be sent out again.

My mother, unused to such sights, wanted to run out and stop the fight, and it took my father all his time to restrain her. At the time I wondered at this because he was such a gentle person and it was only later that I realised he had learned the unwritten rules from his own background. A boy or a man had to fight until he could fight no longer, and it was a father's duty to see his sons learned the lesson. Otherwise there was no survival in the working class jungle he had known.

So the fight went on until Arthur could no longer stand. After making certain of that, his father shook hands with Sellars senior and then carried the bleeding and exhausted boy back into the house.

It was my first real encounter of the tough

new world in which we now lived and I tend to think it had a profound effect on me. At the time, however, the memories soon faded and within a few days Sellars, Marsden and I were all playing together again as if nothing had happened.

One of the highlights of the year for us children was the Hull Fair, which takes place for one week in early October. Centuries old, only rivalled by the Nottingham Goose Fair, it is, I believe, still held on the Corporation Field, a huge cindered area of ten acres near the heart of the city. That such a valuable piece of real estate is kept solely for one week's use in October says much for the size of the Fair and its importance to the city's economy. Certainly no child would have felt his life complete unless he had not been taken at least once to the huge, noisy, and exciting jamboree.

To approach it one went on foot down Walton Street, a journey that often took twenty minutes because of the dense crowds that shuffled along the narrow road. On either side rickety stalls, lit by naphtha flares and manned by brass-lunged vendors, sold everything a child could desire. There were coconuts, sarsaparilla and brandy snap, pomegranates, balloons, toys of every description and, of course, fish and chips. Other stalls held lotteries, while in the distance the lights of the fairground proper could be seen glowing crimson through the October mist.

It was there the full excitement burst upon one. Lights blazed everywhere, circling on roundabouts, running up big dippers, and flashing down from the helter-skelter. There was the great circus tent of Bostock and Womwells, there were steamboats, cake-walks, fat lady shows, and boxing booths where a young man who fancied his chance could win a whole twenty shillings if he kept on his feet for three rounds against the resident pugs. Among all these attractions and many more, crowds surged, swayed, laughed, and sang. Boys chased squealing girls and blew toy snakes into their faces. The ambience was joyous and the goodwill unrestrained.

For me the main attraction was the steam engines that provided the power for the entire circus. I could stand for hours watching them puffing out steam and listening to the raucous barrel-organ music they provided. I was not so happy among the crowds. I had always felt panic-stricken when people hemmed me in, and my father once had to restrain me when a dense crowd formed around us and I suddenly began kicking out at people's shins.

Nevertheless, I enjoyed my visits to the Fair and it was there that I found another hobby. Mother was with us that night and as we passed a shooting gallery, she urged my father to try to win a prize for me. Until then I hadn't known what an excellent shot he was and I was most impressed (as was the stall attendant, although for a different reason) when we left with half a dozen prizes.

After that I wanted to shoot as well as my father and that Christmas I was given a Diana air rifle with the appropriate warnings how to use it, or, perhaps more fittingly, how not to use it.

In my parents' circumstances it was an expensive present and I remember my intense joy and pride in showing it to my friends. My father helped me to build a safe rifle range in our back garden and my time was now divided between building model aircraft and imagining myself Albert Ball of the RFC, or firing at Red Indians and imagining myself General Custer or Buffalo Bill.

I was very close to my father by this time. He taught me how to shoot at moving targets by keeping both eyes open and soon I began developing the same skill with the rifle that I had achieved with the bow and arrow. Some of the things he and I did sound as if memory has exaggerated them but I can vouch for their truth. We would line up a row of red-tipped matches and from a distance of ten yards set a high percentage alight with the lead pellets we fired. Another trick was to hang a coin on a string, then set it swinging. This we used to hit nine times out of ten by using the open eye technique my father taught me.

However, our pièce de résistance came the following year. We had been to the cinema and in a film had seen a man shoot the ash off another man's cigarette. Afterwards I put up my nose and said that it wasn't so wonderful; we were doing far more difficult things ourselves than that. My father agreed and to my mother's horror he took me outside, lit a cigarette, and invited me to peform the feat from about twenty feet.

Needless to say I was only too willing. Ignoring my poor mother, I lined up and fired, and off went the ash.

Of course, there was hardly any danger. The cigarette was over three inches long and at twenty feet I was hardly likely to miss by that much and hit my father. At the same time it showed what confidence he had in me and also what good nerves he had to stand so still while I fired.

Later we refined this act into what I believe was something of a feat. While he stood with a cigarette in his mouth, I would stand with my back to him and line up the sights of the shoulder-held rifle in a mirror held in my left hand. Then I would pull the trigger with my right thumb and off would go the ash. This trick did make friends and relatives gasp and showed even more what a steady nerve my father had.

One of the happiest memories I shared with him were the days we used to go fishing in the canal at Leven. I can't remember how we got there. Having no car, we must have gone by public transport although I've no memory of this.

But the canal I remember well. I doubt if I used a fishing rod. More likely I used a net because I can remember lying on the bank side and gazing down into the water at the fish swimming below. They often passed in shoals and looked beautiful in the sunlight that reached down to them. As they glided along in rainbow colours, I used to think of Kingsley's WATER BABIES that mother had read to me before I could read myself.

I don't think we ever killed any of the fish we caught. We brought them back in a bowl with a fitted lid and put them into a small fishpond my father had built for me at the bottom of the garden.

During this time I was still visiting the airfield at Hedon. By now I had been seen so often that I had almost become a mascot and one day the pilot who had given me my first flight asked if I would like to loop the loop with him. Thrilled, I said yes and off we went. Clinging to my seat, although I had no need, I watched the earth and sky revolve over me and felt I was the luckiest boy in the world.

I had noticed one thing however as we had

pulled out of our dive. A wrinkle had appeared for a few seconds in the fabric of the starboard lower wing and on landing I suggested to the pilot that the main spar of that wing might have a fracture. Not surprisingly he laughed at me, cuffed my ears, and told me he'd give me another flight when he had the time.

Two days later I saw the picture of a crashed Tiger Moth in my father's newspaper. Recognising from the identification letters on the fuselage that it was the plane I had flown in, I read that the pilot and a passenger had taken off to fly to another airfield when the starboard wings had broken away in mid air and both men had been killed.

At first I dared not tell my parents and it was only because of my distress at the loss of my pilot friend that they heard the full story. To their eternal credit they did not forbid me to fly again but only asked that I should tell them first.

EIGHT

We had not been in Downing Grove very long before my parents had another blow. George Bean, now ailing and with his business in decline, decided to sell the warehouse and his stock. I have no knowledge who took the warehouse over but this new owner had no work for my father and so he was given his cards.

To my mother's dismay this meant the contingency fund had at last to be raided while my father searched for another job. The blow could not have come at a worst time because the Wall Street crash was just beginning to cripple Britain and Europe as American banks and businesses began withdrawing their overseas investments. The knock-on affects were long queues of men outside factory gates all over the nation. With few goods to sell and fewer customers to buy them, salesmen were the first to become redundant and my father was among them. There was no sparing the contingency fund now and even although my mother tightened our expenditure in every way possible, even I as a child could see the harrowing effect on both her and father as the fund shrank lower and lower.

At that time my brother was the only one earning a wage although because he was learning a trade it was only a few shillings a week. And even that pittance was denied my parents because some weeks before my father lost his job, he had moved back to Alice. She had complained about her loneliness and when Raymond began worrying about her, my parents felt they had no alternative but to let him go.

Now that we were living on our savings and every penny had to be counted it was agreed that I could continue taking the bus to school, which was a sacrifice in itself, but public transport was not to be used on any other occasion. This included my weekly sports' day excursions because our school playing fields were a long way from the school's busy urban site. Going to them from school presented no problem because a school bus took us there but once the afternoon sports ended, we had to find our way home as best we could.

How I hated those afternoons. I was still small in stature and, much worse, still under the strange, baleful influence that school held over me. My memory of them are the winter days when the playing field was swept by icy winds and its surface disfigured with sheets of water or ice. We would change in a rickety old shed whose missing planks barely hid our shivering limbs and then sides would be chosen to play one another

Although it cannot have happened every week, memory insists that I was always put into the team that faced the onslaughts of McCloud and Scargill. Moreover, I seemed always to be chosen for right wing whereas McCloud, being built like a brick wall, was always the left back of the opposing team.

The result was mayhem. What with leather

footballs that became as heavy as cannon-balls in wet weather and with McCloud's gleeful attention, for the next eighty minutes I was charged, thumped, and knocked down into every pool of water or ice on the field. Nor did it end there when the match was over. There was still McCloud and Scargill to face in the shed and the miserable business of recovering sodden clothes from the mud where they were invariably thrown when the sports master was not looking.

After that there was the walk home to face. I remember that as painfully as the football itself. In real terms it cannot have been more than three miles to Downing Grove, but in the state I was always in, it seemed like twenty.

Of course my mother would have given me the bus fare had I complained but I doubt if any of us did that. In some ways if not in others we became adults at quite an early age.

To me those memories emphasise the effect environment can have on some children. At Eversleigh High School I had been good at both study and sport: indeed I could truthfully say I had been among the best. At Craven Street I had become a different boy. It was no consolation that at this time I was sharing the top place in my class with another boy (also called Smith). To be good at class work was only to be called a swot, which only added to one's sense of inferiority. To be fair, I can't say the majority of the children treated me badly. Nor were the teachers anything but helpful and encouraging. But after my successes at Eversleigh High school, I despised everything about myself and in modern terms thought myself a pathetic wimp.

By the time 1931 passed into 1932 the problems facing my parents were becoming a full-blown crisis. My mother had used up so much of the contingency fund to clothe and feed us that we were rapidly approaching the point of no return. If we went on much longer without a wage coming in, there would not be enough money left to take a shop, which was the only alternative if we were to escape the rigours of the Means Test to claim State charity, which was an option unthinkable to my parents.

A shop, then, was found at number 739 Holderness Road, on the east side of the city. It boasted two windows and was set back a few yards from the pavement. Basically it was a pastry shop but it also sold sweets and tobacco.

It was not an ideal choice by any means because my parents knew absolutely nothing about the bakery business. Their reason for taking it was its price, which I believe was under two hundred pounds. Moreover, the present bakeress, a Miss Barry, was willing to stay on and give advice on procedure and prices.

Deciding they would have just enough money left over to buy a second-hand van, a necessity in such a business, my parents made the fateful decision and we moved into the new premise in early 1932. I don't think any of us were happy about the move. We had all made friends locally and my parents must have felt nervous at committing themselves to such a risky enterprise.

However, we had no choice and the move was made. The new accommodation consisted of a living room behind the shop, a small dining room, a corridor containing a toilet and a coke bunker and finally the bakery at the back which contained two ovens and pine bench tables.

Above, there was a room over the shop which was to become my mother's 'Front Room', a main bedroom which my parents were to use, a small landing, and then a general purpose room containing the hot water cylinder, a bath and a wash basin. This room had just enough room for a double bed and eventually become the bedroom for my brother and myself when Raymond returned to us. This return happened very soon after our move because Alice had decided to visit Canada yet again. As help was needed to run the shop, Raymond gave up his job in the men's outfitters which he had never liked and became Mother's assistant. At first I believe he was glad of the move.

So our new life began. The day started at five thirty when my father had to wrestle out the clinkers from the coke ovens and then light the ovens so they would be at the right temperature when Miss Barry arrived at six thirty. While she prepared bread, meat pies and general confectionery, my mother and brother would begin cleaning and preparing the shop for its opening at eight thirty.

In the meantime, when the bread and confectionery were ready, my father would stock up his old Trojan van and begin his rounds to outlying districts. I, the only pampered one of the family at this time, would be given breakfast around seven-thirty and later take the tram to school.

A word or two about the van my father had bought might not be wasted. With the shop taking all but a few pounds from the contingency fund, he had been forced to buy the cheapest serviceable one he could find and the Trojan had been the result. Serviceable, however, is a relative word and in this case I doubt if many men other than my father could have driven it. He had learned to drive on the primitive crash-geared wagons of the First World War and so was well equipped to handle vehicles that others would have found fit only for the knackers yard.

Not that the Trojan had crash gears. It boasted a belt drive that hissed and whined quite alarmingly, and with its two stroke engine adding to the din, it could be heard miles away. It smoked and rattled but once it got into motion it did keep going.

The trouble here, of course, was that with his deliveries to make, my father could not keep it going. Every time he had to re-start it, he would have to juggle with the starting handle and then race back into the cab before the engine choked itself. Patient man though he was, he limped home one day with the confession that he had kicked the creature so hard he thought he had broken his toe. Later a customer who had witnessed the deed came into the shop and said he had laughed so much he had cried. It seems after my father had damaged his foot, he had swung round on the amused onlookers and with the sincerity born of pain had offered to give the van away for a box of matches. The fact no one had taken up his offer was perhaps some indication of the creature's appearance and value.

This happened in the first year of its reign with us. In the way of machinery, things got steadily worse in the months that followed. It was not until many years later, when I remembered the van and asked my father how he had suffered it, that I learned the truth. The culprit had not been the Trojan itself but only its battery. But because we were living from hand to mouth at that time, even the few shillings that batteries cost in those days could not be found.

NINE

In spite of everything, our Trojan brought us one great asset. By saving our pennies for petrol, which was cheap those days, we were able to visit places previously denied us.

We could not make these trips often because, apart from the expense, my mother was usually busy at the weekends. But three or four times a year, with my brother and I squashed in the back of the tiny van, we managed to visit our Aunt Hannah and Uncle William in the country.

Hannah was the sister of my father's mother who had died in middle age. Although Hannah's face was as wrinkled as a walnut, she had a heart as big as her body was small. She always wore an apron – at least I never saw her without one – and, like my mother, never seemed to stop working. If she wasn't churning butter in the kitchen, she would be kneading bread. If she wasn't darning William's socks, she would be repairing his britches. With no natural children of her own, although she had adopted one, she clearly loved our visits and as soon as the van stopped and the engine died, Raymond and I in the back of the van would hear her loud cry of delight, followed by her Yorkshire voice welcoming our parents. Then, as we tumbled out, blinking our eyes in the sunlight, she would give another whoop of joy and run forward to kiss us. As she did, I would catch the smell of newly-baked bread that always seemed to hang around her.

In the meantime, William would be standing behind her, grinning and puffing on his pipe. If Hannah always wore a pinny, William always wore a collarless shirt and an old waistcoat. He had a countryman's weathered features, reddish hair streaked with grey, bushy eyebrows and blue eyes that twinkled mischievously. Rumour had it that William Leason had been a lad with women in his younger days and as I look back now, I can believe it.

He would first hold out his huge gnarled hand to my father and then give my mother a bear hug of a greeting. In every way he was a typical East Yorkshire countryman of his time, blunt, undemonstrative, reliable, relatively uneducated and yet astonishingly knowledgeable in his field. I was with him once when we found a cow on its side suffering the agony of bloat. My father wanted to call for a vet but William gave a disparaging grunt, shook his head, and turned to me. 'Run back home, lad, and ask yer aunt to give you the knife sharpener.'

Obeying, I returned with the dagger shaped implement. Taking it, William measured along the cow's flank with his hand, placed the sharp end of the instrument against the animal's bowels, then turned to us. 'Better stand back or she'll blow yer heads off.'

Unsure of what was happening, I stood back with my father. A moment later William screwed up his horny fist and struck hard at the sharpener. As it drove into the cow's intestines, there was a blast of foul gas that made me retch. Grinning, William drew out the sharpener and slapped the cow across the rump. 'Come on, y'old bugger. Yer'll be all reet now.'

Astonishingly the cow lumbered to its feet, moved away and within minutes was cropping grass again.

Such were Hannah and William. They had only to hear that noisy little van chugging down the hill towards the village and they would be out in the lane waiting for us with their arms unfurled.

Their village, Ruston Parva, stood just off the main road to the seaside town of Bridlington. Their cottage was one of a dozen that faced a shallow hill called by the locals 'Hilly-Holey' because of its bumps and hollows. A tiny chapel, no bigger than a cottage itself, stood in the row and on a Sunday the sound of singing would drift across the surrounding fields.

William's cottage was a treasure in itself. Sitting sideways to the others in the row, it had been built during the seventeenth century over a natural spring. This precluded any need to fetch water from the village pump, which other villagers had to do at that time. One had only to descend the stone steps into a cellar, whose coolness made it a natural refrigerator, to fill a pail with water that tasted like nectar.

William's garden rose steeply from a small barn to a tiny church that stood on the hill behind him. At that time it was the smallest church I had ever seen and I doubt whether twenty people could have worshipped there without discomfort. Apart from William's garden, it could be reached by a narrow gravelled path that ran alongside it. It was many years before I learned it was one of the few churches in England that had preserved its sacrificial stone from Cromwell. Apparently it had been hidden beneath the altar to escape detection.

One of the delights of our visits was the food the old couple provided. Everything would come from the garden, the chicken (a great treat in those days) the peas, the beans, the new potatoes, all full of the sweetness of home-grown food. Even the apples of Hannah's delicious pies came from William's half dozen fruit trees.

But the greatest joy of all was the old couple themselves. (I say old because they seemed that to me, although at that time I doubt if they were more than fifty). Sometimes we would go on a Saturday night after the shop was closed and stay the night with them. These were my favourite visits because I loved the evenings there. Like most country people of that period, they lived in their kitchen where a fire always seemed to be burning. The only other light came from a paraffin lamp whose mellow glow took one back to another age.

I liked to listen to the old couple talking to my parents. Not for what they said but for the richness and tempo of their dialect. There was no hurry in their speech: there was no hurry in anything they did. They seemed to have a rhythm that matched the slow passage of the seasons. Even as a child I could feel the tension in me unwinding as I listened and took in their way of life.

There were other things I would watch with fascination. Hannah nearly always had something simmering on the hob, either a large kettle or one of her huge cooking pots, and the presence of these was a source of conflict between her and William. The old man, who always sat in the same chair at the side of the fireplace, smoked some foul smelling shag tobacco which every now and then necessitated his releasing a gob of saliva into the fire. Leaning forward and taking aim, he would fire these bullets with unerring accuracy through the handles of whichever pot Hannah was using that day.

The result was hilarious. Hannah would stiffen and cry: 'You dirty old man! How can you do such things, and in front of visitors too?'

William would give a somewhat sheepish grin, mutter something remotely apologetic, but within a few minutes would forget himself and send another bullet hissing into the fire. My mother, in trying to hide her laughter, would go into hysterics and sometimes have to flee from the room. I, boy-like, was fascinated by such skill and would ask William to do it again.

There was a room in the cottage I loved to creep into. Like other selected rooms of Northern folk, it was seldom used and so one could nearly always be alone there. Its contents were pure Victoriana: a large stuffed owl in a glass cage, a huge Bible whose cover was green with age standing on a lectern, a print of The Monarch of The Glen framed on the wall, and antimacassars everywhere.

But it was the silence and the stillness of the room that used to fascinate me. I would stand motionless and listen to the blood beating in my ears. And when the evening sun slanted through the mullioned window, I would see the dust motes glinting like minute stars as they floated through the last of the sunbeams. In my mind I called it my Autumn Room, and in some way I cannot explain the recollection of it would bring me comfort whenever I had to face danger or horror. But those days of peril were still in the future and undreamed of at that time.

The old couple emanated the same reassurance. I used to think of them as two old oak trees whose branches were intertwined. To me they had the permanence of trees and brought stability and meaning to life. I am sure my parents felt this too.

Raymond and I used to sleep in the front bedroom with our parents on those weekends. They used the huge double bed with its thick feather mattress. We slept on the floor but as we were given another feather mattress, we were equally comfortable. There was a print on the wall whose legend I forget but its purpose was to show the stony path to heaven and the broad path to hell. As the very first step on the way to hell was the cinema, and as I used to save up my pocket money to go whenever I could, I needed the reassurance from my parents that my afterlife was not already prejudiced.

Although there was no possibility of their taking a holiday at this time, they did occasionally leave me there during my school holidays. I have only to close my eyes today to remember the Monday mornings when they would dress in the darkness and then kiss me goodbye.

I would lie listening to my father trying to start up the old van in the yard outside. When at last he succeeded, I would hear William and Hannah saying goodbye to them and then the chug-chugging of the van as it climbed the hill towards the main road. The sound would carry for minutes in the early morning silence and for a moment I would feel very lonely. Then I would drift off to sleep, to awaken with the sun shining through the window, the sound of a carrier's cart coming along the lane, outside, and warm Yorkshire voices exchanging greetings as it paused outside the cottage.

Unlike my experiences at school, I got on well with the local children. One of our favourite games was to take model airplanes into Hilly Holey and by using the warm rising air from a deep hollow in its centre, we could keep our gliders flying longer and higher than elsewhere. It was a game we never seemed to tire of.

Another joy was picking fruit in Mrs Farthing's garden. Mrs Farthing, a widow, had a huge garden full of fruit bushes and as she had far more fruit than she could use herself, would allow us to help ourselves. As a consequence I and friends would disappear into the great thicket of bushes and clamber out hours later stuffed with raspberries, loganberries, and every berry fruit listed in the gardeners' dictionary.

However, all good things have to end and with the school holidays over it was back to Craven Street again. But not for long. In 1932 something happened that became one of the great turning points of my life.

TEN

The news caused great excitement throughout Craven Street School. The entire staff and pupils were to move to a new school that had been built down James Reckett Avenue in East Hull.

It so happened that this building was not far from us, being at the far side of East Park which lay behind our road. I must have known it was being built but because the thought of moving there had never occurred to me, I can't remember thinking or talking about it before.

But how different the situation was now. On hearing the news I rushed through the huge park to view the imposing building that stood behind it. Tall and stately, lined with shining windows, with flower-filled gardens at its feet, I thought it the most beautiful building I had ever seen.

In fact, it was one of the first grammar schools in England designed to give co-education. As a consequence it was built like a huge letter E with the left wing devoted to boys and the right wing to girls. The two large playgrounds behind the school were divided by the central section, although they did meet where the bicycle sheds stood on the edge of the playing fields.

But all this I was to learn later. At that moment I could only think of leaving Craven Street for ever and moving into this palace. I think I hugged myself with anticipation.

Nor was I disappointed. Every aspect that had marred my life at Craven Street was absent here. There were no iron railings, no dark, claustrophobic classrooms, and no littered streets outside. From my classroom desk I could see no smoking chimneys, only the park with its flowers, its trees and its huge lake shining in the sunlight. I felt reborn.

It was hardly an exaggeration to say that I was. According to my parents I grew nearly three inches in my first full term there. Perhaps it isn't inappropriate to think of myself as a seedling that had been kept too long in a dark shed. Now that I was in the sunlight I was growing apace to make up for lost time.

At first, as such things are subjective, I barely noticed the physical change in myself and the bullying of McCloud and Scargill continued, although perhaps not as frequently as before. Their attacks usually took place around the bicycle sheds on the fringe of the boy's playground. As the area behind them could not be overlooked from the school, it was a favourite place for bullying and fights.

Somewhat naturally I kept away from this area as much as possible, although unless one never took part in the impromptu games that were organised during playtime, it was not always possible to do this. One morning in my second term at the school, McCloud and Scargill pounced on me, dragged me behind the shed, and began trying to tear my school tunic which my mother had saved up to buy me. Knowing what sacrifices she had made, I was frantic to save it and in my struggles I struck McCloud in the face.

This was all he needed to justify a full bloodied fight. Grinning at Scargill and then waving him back, he hit me hard and painfully in the mouth.

What happened after that has only moments of clarity. I must have struck him back because there was a yell of 'fight' and in seconds we were surrounded by a horde of yelling children. We wrestled for a moment and then I felt pain in my jaw and the feel of cold cement on my legs. I must have climbed back on my feet, however, because blows began raining on my face and body again.

But it was no longer one-sided. Suddenly the pain disappeared and a massive desire to defeat him took its place. The harder he hit me, the greater the desire grew until it became overwhelming. Nothing in the world mattered now but that I should win this fight.

I could feel my fists striking him and kept hearing him grunt as they landed. Although he must have been hitting me as hard or even harder, I felt nothing. My hatred of his bullying was giving me a strength I never dreamed that I possessed

We fought throughout that morning break and did not hear the bell that sent the crowd of boys reluctantly back to their classrooms. How our absence was explained to our teacher, I never found out, but nobody came looking for us and so our fight continued. Astonishingly, we were still fighting when the school broke up for lunch although how we kept on our feet I shall never know.

My only realisation that the fight was over was when I could find no one to strike. Being unable to see properly because of my swollen and blood-filled eyes, it took a boy's awed voice to tell me that McCloud had finally turned and run away.

At first I could not believe it and felt sure

he would return with renewed strength. But after a quarter of an hour the truth sank it. My persecution was over: I had defeated my oppressor at last.

My poor mother nearly fainted when I walked into the house and there was little wonder. My upper lip was split, both eyes were nearly closed, and I had gashes and bruises everywhere. But no wounds or pain could compete with my satisfaction and the promise I made myself that day. Never again would I submit to a bully, no matter what weapons he chose to use against me. If I have managed to keep that promise over the years, I believe I owe it to that day in 1932 and to the influence that new school had upon me.

During this time my parents were engaged in a grim battle for financial survival. Although the move to the shop had fended off the spectre of total destitution and had even given them the chance to take us out into the country for a few weekends, these concessions were hard won. I have never seen anyone work as hard as my mother did during the seven years she had that shop. As I have said before, she was always the keystone of the family with all the chores women bore in those days, but now on top of them she had a shop to look after and a demanding one at that. Bakeries demand tight schedules and strict controls if money is not to be wasted, and there was precious little leeway for that in our tight budget.

To me she never seemed to stop working. Not even Sundays brought rest because there were the residual household jobs to complete, then the accounts to be done, then the shop to be prepared for the opening on Monday. An endless cycle of work with her only reward the knowledge that she could feed her family for another week.

To be fair, the rest of us did try to help now. I delivered a few customers' orders before doing my homework but not having a bicycle I was limited to those who lived nearby. My brother was willing enough but not surprisingly it was difficult for a young man of seventeen to put his heart into the small business. My father did his best to increase sales to outlying districts but that did not relieve my mother of her work. To be honest, lovely man though my father was, he did not have a good business head and had my mother allowed him to control our accounts I feel certain we would have gone under.

Nor were we much use on the domestic side of things. Perhaps we made a small effort to do this or that task but I doubt if any of it took an ounce of weight off my mother's shoulders. In short her life was one of back-breaking toil.

Even so, she had begun to make small progress. Our trips to Ruston Parva and my school blazer were evidences of that. But as the years were to show, it seemed that whenever she managed to take one step forward, fate would thrust her one step back again.

In this case the set-back came from our bakeress. Seeing no doubt that the shop turnover was improving, she announced that she needed an assistant to cope with the extra demand or she would not be able to carry on. As that extra demand was still pathetically small, her excuse was invalid but, because of her key role, my parents had no option but to allow her to choose one. The transparency of her ultimatum became evident when she arrived the following Monday morning with her niece, Evelyn.

To be fair, I don't believe Evelyn had any part in the plot. Not more than nineteen or twenty, suffering from some illness that made her badly overweight, she was a sweet and gentle girl destined not to live into middle age. We all liked her and she was a counterweight to her somewhat truculent and acerbic aunt.

But liking her and affording her were two different things. Her wage absorbed all the tiny profits the business was making and put us back again to the days when every penny had to be counted.

Back at school I was now in Wilberforce House, named, of course, after the great Hull parliamentarian whose doughty efforts had freed the Empire's slaves (after my dealings with McCloud, perhaps an appropriate house for me). The other two houses were also named after two of Hull's famous sons: Andrew Marvell and De La Pole. I was pleased at my selection because at that time Wilberforce house was pre-eminent in most fields, particularly sport, and now that Craven Street had lost its baleful influence on me, my keenness on physical activities was growing again.

At home my brother's interest in the theatre was becoming more and more practical. He and a friend named Harold (I don't remember his surname) became interested in tap dancing, which was very popular at the time, and the two of them started practising dancing as a duo. These sessions often took part at home where my mother allowed them to use her sitting room upstairs.

These sessions went on throughout 1933 and today I feel shame for the way I behaved towards my brother. Sissy was the word used for a boy with artistic leanings in those days, and perhaps afraid that my friends would find out about Raymond's theatrical ambitions, I began to make fun of them. (Considering what I was to become myself in later years, it was more than ironic). Nevertheless, I behaved for a while like the kind of macho boy that I had previously disliked, and during that period my brother and I became less than friends.

To make matters worse I think Raymond knew that my parents sided with me, although for different reasons. My mother did not want him to leave home yet and also felt the stage was far too insecure a profession. My father had the same fears for him and although he was too liberal a man to say it, I had the impression he also wished Raymond would choose a more traditional career. As I was to learn to my discomfort many years later, the Andy Capp remark: 'Why doesn't the bugger get a real job?' was a sentiment most Northerners shared in those days.

So my brother gained little support for his ambitions and it's hardly surprising that when he turned 18, he announced he wanted to go to London to try his luck on the stage. To my parents' credit they did not try to stop him, although, apart from my mother's worry at his leaving home so young (18 was young in those days), it also meant she was losing her only shop assistant.

So Raymond went and the work load on my mother increased yet again. For my part I can't say that I missed him as much as I might have done. Because of Alice, he had already spent a great deal of time away from home and her behaviour had never allowed us to be the kind of brothers my parents would have wished. The bitter fruits of this were now apparent.

I would be approaching puberty around this time. It showed only mildly at first, mostly at our watching the girls at playtime. If we went to the bicycle sheds, we could see round the central wing into their playground. In turn they could see us, and I remember how one of them used to position herself at the end of the wing so that the wind could blow up her navy skirt. It did little for me at that time but seemed to do a great deal more for the older boys who would push us out of the way to gain a better view.

There was always great excitement among these older boys at the beginning of every new autumn term. The school policy was to integrate the two sexes from the fourth form onwards, and with every boy hoping his class would contain the prettiest girls of the year, tension ran high on opening day when the headmaster read out the names of the senior classes. No doubt there was similar excitement and anticipation among the girls.

The expressed reason for this policy was to teach both sexes at an early age to live side by side, which in the case of the boys meant losing some of their aggressive ways and improving their manners. What it did not say in those inhibited days was that it also served as an outlet for sexual urges. As I was to learn some years later, it is not always the denial of sex itself that causes frustration. It is also the absence of the other sex in the normal walks of life. Their very presence acts like a safety valve, allowing the more potent pressures of youthful sexuality to ease away. If that safety valve is denied, as in segregated schools, the pressures are more likely to break out in ways that cause private distress and social disruption.

Without labouring the point, I consider grammar schools of this conviction gave us the finest emotional education that a child could get. Certainly I shall always be grateful for the years I spent at that school and the many lessons it taught me.

ELEVEN

Christmas Day 1933 stands out in my mind because it was the day my parents gave me a bicycle. It was new, had a Sturmey-Archer three speed gear, and had cost them a whole two pounds and ten shillings, which meant they must have been saving up for it for the entire year.

Even so, I think they must have thought it worth while when they witnessed my reaction. No wealthy son receiving a Maserati from his parents could have displayed half the joy I felt on coming down the stairs and finding the shining bicycle awaiting me.

I could hardly believe it. Was it really mine? Entirely mine? This beautiful thing with wheels that spun so silkily when I turned it upside down and spun round the pedals? I was in raptures. I could not leave it even to eat my meals. I would take a bite and then run out of the room to make sure it was still there.

I could not ride it yet but that did not matter. For a while I was amply content to look at it, polish it, and imagine all the exciting things it and I would do together. Part of me was that kind of child. One whose imagination could provide adventures that real life found difficult to match.

But there was the other side of me too. My father helped me to learn to ride the bicycle. After I practised in the park for a couple of days (fearful for the precious bike every time I fell off in case it suffered damage) I was finally allowed out on the public roads but only with his driving the old Trojan alongside me as a shield. We practised this way until he was satisfied I was safe to go out alone.

My happiness was now unconfined. My horizons were no longer limited to the distances I could walk or the tram fares we could barely afford. Now I could ride round the city with my friends and even venture as far as the seaside.

It was not many months before I was doing this. Bridlington, a seaside resort I liked, was some thirty miles away. With packed lunches in our saddlebags, a friend and myself would leave by 8 a.m. and arrive there well before noon. We would stay for at least four hours and still be back home before the spring darkness fell.

It was not long before we grew even more ambitious and pedalled all the way to Scarborough, some fifty-five miles away. This was a hard ride because of the undulating country beyond Bridlington but I can't remember either of us feeling distressed or over-tired.

Years later when I had sons of my own and they had bicycles, they used to tease me when I told them of the distances we used to ride. 'Don't give us that, Dad. You never did 110 miles in a day. Not when you were only fourteen.'

I couldn't blame them for their scepticism. As the demands on each generation lessens, the physical need to meet those demands lessens with it. It makes one wonder what will be the physical outcome if western nations continue to improve their standard of living.

There was a practical use for my bicycle which I'm certain my parents had never considered when they bought it but which gave me considerable satisfaction. I could now make deliveries to customers well out of walking distance. This I began to do in the evenings before starting my homework and also on Saturday mornings. It helped both my parents and I enjoyed doing it.

It was around this time that an unpleasant rash appeared between my fingers and my toes. I was the first to complain about it but soon my mother and father developed the same symptoms. It meant seeing the doctor – a procedure one avoided whenever possible because of the cost – and he pronounced it scabies – almost certainly caught from coins handed in by shop customers. The answer was a course of treatment at the City Sulphur baths, which were maintained for this purpose, and we were given authority to attend them.

I found my first trip to them quite intimidating. The building seemed huge to my eyes and with steam everywhere and attendants walking about in caps and aprons I thought of horror films in which one was at the mercy of zombies. I had to leave my clothes in a cubicle and walk naked down a stone corridor into a large tiled room full of sulphur fumes. A large bath full of steaming water stood in the centre and an attendant told me to jump into it.

The water was very hot and I lowered myself down gingerly. The fumes made me cough and for a moment I thought I was going to choke. The attendant handed me a piece of rough antiseptic soap and told me to wash myself all over and particularly between my fingers and toes. Then he left me for what seemed an interminable time. I remember my throat feeling quite sore when I emerged into the fresh air at last.

We all had to go three or four times before the contagion was cured. My mother was quite horrified by the experience. She said it made her feel unclean and I'm sure she felt in some way it was all her fault.

Meanwhile, after the set back over the bakeress, the shop was slowly making headway again and with their hard-won gains my parents took on a shop assistant. I doubt if they could really afford her but with my brother now in London, my mother could not handle the extra work any longer.

So Sadie came into our lives. She was in her early twenties, a brunette of average height and build, quite pretty, and, most of all, full of fun.

Sadie became my first love. I was fourteen when it happened, with all the mysterious emotions of puberty stirring within me, and they focussed on the cheerful, laughing lass who brought gaiety into the house. Until then the sheer hard work my mother had faced, the dreaded bills that had to be met, and the almost daily complaints from Miss Barry, had made it a somewhat joyless household.

This was perhaps one reason why my father was going out more in the evenings to the local pubs (although it must be said that this was common practice among Northerners at that time). He was a man who loved life and gaiety and yet life had given him precious little return for his affection. Since the war, the years of struggle must have seemed endlessly grey to him and I think he needed those few hours of escape each night to enable him to carry on.

My mother, on the other hand, was basically a shy and more serious-minded person who found little pleasure in pubs and noisy company. This is not to suggest she was a killjoy who was never heard to laugh or sing, but there is no doubt she saw life differently to my father. As this trait had held the family together through all its traumas and provided me with everything a young boy could need, I am the last one to be critical but at the same time I can understand my father's need to find relaxation outside the family. I believe it was this difference in their temperaments that explains what was to happen later.

Whatever the reasons – and who knows what is in anyone's mind even when they are as close as we were – there was not much gaiety in the house until Sadie arrived. Then there was laughter again and even Miss Barry was seen to smile now and then.

My parents liked her so much that sometimes they invited her and her boy friend to go out with us on Sundays. By this time we were the proud owners of a bull-nosed Morris which we owed to a surprising burst of generosity by Alice, who had lent my mother £40 to replace the old Trojan. With this windfall, my father had bought the second-hand Morris and after chugging about in the old van, we felt like royalty riding in a real car. Our Sunday trips usually took us to Thornwick Bay where I would spend the day climbing the chalk cliffs and exploring the caves.

On our return home, Sadie would sit next to me, and as I was usually sleepy after my exertions, she would put her arm around me and draw my head down to her breast. I was old enough now to know something about a woman's body and would feel all kind of mysterious but exciting sensations as the car ran us back home.

Was she aware what I was feeling? She must have noticed how my young eyes used to follow her about and rest on her. If she was aware of my young infatuation, she handled it with kindness and discretion and in ways that made me like and trust women.

I had never ceased to enjoy books but at this time my favourite reading became the popular magazines written by Frank Richards. These were the Magnet and the Gem and dealt with the adventures and escapades of youngsters at public schools. In the case of the Magnet it was the Famous Five led by the peerless Harry Wharton. Their school was Greyfriars and populated by such immortal figures as Billy Bunter, Bolsover, and cads like Skinner and Co.

I used to love these yarns and had no problem whatever in reader identification. Locked in my room, I would share their problems and their successes. I would score the winning goals with Bob Cherry when the match had seemed lost and knock a century at cricket with Hurree Singh to put Greyfriars at the top of the league. And when the Famous Five went on holiday in the country, as they invariably did, I would share the leafy lanes of England with them.

I have often pondered on the effect these yarns had on our young minds. Popular magazines though they were, a strong moral theme ran through them all. The Famous Five never cheated to get their ends – only Skinner and his fellow cads attempted that and they were always found out and punished. None of the Five ever struck below the belt and none of them would dream of harming his moral or physical health by betting, drinking, or smoking. And all were loyal to one another, sometimes to the point of foolishness.

It all sounds very priggish on present day standards and of course it is easy to find faults. They were stories about privileged boys and how much easier it is to hold up the banner of righteousness when one has enough food in one's stomach to support its weight. And I'm sure if I were to read them again I would find tinges of snobbishness and racism that went quite unnoticed in those days.

Nevertheless, most of us boys read them, wealthy or poor, and I don't think many of us felt envy or resentment that we could not share their privileged world. I know I did not. I admired their moral standards and although it was more of a subconscious ideal than an expressed one, I think there was a vague hope in me that my life style would be acceptable to them if ever we met.

Whatever other effects they had, they certainly generated in me a love for the English countryside. One story comes readily to mind. The Famous Five bought an old motor tricycle and took it on holiday in the south of England. From then on, as in Jeffrey Farnell's novels, the pages were full of descriptions of leafy lanes, sunlit ponds, and old world villages. They fired my imagination and when my bicycle arrived, I rode out to find these English treasures. My love of the countryside has survived to this day and I believe I owe that in no small measure to Frank Richards' comics that, whatever their triteness elsewhere, possessed qualities that all literature for the young should possess.

There is one other book I must mention: Bevis by Richard Jeffries. To me it is the greatest book ever written about young boys and their aspirations. I must have read it twenty times when I was around the same age as Bevis and his friend Mark, and in the few cubic inches of my mind I ran with them across sunlit fields, sailed in their homemade boat to their secret island, and shared their every dream. No boy should be allowed to grow up until a copy of this wonderful book has been given to him.

TWELVE

My days at school were relatively uneventful now until I reached the Fourth form. All the bullying from McCloud and Scargill had long ceased and indeed my only sight of them now was in the playground. A system of selection existed that at a certain age put pupils into four classes according to their academic progress, and as the brains of these two were in their hands and feet, they were now in the lowest form of their age group.

For myself, I had continued to grow, although not quite as startling as in my first year, and was now at least fully comparable in height to most of the boys of my age and more muscular than most. One way and another, the athletic promise I had shown when a small child at Eversleigh High School was becoming evident again now that I had regained my confidence. I could not help noticing that I was stronger than most other boys and could run faster than them.

This discovery was reinforced by our gymnasium instructor, an ex-sergeant major named Hankinson, who told me that I could do extremely well at athletic sports, particularly at sprinting, if I put my mind to it. Because he saw this promise in me, he tended to give me more attention than he gave other boys under his tuition.

In some ways this was not a good thing for me. Tending to have a multi-sided nature, and having been small for so long and suffering because of it, I was now revelling in my newly-found strength and began devoting more time to sport than to my studies.

There was, however, another more aesthetic reason for this desire to build up my physique. Having seen photographs of Greek statues in the many books I had read, I felt a desire to build a body with similar proportions.

It sounds a narcissine wish but I did have a predilection for shape and beauty, and it seemed the most natural thing in the world to try to build one's body in the mould of those superb statues that I admired so much.

In hindsight I suspect this wish might have come from a copy of Richard Jefferies' work 'The Story of my Heart' in which he expresses a similar wish to achieve physical symmetry when he was young. As he was my favourite author at that time, perhaps it was his book that gave me the same youthful aspirations.

Whatever the motivation, I joined a body-building club, became a useful member of the school football and cricket teams, and could not wait for the annual sports day to come round. It was all a far cry from my winter ordeals at Craven Street.

Girls were now taking up a greater part of our thoughts and as this was our first year of mixed education, excitement ran high when the names of the girls who were to share our classroom were read out. When the list was completed and we put our heads together, it was generally agreed that we were lucky and had secured more than our share of the belles of the school. Among them was Becky Davidson whose beauty and gaiety made her as popular with the girls as the boys. As Becky seemed oblivious of me, I had no hint at that time of the part she was eventually to play in my young life.

Although I suppose we boasted of our successes with girls as boys tend to do, in fact we were extremely naive and backward in our dealings with them. At least I was. I never seemed to have the courage to ask a girl to go out with me, and had to be content with admiring them from afar or riding behind them on my bicycle when coming or going to school. Indeed, one could do little else on these occasions because fraternisation was frowned on and it was forbidden to escort girls to school.

It was in the evenings when the flirting was done. East Park was the favourite spot. It had a tracked road that ran in a huge circle inside it, and on summer nights local girls would ride round it with boys cycling in pursuit. I say in pursuit but the girls had only to dismount and in nine cases out of ten the boys would lose their courage and cycle a few yards past them before dismounting. Then they would talk loudly among themselves and pretend that girls were the last thing in the world that interested them.

I have often wondered why we were so shy of them. Receiving no sex education whatever, we did not know they were as eager to make contact as we were. It is true that exceptional cases occurred and one heard rumours that this boy or that boy had got into trouble with a girl. But on the whole we treated them with shyness and diffidence and they, wily creatures that they are, took full advantage of our naivety.

To a modern teenager, this shyness would seem a huge handicap in achieving satisfactory relations between the sexes, and if one is thinking only in terms of sex, it certainly was. But there is more to man than his body, and in a teenager the romantic side often exists in inverse ratio to his sexual satisfaction. When such a teenager is denied sex with his personal goddess, his imagination tends to glorify it into pure ecstasy. Conversely if he is allowed sex, the outcome is often a let-down, for reality seldom matches anticipation, particularly when indulged in by a young and clumsy lover. To put it another way, what we lost on the roundabouts we gained on the swings. Indeed, I believe that some of us gained more. There were never any disappointments in our mental sexual relations. Every act was perfect, with romantic music playing in the background and the scent of roses redolent in the air. And afterwards no fears of pregnancy, with all the disgrace for the boy and the girl that that entailed.

There is no doubt this fear was a powerful deterrent. To give a girl a child in those days could mean the ruination of one's life. Although girls were not being expelled from their families as frequently as their mothers' generation had been, they were nevertheless totally disgraced. In turn the boy was expected to marry her when both came of age and with both carrying the scars of guilt, such marriages often became private hells without hope of escape, because divorces were both expensive and difficult to obtain.

This fear was reinforced by our sexual ignorance. In spite of all our talk, I doubt if many of us knew what was safe and what was dangerous, and so even 'heavy petting' was a risk we were afraid to take. No doubt some couples practised it and one heard stories about girls who allowed boys certain latitudes, but in general our sex was limited to kissing, cuddling, and the occasional fumble which the girls would enjoy for a few seconds before pulling our hands away.

Nevertheless I can't remember any feelings of frustration because of the way the young mind romanticises the unattainable. I remember vividly a dark-haired beauty in the 5th form when I was in the 4th – a gap of a whole year that put her way beyond my reach. She lived in a village twenty miles from Hull, yet every Saturday that summer, after I had done my errands for the shop, I would cycle out to the village in the hope of seeing her.

I never did see her there and I would probably have run a mile if I had. Nor did she ever know about the boy who thought her so beautiful. But with my young mind inventing all kinds of romantic adventures on my journeys to the village, they remain some of my happy memories of that year. Perhaps it all goes to show that the only real experiences exist in the mind.

It was during this time that my interest in music began to grow, although at first only with the popular variety. Bing Crosby had recently made his debut and one could hardly turn on the wireless without hearing his light but pleasant voice crooning some new song. The first one I remember was 'When the Blue of the Night meets the Gold of the Day'. Soon we were all singing or whistling it and Bing's fame grew apace as he came up with a new song almost every week.

Radio, of course, was our chief source of entertainment and our equivalent to pop music programmes were the dance bands that played every night from one or other of the London hotels. Henry Hall, Roy Fox, Ambrose, were but a few of them and it was their performances that usually introduced us to new songs.

I was greatly enjoying myself at school now. For this a great deal of credit must go to the headmaster, Harry Shoosmith, and his staff. The rules that governed us were strict but fair, and in my experience children, and in particular boys, respect and like living under such a regime.

Certainly this was true of my generation. We knew exactly where the parameters were, which meant the well-behaved or more nervous students had no fear of committing indiscretions by default. Equally the adventurous ones or the rebels were fully aware of their transgressions when they crossed the boundary lines and so felt no resentment when they received the cane or six strokes across the buttocks. I know this from personal experience, for I never felt the slightest hostility towards my headmaster (the only one allowed to use the heavier cane) when he gave me a spanking. I had deserved it and knew it. The affair ended there.

We were, nevertheless, lucky in having excellent teachers. In those days (so I was told in later years by Harry Shoosmith) there was such a glut of teachers and so little employment for them, that a grammar school headmaster could pick and choose among the best. I doubt if we had one teacher without a first honours degree in his subject and all seemed competent in class management.

One thing I never experienced was the 'crush' that some pupils are said to get for teachers of their own sex. My interests were entirely for the opposite sex throughout the whole of my puberty. But then I never encountered any boy at that school who had such a fixation. Perhaps this was another of the advantages gained from that sensible co-educational policy.

At that time we used to have examinations

at the end of each term, enabling the teachers to see what progress we had made. In general they were not popular but I used to look forward to them. Examinations were a challenge and I have always liked challenges.

Not that I could face them with the confidence of high attainment. At this time I was only about halfway between the top and bottom of the class and in one or two subjects, I was relatively weak. But I had one asset. Because of my Eversleigh High School background, I was good at written English and because of the amount of reading I had done, I knew how to tell a good tale. As a result I found it easy to camouflage my ignorance with well-sounding phrases. The Armed Services taught me later the catchword for this, which begins with Bull and ended with Brains. There's no doubt I used it to good effect throughout the whole of my academic career.

THIRTEEN

A significant thing happened to me towards the middle of my year in the 4th Form although at the time I had no idea of its effect on my future. It was a wet winter day and from my desk alongside the window I could hear the splash of rain on the paths that led up to the school. I remember feeling disappointed because we were due to play a Beverley team at football that afternoon and as their ground was badly drained, they cancelled matches in bad weather.

The lesson that morning dealt with lesser English essayists and my inattention was noticed by Miss Fawcett. 'Smith boy,' she complained, an address she always used as if it were necessary to distinguish us from the girls at the other side of the classroom. 'Stop looking out of the window and pay attention!'

How often it is in life that small things have the greatest significance. Had she not noticed my wool gathering that morning, I might never have paid attention to the essay that was under analysis, which in turn might have changed the entire tenor of my life.

I believe the essay was entitled RAIN and written by Robert Lynd. At first no title could have seemed less appropriate that day. Determined that I should not backslide again, Miss Fawcett made me stand up and read a few paragraphs aloud.

At first they were just words that I read. Then, quite suddenly, they became alive. The raindrops on the window became tiny tadpoles that squirmed and ran down the glass. The paths and pavements below turned into silken carpets that reflected the sky. I saw rain as I had never seen rain before and barely heard Miss Fawcett congratulating me on my reading as I sat down with the book still in my hand. Gazing out of the window again I realised there was beauty out there and not just disappointment.

Looking back, it is odd why that essay affected me so much. After all, I had been an avid reader all my young life and my imagination had found no difficulty in turning words into vision and sometimes into experiences more real than reality. Then why did I find those particular words so graphic and why did I suddenly think it wonderful that words could transform an everyday scene into fairyland?

I must have taken it all for granted before. Now my maturing mind was beginning to understand the art and music that lay behind carefully chosen words. I remember thinking all that day how wonderful it must be to have the power to use words so expressively.

At the same time I don't think I suddenly wanted to be a writer. Writers were like film stars and dance band leaders: exotic creatures who lived in another world to ourselves. Perhaps that was another way in which we differed from youngsters today. The ambience of our lives did not allow us the confidence to believe we could ever become such people. But admiration we could have and from that day I made careful note of the author's names on all the books I read and loved.

Some time during that term there was a boxing championship held at the school and I entered it. I got through the first and second fights comfortably enough but in the third I had the misfortune to meet a boy whose father had been an ABA champion. Naturally enough he had passed on his skills to his son, who in build and style looked more like a professional welterweight than a schoolboy.

I survived the first two minutes more by good luck than skill but towards the end of the round received a blow to the chin that put me down on the canvas. My next conscious moment came in the dressing room with the sergeant major bathing my face. Naturally enough, I thought I had been knocked out and carried there. When I spoke in those terms Hankinson showed surprise. 'Of course you weren't knocked out, lad. How could you have been? You fought on for the next two rounds.'

Later I learned it was true and that I had performed reasonably well into the bargain. At the time, however, it sounded like nonsense and I said so. Believing no doubt that my mind was fuddled by the beating I'd received – and from my appearance it had been the granddaddy of a beating – the sergeant major took no notice of my protests and insisted I had put up a splendid fight.

He never believed my explanation and the fight became one of his favourite stories. It was acclaim totally undeserved because not a vestige of courage was involved. I had been as unconscious of what was happening as if I had been anaesthetised.

It was around this time that my school friendships began to crystallise. Until then I can't remember any name standing out more than another, but by that winter there were some whose friendship was to last a lifetime. Two, Stewart Cottingham and Frank Holland, were in the same year. As all three of us were members of Wilberforce House, we played in the same football team, Stewart in goal and Frank and myself on the left and right wings respectively. On one great occasion, because Wilberforce house had a particularly strong football team, we were lined up against the combined strength of both the other houses. We not only won this game but Frank and I scored the two winning goals! Friendships, I am sure, have been forged on lesser triumphs!

My keenness of sport led me to try all that were available. I can remember playing a kind of makeshift ice hockey on the park boating lake. This makes one wonder if the winters were colder than they are today, as I have not heard of ice being thick enough to take the weight of so many youngsters since. On the other hand it might have been a freak winter when we played.

Unlike my days at Craven Street, when the reverse was true, I find it more difficult to remember what we did during those winters of the Thirties than in the summers. Reading was certainly one of my chief pastimes. Apart from the Public Libraries, which I used a great deal, there was also the Green Circle Libraries chain which existed. Devoted to books which, for a few pence could be taken out on loan, they were usually well patronised because they bought the latest publications.

The cinema was another popular entertainment. Most charged from nine pence to one and sixpence a seat and changed its programmes twice a week. The contents of these films, however, are worth a mention in today's climate.

Married couples never shared the same bed. If hubby wanted to kiss his wife he had to keep one foot firmly anchored to the floor which must have made procreation an acrobatic miracle. Single lovers were even less fortunate. A soft pressure of the lips was their only consolation before they were shooed off to their lonely beds. As for sexual relationships, which at the best were only inferred, a mistress was always a baddie and the wronged wife invariably a suffering angel.

Violence was always sanitised: one rarely saw blood on the screen. If a film contained any scene resembling blood, an announcement would be made beforehand giving the assurance that a nurse was available should anyone be overcome. Even then any blood shown would be no more than a small dark stain on a man's shirt.

Blows never broke a man's chin; they merely made him shake his head and come back for more. Villains were always ugly or at least had sardonic lips while heroes were Anglo-Saxon Aryans with godlike features. Villains, who always got their comeuppances, were also very bad shots while heroes always hit their target. And lovers always won through in the end no matter how heavy the odds.

What did all this unreality do to my generation? Why has no in-depth study of its effects been made? After all, the cinema was one of our major forms of entertainment and yet on its tinsel screen we saw life not as it is but as its Hayes Committee felt it should be. Not once a week but twice if we were lucky.

It must have had some effect on us. The question is what. Did it make us reckless and braver, remembering how Douglas Fairbanks could fight a dozen rogues single-handed and still emerge unscathed to embrace his sweetheart? Or did it have the reverse effect and turn us into cowards when we discovered a blow to the chin with a hard fist did much more than knock the smile from our faces?

Did it make us more moral sexually when we saw our heroes behaving with such gentlemanly restraint when they were so obviously fired with passion? Or did it give us an undeserved confidence to know that, whatever the odds, life would always ensure our love affair would be successful and in the end win through?

Did it make us feel better towards life by the promises it gave? It certainly made people forget for a couple of hours the harshness of their lives. Was this soporific a good thing or a bad? Did it make us gentler people by its inferences or did it eventually embitter us when we grew older and discovered its promises were false. I don't profess to know the answers. I only ask the questions.

I can't remember listening to the radio a great deal at this time with the exception of the dance bands and important sporting events. The Cup Final comes to mind here. The Radio Times and some of the newspapers used to print a map of Wembley with the pitch itself sectioned into squares – from memory it was eight. These were for reference when the commentator began his description of the game. As the ball was kicked from one imaginary square to another, he would give the number from his own chart. It worked quite well and had one great advantage over television. Because one never saw the players make mistakes or commit fouls, they were always chivalrous and charismatic. Television might have lined their pockets far more since those days but it has done precious little for their image. It seems that life must always balance the scales.

FOURTEEN

By this time the hard work my parents had put into the shop was beginning to show results. We were not comfortable yet but at least bills could be paid and there was enough money over for us to afford a few more Sunday trips in the bull-nosed Morris. Sadie was still with us and along with her boy friend we did a number of trips to Flamborough that summer.

In my memory it never rained on those days. The sun shone from a cloudless sky, the gulls wheeled lazily over the white cliffs, and the sea was like blue satin.

In retrospect this was perhaps the golden year of my youth. My parents had lost their worried appearance and the feeling of strain that had haunted the house for so long had disappeared. I found this an immense relief.

To add to this I had never been happier at school or at play. Life seemed full of promise as in the summer evenings we cycled round East Park, either racing one another or looking for girls. At other times we would organise games of cricket or, if we had the money, hire a rowing boat and spend an hour rowing round the huge lake that ran the full width of the park.

Then there were bicycle trips out into the country. A friend and I would take food with us and after a couple of hours of cycling sink down among the cow parsley on the roadside and have our lunch. Apart from the local seaside resorts, we would go to the dales that surround Hull and sometimes even as far as Weedley or Millington Springs where we would pick and eat watercress.

To me the beauty of cycling, apart from the physical exercise that I enjoyed, was one's intimacy with the countryside. You could smell the hedges as you rode past, hear the birds, feel the wind on your cheeks. Much as I enjoyed our outings in the car I could not help noticing how one was insulated from the scents and vibrancies of a summer's day.

Not that it was all sunshine and sweetness. With little or no insecticides in use, the insect population was controlled only by the birds, and on a summer day the sound of insects in the country was like an insistent organ note. We had no trouble from them when cycling but they could be a harassment during a picnic. On one occasion my uncle, Harold Wilson, who was now working for the manufacturers of Fairy Soap, took me and a friend out in his small car to a local beauty spot by a river. In the fashion of the time he groomed his hair with brilliantine and its scent must have resembled the sexual pheromones of flies. For no sooner had he stepped out of the car than a buzzing black cloud settled on his head.

We tried to help him but in vain. With a yell of dismay he fled to the river, there to bury his head in the water. Only when the last scent of that aphrodiastic grooming had been washed away could he return to us. It was noticeable that the next time we met, the scent of his brilliantine had markedly changed.

During that summer there was a professional sports meeting held at a venue not far from Beverley and one of the boys at school, named Samuels, with athletic ambitions like myself suggested we entered it, he in the mile race and I in the 220 yards.

It was a reckless idea because the boundaries between amateur and professional sports were strictly defined in those days, and had we been found out it might well have been the end of our sporting ambitions. At the same time there were virtually no opportunities for promising youngsters to gain attention unless they attended the fashionable and expensive public schools. To make matters even worse, we lived in East Yorkshire and if any Northern sportsman today thinks he is neglected, he should have lived in the Thirties. It's highly debatable whether the sporting hierarchy in the south had heard there was an England north of the Watford Gap, much less young people there with athletic promise.

So this was a chance to test ourselves against some of the best athletes in the land and the temptation proved too much. Sammy and I saved up our pocket money for the entrance fee and posted it off with our entry forms signed by pseudonyms.

I should mention here that neither of my parents knew anything about the risks involved. Neither had played any athletic sports: my mother because it had not been fashionable for young ladies at her private school to gallop around a hockey pitch and my father because all his youthful energy had gone into supporting his widowed mother and family. Consequently they were ignorant about the amateur and professional divide and thought my entry was nothing more than a schoolboy prank.

Indeed, my father drove us to the venue. I

think both Sammy and I had a twinge of apprehension at our first sight of the field. There was a huge marquee, a number of smaller tents, and a roped off circular track where the sports were to take place. Hundreds of people were already there: some lined up along the ropes that ran round the track, some relaxing on the grass, and others quaffing beer in the marquee. But what caught our eyes were the men standing on tables shouting and waving their arms. Having no idea what they were doing, I had to ask my father. Looking concerned for the first time, he told us they were bookies taking bets on the competitors.

Because there was money involved, a handicap system operated. To my disgust I was given only a yard and a half start in my 220 yards and Sammy had a similarly poor handicap. When my father complained, pointing out we were only schoolboys, he was told it was the custom to give all unknown entrants a minimum handicap in case they were professionals entering under assumed names. As there was no answer to that, we left to get ready.

The smaller tents served as changing rooms for the various disciplines and mine was full of huge muscular men, as sprinters tend to be. The air stank of strong liniment and made me cough. I remember feeling very much a schoolboy as I changed into my strip and the running spikes that my parents had bought me the previous Christmas. I saw men eyeing me and a huge one with a yellow headband asked me who I was. When they discovered I was only a schoolboy at my first games they became very friendly, and one stocky man wearing a blue vest slapped me across the back and wished me luck.

I felt very nervous when we lined up for the first heat. The crowd surrounding the track was huge now and I could hear the bookies calling out the odds in the pause before the starter fired his gun. Nevertheless, nerves or not, it was a new and exciting experience and I knew I was enjoying it.

The gun went off and I ran as hard as I could. That is all I remember about that heat and the one that followed. I must have been among the leaders, however, because I qualified for the final that was scheduled towards the end of the meeting.

I don't remember feeling particularly elated. By this time I'd heard so many stories, either from other competitors or members of the crowd about races being rigged, about runners sewing lead into their spikes in order to gain greater handicaps at other meetings, that I began to feel this was the only reason I had qualified.

My father did not agree with me because by this time the bookies had taken notice of my name and were shortening the odds. I remained unconvinced and went to watch Sammy run the mile.

With his poor handicap he stood no chance. He was in an event that called for the stamina that comes with maturity and like myself he was only sixteen. Even so, although he did not qualify for the final, he told me he enjoyed the experience. After changing he came to watch my final.

I believe there were eight men in it, although I can't be certain of this. As the quarter mile track was circular in shape we had to run round two bends. There were no lanes provided but as our handicaps staggered us, this would cause no problems at the start. The problems would come on the bends when the handicaps began to cancel out.

If I had remembered nothing about the heats, I remembered every detail of that final. Because I had such a poor handicap, I was behind everyone but the scratch man when the gun went off and so could see nearly everything that happened from beginning to end. And what I saw both astonished and scared me.

The first incident came on the foremost bend. One man was running on the very inside of the track and a short stocky sprinter edged past him and then cut in sharply, causing the other to chop his stride. It was deliberately done and I heard the offended man curse and shout something out.

Nevertheless he recovered, held his ground, and as we approached the second bend he began to catch up with the stocky man. As he drew level with him he somehow flicked the spikes of his outer foot behind and across, catching the stocky man in his calf. From the corner of my eye I saw blood spurt as the spikes tore the man's leg and then saw him hurtle through the ropes into the spectators.

While I was seeing this I was catching up with both men and knew that if I was to gain a place, I had to pass this acrobat who could perform such an astonishing feat while running at top speed. It was obviously something he must have practised many times, making me wonder if he would allow a mere schoolboy to pass him.

I had to try and so put my foot down. For a moment we were running side by side and any second I expected to feel his spikes in my leg. Instead he began to fall behind and I knew I was safe. After the race was over this same man walked over and congratulated me.

I was so relieved to finish the race in one piece that I was some time realising I had come first and won the fortune of twenty pounds. To add to the unreality I was told that the man who had come second had won at Powderhall the previous year. Reality only began to sink in when trainers began to crowd around me. I suppose they saw money in me if I were properly trained and questions and invitations were flung at me from all sides.

My father rescued me and after collecting my prize, we drove away. For days I found it difficult to believe what had happened. How had that man performed such a vindictive feat while running at top speed? And had I really won a race against some of the best sprinters in the land?

It was my father who laughed at my fears that the race had been rigged. He had spoken to the timekeepers and one had told him that two watches had clocked me at 22.00 seconds. Or, if scaled down to 200 metres, 21.66 seconds. Even allowing for stop watch errors, it did seem an exceptional time for a boy of sixteen and promised much faster times when I was older and properly trained.

Certainly, as the more graphic details of the race began to fade in my mind, my feelings were strengthened that I could win the school championship if I were to stay at school one more year, when my strength would began to match that of boys of eighteen years and more.

To spend another year at school, however, meant one of two very different things. If I were to pass my matriculation in the major exams due in the late summer, I could move up into the Sixth Form and take my Higher

School Examination. Success here meant entrance to university if one's parents could afford it. This I thought unrealistic and I put it out of my mind.

The other possibility was a less glorious one. If I failed my Matriculation, the educational system would allow me a further year in the Fifth Form to take it again.

To be fair to myself, this was what usually happened. To obtain one's Oxford Certificate, one had to obtain a pass in all subjects. To gain Matriculation in the same examination, one had to obtain a credit in all subjects, which few did. The norm was to stay on for a further year in the Fifth Form to gain those extra credits.

To my horror, on my first attempt I nearly failed my Oxford Certificate altogether. Although I gained credits in all other subjects, I failed abysmally in French. (Foreign languages were always my weakness). However, I was saved by a special dispensation that granted me the Oxford Certificate because I had done exceptionally well in English and Physics.

This meant, of course, that to obtain Matriculation I would have to pass every subject with a credit again, which was the somewhat harsh rule in those days. As it meant another year in the Fifth form, I cared little about that but it seemed hard on my parents to have to pay my fees for another year, and I wasn't happy in putting the case to them.

The result was never in doubt. They would not hear of my leaving school without the advantages of matriculation and so to my secret delight I found myself with another year of school ahead of me and with it the possibility of winning the school sports championship.

1935, then, was a good year for me in which even my failures brought me profit. I look back on it as the sunlit year of my youth, the year without the shadows that were soon to fall upon my family.

FIFTEEN

1936 started auspiciously enough. Our neighbour Mr Fox, being appropriately dark-haired as the custom demanded and a coal merchant to boot, brought in the New Year for us by knocking on the shop door as the church bells and the ship sirens sounded. He then presented us with a slice of bread and a piece of coal. My mother, in some ways more traditional than my father, would, I think, have felt unease if the age-old ceremony had not taken place.

It was a New Year when we thought ourselves fortunate. Shop trade was improving, Raymond had written to say he had found work with a Repertory Company, which he was enjoying, and I was to stay at school until September. In all it looked like being a second good year.

Yet it proved to be a false dawn. Our first hint of this came when my mother saw a man standing outside the shop window and writing down prices on a pad. When she went outside and asked if she could help him, he gave a somewhat sheepish shake of the head and walked away. I could not miss the apprehension of both parents when they discussed the incident over supper that night.

The next shadow appeared when Sadie gave in her notice. Her reason was innocent enough: she and her boy friend were to be married within the next few weeks and she wanted time to make her preparations.

We were all sorry to see her go. Her fun-loving ways had helped my parents to survive the difficult days of the past, and although I had now reached the age when girls of my own age attracted me, I knew I would always remember her for the way she had understood my youthful infatuation and handled it so gently.

Her replacement was a woman named Elsie. Although I doubt that she was more than thirty, to me she seemed much older than Sadie. She had lived for many years in Detroit (although I don't think she was American by birth) and I took advantage of this by asking all kinds of questions about the USA. She was a pleasant enough woman but I think we all missed Sadie's laughter.

But the real blow was to fall a few weeks later. I came home from school to find my mother in tears and was told that the large grocery and off-licence shop fifty yards away had opened out as a confectioners. Ovens had been installed and the owner was selling bread and pastry at a totally uncompetitive price.

I ran to the shop and saw she was right. The intention was clear enough, to drive us into insolvency or bankruptcy and then take over all our trade.

It was my first experience of the cut-throat world of business. I had already learned that life could be a struggle but until then I think I had put it down to luck or fate and not to the ruthless greed of my own kind.

From information my father received later, the move had been no snap decision. The owner, an alderman, a churchgoer and already a wealthy man, had been watching our shop ever since we moved in. During the time it had barely paid its way, he had held his hand. When it had turned the corner, his interest had sharpened. He had waited until he felt the pickings were worthwhile and then reached out to grab them.

Another bitter lesson I learned was how frail loyalty can be. Because of her nature, my mother had often been her own enemy in her treatment to customers. She had often given credit when the business could not afford it, and many a distressed housewife whose husband had lost his job had had a free bread loaf or bar of chocolate slipped into her carrier bag.

From the autobiography she was to write many years later, it was the loss of such customers that hurt her most because she had thought of them as friends. With times being hard, she could understand their saving pennies wherever they could, but to see them avoiding her gaze as they hurried past the shop caused her considerable distress.

But to the young all experiences are lessons and this one taught me the vulnerability of a small shop as a source of income for those with limited means. Fixed on one site, it is at the mercy of those that patronise it. It also acts as a trial kite for the business hounds whose appetites are insatiable. If the shop fails, they search elsewhere. If it succeeds, they bound in and take its business over.

Not that our shop collapsed at once. After three to four weeks our alderman had to raise his prices to our own level and so the massive haemorrhage ceased.

But the damage had been done. Not only did he keep a number of our customers by offering them certain 'loss leaders' but his earlier tactics had drained away the small cushion of reserves my parents had built up so painfully over the last years. We were back to living a hand to mouth existence again, with every penny having to be counted. Inevitably Elsie's position became precarious. My mother argued she could manage on her own again but, worried about her health, my father fought against the idea and so for the moment Elsie stayed with us.

I was old enough now to feel some responsibility for my board and lodgings, and in spite of the forthcoming school championships, felt I had to offer to leave school and look for a job.

My parents would not hear of it. They had already paid the two pounds ten shilling for the winter term and would somehow find the money for the summer term when I would sit for my Matriculation again.

Although nothing was said to me, I knew this meant one thing. Whatever my athletic ambitions, I must now put my academic studies first. It was the least I owed my parents.

Although it was not a prospect I relished, I need not have fretted over it because fate was shortly to take from me the need for painful decisions. It happened on a bitter windswept day during a football match in March.

We were playing away on a pitch that was hardly fit for a clash of arms, much less a football match. Indeed, for me it had the undertones of battle because the full back who was marking me was an enormous lad, well over six feet in height and built like a Sumo wrestler. Every time I was given the ball he would hurl himself at me like a bull charging a red flag. Most times I was quick enough to elude him but the few times he caught me I was sent hurtling yards into the mud. Before the interval came, my feelings about him were on a par with my one-time feelings about McCloud.

But the real disaster of the day happened just before halftime. As I received a pass and turned with the ball, my right foot dropped into a hole in the ground, possibly made by a rabbit. At the same moment the bull's huge knee hit the same bent leg and we both spun round on the trapped limb.

I heard a loud crack, felt a shock of pain, and fell in a heap to the ground. As I was trying to rise, the whistle went for halftime.

I was helped to a bench and the referee, one of the teachers from our opponents' school, came over to ask if I was all right. Feeling no pain from my knee, I told him that I was.

What follows makes little sense to me although no doubt a modern sports physiotherapist could explain it. The lack of pain was no doubt the sign of a serious injury but my ability to walk on the damaged knee becomes something of a mystery when the true seriousness of the injury was eventually diagnosed.

Nevertheless, when the whistle sounded, I was able to return to the field without help. It is true I was limping a little and my knee felt numb but that seemed only natural after the punishment it had received. I even ran on the leg when the ball was sent in my direction.

It was only when I kicked the ball that the thing exploded. I felt a quite horrendous shock of pain and my leg felt as if it had come apart. There was no standing up and walking this time. I had to be carried off the field into the dressing room. Although I remember little about it, I was told later the knee had swollen so much by this time that my shorts had to be cut to remove them.

So I was taken home and a doctor was called in. He, foolish man, decided that I was suffering from a bad sprain and would be all right in a week or two if I rested the leg. For that he took a fee that must have caused my parents even more problems.

The leg was no better after a fortnight's rest. The knee remained swollen and I found it quite impossible to walk. After the doctor was called in again, to give a similar idiotic diagnosis, it became clear a specialist's opinion was necessary but now there was the problem of finding the money for one.

After another two weeks resting the leg, during which time I was falling behind in my school lessons, three old people to whom I had delivered confectionery prior to my injury, offered to help. From county stock, they consisted of two spinster sisters and a brother. He, the brother, was becoming incontinent and the two old ladies were finding it increasingly difficult to nurse him throughout the night.

So they made a deal with my mother. If she would help to nurse the brother for six nights a week, they would pay for me to see a specialist. They would also pay her the princely sum of ten shillings a week for her attendance.

Incredibly my mother agreed. Fortunately Elsie was still with us but even so my mother was needed in the shop during the day, both to handle problems and to keep Miss Barry from dominating the shop girl.

How she fitted all these duties in I'll never know. When she slept, I'll never know. But in the evenings after supper, she would pick up her holdall, kiss us goodnight, and make her way down Holderness Road to the old folks' house. I'm not certain what time she arrived back in the mornings but she was always there to give me breakfast. She continued doing this for the rest of that year and long into the next. How she did it only God knows.

In the meantime I was taken to a specialist who X-rayed my knee. He said that not only had ligaments been badly stretched and the outer cartilage torn but there had been damage to the bone itself. Fortunately this bone damage had now healed relatively well but it would be months before the joint would bear my weight again. In the meantime I would have to wear a steel knee bandage if I were to continue at school. From the look he gave my father when I asked how long it would be before I could sprint again, I knew that my athletic ambitions could now be forgotten.

It will be noted that there was no mention of removing the cartilage whose torn condition was to plague me at intervals throughout my life. Non-critical operations of this nature were not even suggested to those who clearly could not afford them.

So I returned to school a virtual cripple and when sports day came I watched the events with my father from the sidelines. I can't deny shedding a tear or two that night but when I thought about the sacrifice my mother was making for me, they had to be shed in private. She was, without any question at all, a woman in a million.

I had one consolation during this time, Becky Davidson, whom I had previously admired without receiving the slightest hint of encouragement, eyed me sympathetically when at last I limped into the classroom and actually spoke to me at break time. It was little more than 'I'm sorry to hear about your accident,' but she did keep enquiring about my leg in the days ahead and although there was nothing in them to give me hope of a deeper relationship, they did provide a few shafts of sunlight in the gloom of that year

For a while I was very sorry for myself. I couldn't cycle into the park to see my friends and flirt with girls; I couldn't go out into the country; I couldn't even walk fifty yards. With my horizons suddenly tight around me, I had no choice but to open my text books and study, particularly French.

Yet it is interesting to speculate on the role that misfortunes play in our lives. In mine, events that seemed absolute disasters at the time have so often turned out blessings in disguise. To a boy of sixteen with athletic ambitions, a crippling leg injury seemed almost the end of the world, and yet it not only concentrated my mind on my studies but it also showed me the lengths my mother would go to help me. That knowledge not only deepened our relationship but also seemed to promote my maturity. I became much more aware of my parents' struggle for survival and for the first time I genuinely wanted to leave school and to find a job.

At the same time, this increased awareness

posed its own problems. Once I had enjoyed the challenge of examinations. Now, more conscious of their importance, I felt nervous when the big three days arrived and we sat at desks moved into the gymnasium under the supervision of scrutinisers.

Although I had prepared well enough, this nervousness left me feeling my papers were inadequate, and during the interminable four weeks' wait for results, I was very apprehensive. When the results finally appeared in the newspapers, my misgivings seemed justified. Although I had done very well in the other subjects, I had still only received a pass in French.

In the normal run of things this meant I had failed Matriculation again. And this was my last chance! I had not only failed myself but I had failed my parents too. I was quite shattered.

Then came the glorious reprieve. Because I had done so well in the other subjects, the Examiners decided to give me yet another dispensation. I was awarded Matriculation after all.

So my school days ended. I had first enjoyed them, then hated them, and finally enjoyed them again. Now I had to enrol in that big, somewhat mysterious world outside where failure was not a reproving word from a well-meaning school teacher but often a brutal dismissal. I think that but for my parents' experiences in business, I would have looked forward to the challenge. As it was, I could not help feeling some apprehension.

SIXTEEN

For my first job I tried to get into the Police Force. I can't think why but whatever the reason, I failed. In those days one had to be six feet in height and at that time I was half an inch short and did not reach my full growth for another three years.

With the labour market still stagnant, jobs were few and far between but one day my father noticed that there was a vacancy in the City Guildhall for a junior clerk and told me to apply for it.

At the time it seemed a long shot because in those days City Hall jobs were called 'plum jobs' and consequently there was a long queue of young hopefuls inside the Guildhall when I arrived for my interview. My heart sank when I saw them and not only because of their numbers. Every one was wearing a suit and not possessing one I was dressed in a sports coat and grey flannels. It seemed my cause was lost before it had begun.

One by one we were called in to face the

Great Man, the City Treasurer. I remember little of the interview except his interest in my name. 'F.E. Smith', he said. 'Ah, yes. You bear an illustrious name, Smith. Do you realise that?'

As a matter of fact, I did. Since my very first days at school, my teachers had commented on or teased me about my name, for in those days Lord Birkenhead's doings, anecdotes, and escapades were newsworthy and my name never failed to raise a comment. In fact, my nickname at school was F.E., and I was known as FE right throughout my school years.

So the Great One's comment came as no surprise and after he mentioned its similarity to my famous forebear, I thought the matter ended there.

But not so. A week later I received a letter saying my application was successful. My wage as a junior clerk would be fifteen shillings a week, paid monthly, and I would work five and a half days a week, beginning on weekdays at nine o'clock and ending at five thirty, with one and a half hours for lunch. Saturdays would be from nine to twelve thirty.

In those days these were good hours. After my initial astonishment I wondered why I had been given the job. Had it been my different appearance or had it been my name? Whatever the reason I began work in the Hull Guildhall two weeks later.

The office given me handled wages, insurance, and superannuating. At the time it was run by five clerks with its chief, Frank Gosling.

Frank Gosling was in his middle forties, a stocky man with the gruffish voice and blunt manner that some Yorkshiremen possess and which can hide basic geniality. He wore reading glasses and, as he made a point, he would give one a long stare over them.

But my assessment of him and my other colleagues was to come later. All my attention that morning was needed for the jobs I was given. In short they were to keep the insurance cards of all the city's municipal workers up to date by stamping them with the insurance contributions deducted from their wages. These would vary according to the age of the worker, but for an adult man they were one shilling and eight pence for health insurance and one shilling and sixpence for unemployment.

A second job was to help the rest of the office staff to pay the workers their weekly wages. But the third job I must mention in some detail because of the difference it shows in yesterday's climate and that of today. It was to accompany one George Claude Brown on every Thursday to buy the aforementioned health and insurance stamps. The average weekly sum to buy the stamps was never less than four thousand pounds, the equivalent today of perhaps eighty thousand. And who was detailed to take this money to the General Post office? George Claude Brown, who although as pleasant a man as one could find, would have been hard pressed to fend off the attack of a stunted pygmy. And who was sent to be his guardian? The youngest junior in the office.

From a work point of view it made sense. From a security aspect it was absurd. And yet was it? For years, and for all I know for centuries, this practice of sending unarmed and ingenuous couriers to the Post Office had been in vogue without a single case of assault and theft being known.

Nor was the outing merely to the Post Office and back. As it was the only time any of us escaped from the building during our working week, we couriers were honour bound not to spoil it for our successors. Which meant that after buying the stamps, George Claude would lead me into the City Market where we would listen to the brass-voiced vendors selling their wares and then on to the local Kardomah café where he would buy us both a coffee before glancing at his watch and suggesting it might be a good idea to get back to the office. All this with a briefcase stuffed with four thousand pounds of legal currency tucked under his arm.

A new boy to the game, I was sweating not

in fear of being robbed but what Frank Gosling would say to us on our return. But even Gosling knew his role in the weekly ritual. He swung round in his revolving chair to stare at us over his glasses but George Claude had savoir faire. Without batting an eyelash, he deposited the stamps into a metal cabinet, thanking me for accompanying him, and then took his seat without a hair on his head out of place.

To me nothing has ever illustrated more the difference between then and now. How long would such a couple last today? Two weeks perhaps. One week for their task to be identified and another for a hit to be arranged. Yet I was to escort Claude Brown for over two years every Thursday and we had not one moment of unease.

The innocence of those days also showed in our office on Fridays. Being the pay point for all the various workers within reach of the Guildhall, we received trays of sealed packets first thing in the morning, a tray for the workers of each department. While it was true that the average wage in each packet would be little more than two pounds ten shillings (£2.50), by the time all the trays were in the office there were thousands of pounds lying on tables in full view of anyone who entered. Yet to my knowledge there had never been a robbery since the practice began.

In fact, I was never shown where the alarm bell was and only found out when I caught sight of a rusted metal stud at the foot of the counter and asked its purpose. Later, when someone decided it might be prudent to see if it still worked, it was discovered that the electric cable from it had long been disconnected.

Nor can I forget the honesty of the workmen we served. Because glue was used to seal down the pay envelopes, it sometimes happened that two envelopes would stick together and during the hectic Friday afternoons it was easy to give a man two packets instead of one. Yet in my entire time in that office I never knew a case when a man who had been given two packets inadvertently did not return the extra packet to us. These were men who in most cases were having a difficult struggle in feeding and clothing their families, with no social security to back up their efforts. Their honesty renewed my affection for the working class that I had gained during my Sterling Street days.

The same disciplines held at the football matches that my father and I sometimes attended. It is true that he was a fan of rugby league: a code that has kept its harmony between spectators to this day, but I never saw or heard of any trouble between soccer fans either. There was no segregation of spectators. Everyone mixed in together, indeed listening to the wits cracking sardonic jokes about their neighbour's team was often more enjoyable than the match that followed.

Why was there this general lack of malice in spectators? Did they have a better assessment of sport in relation to the harsh world around them? If they had, it seems strange when one remembers that a football match was often the only pleasure many workmen enjoyed throughout their entire working week.

The accusation of looking back though rose-tinted spectacles is a criticism a man always receives when discussing his early years. Yet what is he to do? To deny what he saw in order to appease his critics?

Perhaps the harsh conditions of those days burned up the aggressive tendencies of people. Perhaps the general poverty met everywhere gave them more sympathy for their own kind. Whatever the reason, the facts argue against the belief, so prevalent today, that crime is the first child of poverty. Indeed, if social conditions alone are allowed to dictate judgements, then the Western world today could argue with total justification that wealth, not poverty, is the father of crime. (What a cat that would be to throw in among the pigeons!)

I soon found the worst part of my job came after the insurance stamps had been bought.

They had then to be affixed to every worker's card and that took up three days of every week. During these days the hands of the round-faced clock on the opposite wall would creep along like some sadistic snail, pausing at intervals to show me it was the master and it would dictate when my boredom would end.

But of course there were compensations. The outstanding one was returning home with my first pay packet. For the first time I was contributing money to my parents instead of taking it from them. That was a feeling to remember. I felt a grown up man that night.

I believe my mother gave me back five shillings of every pound I earned. It was more than most of my friends were given and I felt like a millionaire with it. I could go to the cinema more often, take out more library books, and even afford to take a girl out occasionally. This I did as often as possible because my interest in girls was now at its peak. At the same time I think I still laboured under the fear that one passionate hug might break them in half. I had a year or two to go yet before I was to learn they are made of much sterner stuff than that.

SEVENTEEN

My first year in the Guildhall was uneventful but it was not so at home. Although my contribution had helped a little, the finances of the shop were in steady decline and it was becoming obvious that unless some drastic action was taken soon, the business might go bankrupt.

To my parents, and particularly my mother, bankruptcy was the ultimate disgrace. It meant in effect that one had taken goods without the means to pay for them, and in their code that was dishonest, no matter what circumstances had driven them to it. To avoid this stigma, every effort, no matter how self-punitive, had to be made.

Every effort was made, even, I understand, to the point of my mother asking Alice for a loan to tide things over. I was not told the result but when there was no improvement in our life style I had to assume the answer had been negative

At this point my mother was still nursing the old man in spite of our efforts to dissuade her. The ten shillings a week she was earning had become an essential part of our income. I believe, or like to believe, that I offered her more of my salary at this time but can't remember her taking it.

So tension was growing at home as the weeks passed by but I can't lie and say that the problem was casting too great a shadow over me. I had reached those teenage years when the body is thrilling to new strengths and sensations and the mind is intoxicated by them. In other words I had entered the golden meadowlands of youth when the world centres around one. A time of selfishness when creation itself seems designed for one's pleasure.

God knows, it does not last. Soon the misfortunes of others return to cloud one's consciousness and rain begins to fall in dreamland. But how ironical and contradictory it is that self-gratification should come from self-interest. Perhaps it is not a thought to be dwelt on too deeply.

It was during this time that I became interested in the guitar. Why the guitar, I have no idea. I had always enjoyed listening to my mother play the piano and for a while had tinkered with the thought of learning to play it. So why my allegiance had changed is a mystery. Perhaps I had heard a guitar played solo on the radio or perhaps I had heard the 'Hot Club of France' who were making their debut around this time. Whatever the reason, the guitar it was, and I did not rest until I had saved enough pocket money to buy a cheap, second-hand one. I also bought a course on guitar playing and from then on, in my somewhat obsessional way, spent much of my spare time learning how to play it by taking lessons from a professional player called Roland Ford. These lessons enabled me to play the instrument solo and not merely to twang chords. Encouraged by this, I asked my mother if she would accompany me.

At first she was reluctant. Since taking the shop, she had hardly had time to touch the keyboard. However, I kept on nagging at her and soon she began to enjoy playing again. Having learned the theory of music from my tutor I was able to transpose sheet piano music into music for the guitar. As in those days popular tunes were released as sheet music at sixpence a time and as often there would be one or two new releases a week I was soon spending most of my pocket money on them.

As this sheet music meant my mother and I could now play together. I practised harder than ever and soon we were playing duets two and sometimes three evenings a week. I know she enjoyed these evenings as much as I did, and they remain some of the happiest memories of my youth.

It is, however, fascinating to compare the popular music of those days with its equivalent today. In the main the accent then was romantic. Music that caressed rather than inflamed the passions. Today it is often aggressive. It does not soften the emotions, it hardens them with its pounding beat. To us who have lived in many places it is the music that primitives use to incite.

One wonders why. Contemporaries say it is a manifestation of the times but that is not born out by the facts. When romantic and emotional music ruled the world, the two bloodiest and most destructive wars in history were fought by the very people who whistled or sang those songs.

So why has there been such a violent change? Is it because the aggressiveness of man must always come out and if there are no wars to indulge it, it must surface in other ways? Or is it because the sexual revolution has killed romance and so killed the songs it created? As so often happens, I do not venture to answer. I only ask the question.

A new man moved into my Guildhall office at this time. Named John Gemmell, twenty-six years old, a small man wearing glasses almost as thick as pebbles, he was not an impressive figure until one noticed the eyes behind those glasses. They were as shiny and bright as polished buttons. Moreover I noticed that Frank Gosling, that most un-demonstrative of men, arranged for a desk to be drawn up alongside his own which even I recognised as a kind of accolade. Gemmell was clearly regarded as an asset to our office.

A word should be said here about Frank Gosling. On my first day in the office, I received a lecture from him about my duties to the general public. We were, he told me, their servants. If they happened to be artisans or labourers, the fact we enjoyed better conditions than they was due to circumstance, not to some imagined superiority. They all paid our wages, either from their rates or from their taxes, and it was our obligation and duty to be attentive and polite to them at all times.

It was a directive he made certain we carried out. If we did not jump to our feet and go to the counter the moment a man or woman appeared, he would turn and glare at us over his spectacles.

His directives did not stop there. At all times we had to be thorough. Slipshod work he would not tolerate. In this he reminded me of my father's dictum: that if a job was worth doing, it was worth doing well.

Of course we used to think his behaviour impossibly authoritarian, particularly when he would time how long we spent in the toilet, which he quite often did. At such times we called him a grumpy old bastard and worse.

But he knew that once a good habit is drilled into the young, it is harder to remove it than to practise it. Frank Gosling was a superb chief for a young man to have in his formative years, and whenever I go into a public office today or find myself waiting in a store for someone to serve me, I find myself wishing to God his kind were alive and managing the world today.

Switching back to Johnnie Gemmell it was not until I made an enquiry about our pensioners that he took real notice of me. I had noticed that workmen who had been hale and hearty all their lives had a high death rate after going on pension. It happened so often that one day I asked Gemmell what the statistics were. He looked at me with those bright, intelligent eyes as if he had not seen me before, and told me that statistically one pensioner in two died within the first six months of his retirement.

I remember feeling quite shocked at this figure. I don't know what I replied but after that day John Gemmell took more notice of me and sometimes chatted to me when Gosling was out of the office. It was the beginning of a friendship that was to last a lifetime.

However I was never able to forget those statistics. In spite of their longing to retire, did those men die because somewhere in their subconscious a tolling bell told them they were now only wastage, that the world no longer required them? Did that in turn set off a chain reaction that eroded and destroyed bodies that previously had been strong and upright? The more I thought about it the more I decided that somehow or other I would never retire.

Nevertheless it is very likely that I might have remained in the Guildhall and had to accept retirement had not Hitler been busy inciting and fostering German aggression on the other side of the Channel. Ever since 1934 we had kept hearing his voice on the radio, haranguing or cajoling at one of his rallies, and more and more the threat from Germany had grown in our minds. There are those who say that, because of the way our newspapers tended to play down the dangers, the general public had no suspicion of the holocaust to come, but that did not apply to me and my close friends. Even in my last year at school I remember discussing the possibility of another war, although in those days and indeed in the two years that followed, our inclinations were pacifist.

This was hardly surprising. Most of us had fathers who had fought in the First World War and few of them had emerged with anything else but disgust at the carnage and cynicism at the broken promises that followed. If they did not actually tell us that men were fools to fight for capitalism, it was implicit in their expressions. If it had been suggested to them there could be such a thing as a 'good' war', fought for something other than profit, I feel most would have laughed at our naivety.

Perhaps they were right and it is impossible. The depths of moral judgements tend to be in direct ratio to one's distance from the killing fields. Certainly at this point in time we tended to side with our fathers, particularly when our headmaster, a veteran himself, enrolled many of us into the League of Nations Union, whose purpose was to proscribe war as a means of settling differences between nations.

It was while taking round leaflets for this union that I was to see the poverty that existed at that time. Prior to it, I had thought my family had suffered hardship, but I was soon to learn the lesson that there are always people far worse off than oneself.

I met them in the Stoneferry district of Hull. Our task was to urge people to sign the anti-war leaflets we carried, which meant knocking on doors and asking to see the adult member of the household.

The sights we saw are hard to believe. One would knock on a door, a gruff voice would shout out, then the door would swing open and light flood out into the darkened street.

The first impression would be the smell.

Thick and fetid, it sometimes made me retch. But the sight inside was often worse. Adults and children would be everywhere, sitting on broken-down furniture, on tea chests, and often on the floor. Washing would be hanging down from string tied from wall to wall. Mould from steam and moisture stained the walls. To add to a surrealistic nightmare, unwashed babies would be wailing and adults often screaming at one another.

To me it was like looking into hell but it was undoubtedly the way some people lived in the Thirties. Needless to say our petitions did not fare well in this area. We were not attacked for our temerity, which gave credit to their tolerance, but I did learn words that were to stand me in good stead some four years later.

So we were not warlike youngsters in the Thirties. I mention this because not long after the war the absurd assertion was heard that we who had served in the RAF were a bloodthirsty generation who had enjoyed dropping bombs on women and children. How little they knew of the mental conflicts we went through before deciding we had no option but to fight.

Not that this means we spent our entire time discussing the possibility of war and the role we should play if it came. We were still teenagers and who at that age can really believe that one's dreams might soon end in mud and blood? The spring is too exciting, the sky is too blue, and girls are too beautiful. One is too full of the songs of youth to hear the distant drums.

EIGHTEEN

1938 was the year when the shell of my euphoria was broken open, and it happened in ways I would never have thought possible.

It began as such things often do, on a muted and seemingly harmless note. By this time our office paying out procedures on Fridays had been changed. To ease the congestion, a table was set up in the adjacent office and certain sections of the public were paid there. Among them were the Home Helps. These were women of all ages and as I was given the task of paying them, the younger ones often used to tease me. I was embarrassed at first but soon learned how to hold my own.

There was one woman, however, whose behaviour I could not understand. About forty, she was slim with dark hair and attractive features. I noticed her at first because voices have always been an important feature to me and she had a quiet, well-modulated way of speaking that was quite different to the cheerful but often shrill voices of the others.

But there was more than her voice to catch my attention. I noticed that whenever I handed over her wage packet, she would look at me and give me a smile that seemed to have no connection with the act. It was not a woman's inviting smile, it was a tender one, almost as if she were related to me and longed but was afraid to make that relationship known. Also she would sometimes pause at the door when leaving, and although pretending to check her money, she would keep glancing my way with a look that can only be described as fond.

Although I felt it must be a sexual advance, I also noticed that the moment our eyes met, she would look apprehensive and hurry away. Eric Blackburn, who shared the office with George Claude, had no doubt what it signified. 'She fancies you, Smithy. She likes 'em young. Why don't you do her a favour? She's a good looking woman.'

His teasing was taken up by Claude Brown and I began to dread the woman's appearance. In turn, she must have become conscious of the amusement her behaviour had caused because she ceased looking at me, although I always received a rather sad little smile when I handed over her wage packet.

It was all explained one night that summer. I had been in the park with some friends and it was after ten o' clock when I returned home to find my mother crying bitterly. Believing it was the usual problem, the shop finances, I asked what had happened but she would not tell me. Instead she sobbed and sobbed as if her heart would break. This was not like her because she was a brave woman who sooner or later always came to terms with her problems.

So I continued to question her until finally she broke down and confessed. Someone had come into the shop that day and told her my father was having an affair with a woman who worked in the Home Helps Department.

I was quite stunned. Until then I had never thought of my parents as people with the feelings and desires I was now experiencing myself. If I had given thought to how my brother and I had been conceived – and I had not – it would have been by two people who had become immediately sexless after our birth. People who had become mother and father, whose only function thereafter was to bring up their children. Moreover they were over forty years old!

It was an incredible revelation and at first I could not believe it. But then I remembered the slim woman's behaviour towards me and I realised it might well be true.

Naturally enough I took mother's side and waited up with her to confront my father on his arrival home. I remember how I dreaded the moment, how my mouth was dry, and my heart thumping in my chest and throat. I had to attack the man I loved and I felt as if my world was collapsing around me.

I don't know which one of us suffered more during that confrontation, my mother, my father, or I. Not that there was a quarrel. My father hardly spoke a word while my mother and I made our accusations. His face just seemed to grow paler and more drawn as if we were raining physical blows on him. At the end, still without making any excuses for himself, he picked up his hat and turned away but not before I noticed tears in his eyes. Half a minute later we heard the car drive away.

My mother cried for most of that night and so did I. For a while I hated my father. A full twenty-four hours passed before he came back to tell mother he wanted to see her in private. I remember he tried to grip my arm as he passed by and I shrank back as if he had suddenly become a leper.

I could hear them talking through the wall that separated our bedrooms and it seemed to me they talked most of the night. In the morning my mother drew me aside and told me the matter was closed. She had forgiven my father on his promise never to see the woman again.

I dreaded the next Friday when I would pay the Home Helps again. Perhaps I had a vision of the woman berating me for helping to break up her affair. I wished later that she had done this, because what followed was far worse. She took her pay packet, glanced up at me and then whispered: 'I'm sorry, my dear. I really am so terribly sorry.' Then she hurried from the room and I never saw her again. When I made enquiries I discovered she had resigned from the department.

Although my father's attitude towards me did not change in the slightest way, it took me some time to behave the same way towards him, although no doubt embarrassment at the things I had said was one reason. I was torn with ambivalent feelings because I could not forget that he was the man who had carried me on his back when I was a child; played with me; and given me some of my happiest memories. Whatever his sin and whatever things my mother had the right to say, I began to realise he had not deserved my self-righteous condemnation.

At that time I thought of it in simplistic terms. I had always known women found him attractive. Even as a child I had noticed this and now assumed he had taken advantage of this charisma. When I was told by Eric Blackburn, who handled the woman's resignation, that she was a war widow without children, I was too young to put any significance on this discovery.

It took years and another war for me to

realise what a young prig I had been. My father had been one of that lost generation who, because of his father's early death, had sacrificed his young days to support his mother and family, and as a reward had been given four years of hell in the trenches. Only those who fight in a war understand the changes it can inflict on a man: not only the loss of faith but the change in values and concepts. A man learns to recognise loneliness in others because he has experienced it himself, and nothing can upset social conventions more than pity.

Perhaps I am wrong about my father. Perhaps he was only a man trying to relieve the grey monotony of his days. God knows, there had been precious few rays of sunlight in them, and he was a man who needed fun and laughter as others need food and drink.

But always my mind returns to that woman with that sad, wistful smile. My father was a man who could see into another's heart. He had so often seen into mine and put his arm round my shoulders, as he had done during my days at Craven Street School. Had he seen into this woman's heart too and perceived her racking loneliness? If he had, then he was not a man to count the cost to himself.

In the end a choice had been forced upon him and I wince to think of the miseries it might have caused. What had happened to the woman afterwards? Had she been left imprisoned in some dingy apartment with nothing to look forward to but a future of poverty and loneliness? Was she to blame, as my mother always insisted, or was she, like my father, a victim of a world that cruelly betrays its children but still expects them to obey its self-righteous commandments?

I cannot blame my mother for her reaction. Women were told to link extramarital relations with betrayal and she was a woman of her time in both courage and concepts. She also loved my father very dearly and must have been terrified at the thought of losing him, particularly at that moment.

Yet what a pity it seems that society has never found a way of extending its love and compassion into those realms that belong to that foremost and most precious of all virtues, charity.

If this affair caused a storm in our family it was but a prelude to the hurricane that was to come. It seems that before I had returned home that evening, my mother had phoned Alice to ask for advice. It had been a natural enough act for a daughter in such circumstances, but my grandmother was no comforting parent with suggestions how to settle the affair with the minimum of damage. On the contrary, it simply fed oil on the fire of her dislike of my father, and her advice was draconian. A private detective, whom she would employ herself, must be used at once to obtain evidence, and when that evidence was forthcoming my mother must sue for divorce.

It was the last thing my mother wanted to hear and she had put the phone down. But the damage had been done. Incensed on discovering two days later that my mother had forgiven my father, and no doubt with every self-righteous element in her compact body quivering at his insult to her family, Alice committed an act that I still find hard to believe.

The first hint of it came the following week when Miss Barry gave my mother a week's notice, telling her that she and Evelyn had long wanted to have a shop of their own and at last they had found one suitable. When mother asked if they would not extend their notice to a month or even two weeks, Miss Barry shook her head. The decision was made and was final.

It was a death blow to the business. Miss Barry had never allowed anyone to see her various recipes for cakes and pastry: the books were always taken home at night. Without her, therefore, there was no survival. It was like a strangler's hand on the throat, cutting off all oxygen.

So my mother now had to face that

dreaded bankruptcy at last. Nor can it have been helped by the seeming treachery of the couple she had so often helped in the past.

My father had never liked or trusted Miss Barry, and was curious to know how people who had pleaded poverty so often could suddenly afford a shop. The astonishing answer came from Miss Barry herself. Alice had lent her the money. Not only that, she had also helped her to find suitable premises! As her daughter would not punish Sydney for his affair, Alice had done it for her, no matter whom she hurt in the process.

After that revelation, blows came thick and fast. A new baker was taken on, only to be dismissed when it was found he was stealing goods from both the bakery and the shop. With no money in the bank, unpaid bills were piling up and before long the electricity was cut off. Desperate, my mother sold her engagement and wedding rings and substituted them with a brass ring bought from Woolworths. With this money she paid the rates bill and the rent but, with nothing left for electricity, we spent our evenings in candlelight.

With the business in her name, it meant she had to meet the Official Receiver and eventually to appear in court. I doubt if anyone condemned to face the firing squad could have dreaded this ordeal more than my mother.

It was all such a pathetic affair. She had to

watch while all her hard-won possessions were valued and tagged. Some creditors, who knew the full story and were aware of her honesty, refused to make their claim and wrote the debts off. The Receiver himself, discovering my mother had only fifteen shilling left in the world, took her for a meal out of his own pocket.

Nevertheless, the grisly business had to be gone through. When the possessions were valued, the outstanding debt was £60. Aware by this time that Alice was a relatively wealthy woman, the Receiver suggested that Alice be asked for the money to prevent the bankruptcy order. In view of my mother's horror of bankruptcy, I don't know whether or not she made the request, but in any case Alice never did pay. Instead she had the car taken away to repay the loan that had purchased it.

So the day came when auctioneers arrived to take away our home. I was present at the time and saw my mother's face as one after another of her pathetic possessions were carted away. These included her beloved sideboard which by this time had been squeezed into the small house.

It was only my father's hand on my arm that saved me from attacking those men because that day I knew a hatred that scalds the mind. It was not only for the auctioneer who acted as if he were taking away the possessions of criminals. It was for a system that allows honest people to go to the wall while their exploiters thrive and prosper. If my parents had made the shop a private company, their home would have remained intact. But because they were honest folk with no knowledge of such legal chicanery, they were being crucified. The hatred that I felt that day leaves a scar with dangerously thin tissue, as I was to discover many years later.

The problem facing us now was where to live because our rent expired at the end of the week. A customer who had stayed faithful to my mother came to our rescue. Seeing the auctioneer's van drive away, she came into the shop, threw her arms around my mother, and told her how disgusted she was by all that had happened. She had a large room in her house that we could have rent-free as long as we needed it.

It was a gesture that did more for my mother than just solve an urgent problem. She was near to being destroyed by the recent events and this reminder that there was still charity in the world could not have been more timely, particularly as none of our relations, who no doubt viewed the bankruptcy as a disgrace, offered us help or accommodation.

To my shame I cannot bring to mind this

woman's name. But her honesty was such that before my mother accepted her offer she felt it right to admit she was living with a man to whom she was not married. If my mother felt able to bring her family into such a house, she would be more than welcome.

Such was the convoluted morality of those times. A woman offering sanctuary had first to apologise for her relationship with a man who proved as warm-hearted and hospitable as she herself.

Although too young to appreciate it, I was being given the invaluable lesson that few are so kind to the misfortunate as those who have no spiritual or secular pride. I was also soon to learn that life gives them few rewards for their charity. Jack, as was the man's name, volunteered for the Merchant Navy on the outbreak of war. He was dead six months later when his ship was sunk by a U boat.

NINETEEN

In all we lived for ten weeks with this warm-hearted couple during which time I must have been the only breadwinner of the family. Then my father obtained a job as a traveller and van man for a local sweet wholesaler for a wage of fifty shillings a week. This enabled us to move into a tiny house in a newly-built street quite close to our old shop.

It was during this time that my feelings about Nazi Germany began to surface. Perhaps my recent insight into the way a seemingly stable world could suddenly turn upside down had some bearing on it, or perhaps it was due to a piece I read in a magazine about the brutal way the Jews were being treated. As I had an undoubted neurosis about bullies, which recent events had done nothing to dispel, it was not difficult to associate myself with the Jewish persecution and I began feeling a deepening disgust for Hitler and his 3rd Reich.

Not that there was much on the radio or the Press about the Jewish persecution. How much of this was due to indifference and how much to anti-semitism is open to question but neither is to our national credit. One had to search for information and even when it was found little criticism was made. One had the feeling there was an agreement between both the Government and the Press to offend Hitler and his minions as little as possible. From all I learned later, the same cowardly concordat existed in France.

It was during this time that the German airship, The Hindenburg, flew over Hull. I saw it quite clearly as it flew over Hedon and the docks. Although it was claimed to be on a goodwill mission, rumours spread around that it was photographing the docks for use in case of war. In view of what was to follow, I have little doubt this was true.

Being the junior in my office I was now having to take my summer holidays after my seniors has taken their choice, which left me the second and third weeks of September. As these were spent at Ruston Parva, my memories of those holidays are of ripe corn, huge September moons, and evening mists creeping over fields and berry-laden hedges. My companions on these holidays were usually Stewart Cottingham, Frank Holland, or a new friend from the Guildhall, Arthur Barr. Aunt Hannah would pack us a lunch and we would either cycle about the countryside or take the bus to Bridlington. There, if weather permitted, we would spend the day either on the beach or walking along the promenades checking on the 'talent' available. I use the word available but because of the shyness boys and girls had in those days, it usually took us two or three days to make any contacts.

Even when we did, the affairs were innocent enough. On most days we would hire a tent at sixpence a time and if the weather were suitable attempt to sunbathe. In the evenings, if the girls were brave enough, we might take them along the cliffs towards Flamborough Head. After a mile or so we might suggest taking a rest there. With a huge harvest moon floating in a September sky, the sea murmuring on the sands below, and sometimes the strains of a band drifting towards us from Sewerby Park, there were worse places for romance and just occasionally we might be lucky.

Luck, however, is a relative term. Our luck consisted of embraces, kisses, and a hesitant fumble or two. The extent of these fumbles depended on the girl but at this time I never met one who allowed an eager hand to venture lower than her breasts, unless it was a quick, impulsive touch that was immediately snatched away. The fear of pregnancy could conquer the moon, music, and the stars in those days.

Nevertheless, we felt as successful and puissant as Lothario himself when the brief moments were over, even if our loins did ache and feel as heavy as lead when we started back to Ruston Parva. On arrival we would find an entire chicken waiting for us, along with new potatoes and the sweetest of peas, all from William's garden. As chicken was an expensive delicacy in those days, we felt as rich as princes when at last we sank onto the huge feather mattress in the front bedroom.

It is fascinating to reflect on the different attitudes to sex that existed in those days. One questions whether two young men could take such a holiday today without the immediate assumption they were homosexuals. Yet in most cases nothing could have been farther from the truth. We used the same bed at Ruston Parva because there was no other one available. Nor did anyone think twice about it. It was quite common practice in those days for both children and adults of the same sex to use a common bed, as my brother and I had done for many years.

The truth is that we knew nothing about homosexuality. We were not taught sex at school and I certainly never heard anything about homosexuality from my friends and acquaintances. Indeed the suggestion that men could find sexual pleasure from one another would have seemed absurd to us. Pleasure from sweaty, hairy boys when there were all those gorgeous girls about? The very thought would have my friends roll on the floor with laughter.

No doubt homosexuality did exist but it was not in the public consciousness as today. This meant that young men could go about together without the risk of gossip and misunderstanding. As few human relationships are as satisfying as those that make no demands, this is surely a loss in itself.

It was during one of these holidays that Frank Holland and I had an odd experience. Coming back on the bus from Bridlington late one evening, we dismounted at the wrong stop and found ourselves with over two miles to walk to the village. At first this seemed to present no problem because with a huge harvest moon floating over the fields, it was almost as bright as day.

After walking for about five minutes with fields stretching out on either side of the road, Frank gave a sudden exclamation, caught my arm, and pointed at the field opposite. 'Look! There! Across the road.'

The hedge opposite was low and with the field bathed in moonlight one could see from its stubble that it had been recently harvested. But it was not the field that had caught Frank's attention but a luminous shape suspended over it.

I remember my throat turning dry and the hoarseness of my question. 'What on earth is it?'

We stared at one another and back at the 'thing'. It was between thirty and forty yards from us, a luminous horizontal shape with the configuration of a man floating about six feet above the stubble. The head could be seen quite clearly and although the body shimmered vaporously in the moonlight, its arms seemed folded over its chest in the posture of the dead.

It would be pleasant to record that the two of us climbed the hedge and went over to investigate the vision. The truth is we took one more look at it and then hurried on home.

It was many years before I found a feasible explanation. I say feasible because I still have some reservations. A magazine article stated that in parts of Ireland where the ground is rich in peat it has been known for the peat to interact with the flesh of newly-buried corpses and to produce a phosphorescent vapour. This vapour filters up through the soil and on calm nights will create an image in the shape of the dead below. The effect is known as 'corpse candles'.

I have never been able to find out if this grisly article was scientifically based or written from mere hearsay. But if such things can happen and if it explains the apparition we saw, then whose body was buried in an unmarked and unconsecrated grave in that field? And who had committed the deed? After all this time, we shall never know.

As by this time I was playing the guitar reasonably well, I joined a small semi-professional dance band in which I became the guitarist and the 'crooner'. It was all very small stuff and our fees absurd in modern terms but we enjoyed it enormously and no doubt secretly dreamed that one day we would take the musical world by storm.

I also had the nerve to tutor pupils on the guitar. In all I had three of them during the winter of 1938/39. As I only charged them two shillings an hour, they seemed happy enough to come once a week and the money augmented my pocket money.

We did most of our dancing in a local church hall. The dances were held on Saturday nights and, as a band was provided, they were very popular. Although it was only a tiny 'hop', there was no question of our wearing old slacks and pullovers. We dressed in the best clothes we possessed and even changed into dancing shoes on arrival. From memory we seldom took girls with us. Like ourselves, they went in groups and the intermingling went on during the dancing. There was the usual scramble to dance with the prettiest girls but although there must have been the odd quarrel, I can't remember any fights among the boys, either inside or outside the hall. By and large we did not seem to have been an aggressive generation.

Undoubtedly, the fact we drank little alcohol was one reason. Apart from the odd glass of sherry given me by my parents at Christmas, I never had a drink of any kind nor a cigarette until I entered the RAF and even then I drank very little.

One wonders why. Was it simply that we could not afford drink? It would sound less priggish to give that as the reason, and in some cases it might have been the case, but the truth was that my friends and I really believed that drinking and smoking would damage our health. We had been taught at school that our physical development would suffer if we indulged, and as we were all extremely sports conscious, we felt no temptation to put the matter to the test.

Drug taking, of course, was almost unknown among the middle and lower classes. Even so, I find it difficult to believe that I or any of my friends would have dreamt of risking our health by using them.

It was, I accept, a different world. There was no absurd celebrity culture and no television to exalt the spurious fame of its dubious characters, there were no discos with their aggressive music and strobe lighting to unhinge the mind, and the potent drugs that are so often in the news today were either unheard of or too expensive to buy.

At the same time there was still the tabloid press, the news reels laden with nonsense about film stars, and liquor advertisements on every tram and street hoarding. Beer was only four pence a pint, wine and spirits were absurdly cheap, and pubs were at every street corner. Yet none of my acquaintances used any of them. I have to ask why.

TWENTY

It was in 1938 that the threatening clouds of war were finally to settle overhead. It was the year when Hitler staked his claim for the return of Germans outside the borders of the 3rd Reich, which resulted in Austria being invaded and made a province of Greater Germany. Hitler's move was to extend his 'protection' to the Germans in the Sudetenland and then to hurl a barrage of propaganda at Czechoslovakia, his usual ploy before invasion. With Europe on the brink of war, Chamberlain flew over to Germany and in a settlement supported by Roosevelt and Mussolini, agreed to a partial dismemberment of Czechoslovakia.

I can remember well the hoo-ha when Chamberlain arrived back in England. Cinema newsreels showed him stepping out of his plane and waving his agreement. News papers claimed hysterically that now there would be peace in our time.

I doubt if any thinking man, or teenager for that matter, believed this. If any did, the scales soon fell from their eyes when Hitler broke his pact and annexed the whole of Czechoslovakia. The sands of time were running out fast now and particularly on that grim day in August 1939 when the news came through that Hitler had made the greatest volte-face in history and sealed a pact with the Russians: the race he had denounced until recently as the Bolshevik arch-enemies of civilisation.

It was like a sudden, brutal blow to the stomach. Against Germany, I believed, we might just be able to survive. Against Germany and Russia, we had no hope at all. On all counts it seemed a death sentence for my generation and from that moment on I was convinced that I and my friends had only a short time to live.

Nevertheless, in the way of youth, we went on with our lives. In my case it was to continue my work in the Guildhall. Soon the Conscription Act was passed and just after my twentieth birthday I was called to the local Labour Exchange to put my name down for Military Service. Given a preference I said I would like to be an RAF pilot and was given an enrolment form which had to be filled in and returned in twenty-four hours. This I did, received a badge, and so became a volunteer in the RAF Aircrew Reserve.

At first, expecting to be called up quickly for a medical, I made no plans, but as the weeks passed, I became due for a holiday. As for administrative reasons I had to take them in two parts I decided to spend them with my brother. He was now working in a repertory company touring the British Isles and offered to share his digs with me if I fancied any of the towns the company visited.

At the time it looked unlikely I would get the opportunity because after Hitler threatened to invade Poland unless she surrendered Danzig and with Britain guaranteeing Poland's frontiers, war seemed only a knife edge away. My school friend, Stewart Cottingham, who had joined the Territorial Army a year earlier, was called up and I expected my notice any time.

Events moved even more swiftly now. On the 1st September Hitler invaded Poland and gas masks were issued to the British public, with a warning they should be carried at all times. I remember very clearly the look of horror on my mother's face when we urged her to try hers on.

Back in the Guildhall conditions became chaotic as hundreds of workmen who were members of the Territorial Army came in for their cards. Having to work until nine or ten every night, I can remember feeling so tired that when the news came through that Hitler had carried out his threat and invaded Poland, it was some time before I realised we were virtually at war.

Sunday confirmed it. After solemn warnings on the radio that an important announcement would be made at 11 am, Chamberlain came on the air and, sounding as if he would break down at any moment, announced that we were at war with Germany.

Such moments are never forgotten. My mother, father, and I were grouped around the wireless in the sitting room and as the words 'we are now at war with Germany' were heard my father gave a choking sob and walked from the room.

It was the first and only time in my life that I had seen him break down and it had a greater impact on me than the announcement itself. As an infantryman, he had endured the bloodiest and most brutal war in history, and his thoughts that morning, along with millions of other fathers, would defy description. I wanted desperately to comfort him but, inhibited Yorkshire boy that I was, I did not know how. So instead I kissed my mother, who was weeping bitterly, and walked out into the garden.

It was a day when the very thought of war seemed sacrilegious. To describe it in my diary, I used extracts from that poet of the countryside, Richard Jefferies. 'A sense of rest, not of weariness but of full growth, was in the atmosphere: tree, plants, and grassy things had reached their fullness and their strength. Like a grape, the air was ripe and luscious, and to breathe it was a drowsy joy. For Circe had smoothed her garment and slumbered, and the very sun moved slow'.

September 3rd, 1939, was such a day. The sky was a robin's egg blue and I remember there was a lark fluttering high above the small garden and singing as if to burst its heart. Mixed with my grief for my parents, the sound brought a confusion of thoughts that were incapable of analysis. No young man on the eve of being called up to fight for his country ever felt less like a warrior than I that Sunday morning.

But self-preservation braces the best and the worst of us, and within fifteen minutes of hearing the news all the men nearby were digging a shelter in the field behind us. Because of the Spanish civil war, when the Fascist Air Forces of Germany and Italy had bombed cities and carried out atrocities like Guernica, we had been led to believe that the same death and destruction would rain down on us once war was declared. Consequently our activity was feverish and the trench deepened at extraordinary speed.

Looking back in hindsight, one wonders why it had not been dug earlier. Only two reasons make sense to me. Either the farmer who owned the field had withheld permission or some of our neighbours had refused to believe the worst could happen.

Whatever the reason, everyone was making up for lost time now, although by the middle of the afternoon I was called back to the Guildhall. With the belief that bombs in their hundreds would soon be raining down, the City Fathers had ordered that the Guildhall be evacuated and all its offices transferred to the University buildings on the other side of town.

It was a move that shamed us because it meant all our workmen would have much further to travel. In my case, I think my disgust came from my schoolboy traumas with McCloud and Scargill. From them I had learned that the surest way to make an enemy seem formidable is to run away from him and in my case I was surprised to find that now we were facing up to Hitler at last, I was feeling calmer in mind and body.

Dog tired that night I slept heavily, only to be awakened by a noise that sounded as if all the devils in hell were screaming. It took a few seconds to realise it was the air raid siren.

None of us wasted any time in getting into our makeshift shelter. Brainwashed by the Press, and aware that the huge Hull docks would be a prime target, we had every reason to believe that within a few minutes bombs and gas shells would be raining down on us.

I can believe that for some it was one of the most frightening experiences of the war because that night we were facing the unknown. Led to believe from the Press and the radio that the Nazis might smother us with gas, women were struggling to put the masks on their babies while the rest of us wondered if our courage would be equal to the carnage ahead.

It was a clear, windless night, full of stars and silence. As we listened, we heard a succession of dull thuds in the far distance, which made us believe enemy planes were breaking through the coastal defences. Another fifteen minutes passed and then we heard the drone of an approaching plane. Believing it was the vanguard of the attack, we checked the corrugated iron sheets covering the trench and waited with held breath for the first bombs to fall.

When nothing happened, we peered out and saw the plane flashing its recognition lights. Half a minute later the all clear sounded and we began to climb out of the trench. It was a huge anti-climax and we were all so embarrassed that we laughed and chatted around the dug-out for a good fifteen minutes before returning to bed.

So our first air raid came and went and perhaps, even when the real thing began, we were never quite so apprehensive again.

Back at work the chaos was growing. Not only were workmen finding difficulty in finding us, but even when they did, we found it nearly impossible to meet their needs because of misplaced registers and insurance cards. At the same time new departments were being formed almost daily, such as the Auxiliary Fire Service, the Decontamination Service, the Air Raid Warden service, and the First Aid Emergency Section. It all ensued that the City Treasurer, who had sanctioned the move in the first place, asking if our office was prepared to return to the Guildhall to restore proper services to the public.

As an ex-solder himself, Frank Gosling must have found it embarrassing to make such a melodramatic request to us. Naturally we all 'volunteered' and within a day or two were back in the huge empty building, although now sited in its large front office instead of our previous smaller one.

By this time the rumour that London had been destroyed was scotched, and with our own air raid a fiasco, I don't think any of us felt in any more danger in the Guildhall than in the University. However, there was no sign that the authorities were more sanguine because in the days that followed we saw thousands of stretchers being delivered and carried down into the basements.

It was around this time that I was ordered to take my aircrew medical examination. Given seven days notice, I was granted a week's absence from work and decided to spend it in Glasgow where Ray's company were now playing. By this time we had settled all our past misunderstandings and it was good to see him again. He managed to get me into his 'digs' where I was introduced to the friends who shared the same boarding house. They were Velma Faye, Yvonne Bevis, and Earnie Whitelock. Yvonne and Earnie were members of The Seven Houdinies, a spectacular acrobatic act. Velma's part in the show I can't remember but she was a blonde, willowy American girl with a great deal of charm.

For me it was an exciting five days. Although I can't remember the name of the show, it had all the spectacular glamour associated with variety in these days: indeed its boast was that it had a beautiful girl from every country in the world. How true that was I never found out, but beautiful girls were certainly in abundance and for a virile young man, unused to the theatrical world, it seemed like paradise, particularly because my brother, having the juvenile lead, was able to get me backstage. Moreover at that time Scotland was like a foreign country to me and I enjoyed to the full taking trams here and there and walking for miles along the Clyde. It was during one of these walks, with Ray and Velma, that I saw the Queen Elizabeth under construction. She was only a massive hulk without superstructure at the time and yet only a few months later she was completed and safely docked in New York. War speeds up production in ways that make the mind reel.

There were other things to make my mind reel too. Not only was Yvonne fond of me but, no doubt because of my youth, the other girls used to tease and flirt with me outrageously. I remember standing on the stage one afternoon when six of them were rehearsing an acrobatic act. At one point it involved one girl being swung round and round by her arms and then balancing upside down on the top of a human pyramid. She was a beautiful lithe girl with flowing black hair and I think she had already noticed my admiring glances. Whatever her reason, as the act reached its climax and she balanced upside down, laughs broke out from the girls who were watching and one called out: 'You'd better watch out, F.E., or you might go blind.'

I understood why a moment later. To tease me, my acrobatic beauty had left off her panties and, as she revealed all, she wiggled her legs and winked at me. As these were not everyday sights for young men at that time, perhaps I was lucky to escape with my vision intact.

Still dazed from it all, I returned to the Guildhall on the Monday and on Tuesday I reported to the Metropole Hall at 9.30 for my medical. In all there were ten of us up for medicals and I knew one of them. He was Stan Cook, who had once been a stalwart member of our school football team. The only other whose name I remember was Desmond Matthews. He was a tall lean young man with curly, fair hair. He seemed somewhat curt of speech and I doubt if we passed half a dozen words that morning. Little did I know how our paths would converge in the years ahead.

We had to wait for two hours before our medicals began. Six specialists examined us, each concentrating on one part of our bodies, and in the end, to my relief, I was passed grade A1, which was necessary for air crew trainees. I believe many of the others failed but Stan Cook and Desmond Matthews also passed the aircrew standard.

Our next test was to face an Air Commodore. He asked me only three questions: what is the log of 100, what is a rhomboid, and in what countries were the cities of Prague and Riga. I botched the first question, giving the square root instead, but gave the right answers on the other two. Afraid I might have failed, I was told instead that I was the only applicant to know where Riga was. I remember giving Miss Hesketh a silent benediction.

Before being released we were told we would probably be called up within the next three weeks. When I returned to work and told this to Frank Gosling, he immediately gave me a short holiday from the following Monday. This from the man I had once thought dour and unyielding.

TWENTY-ONE

Before I was called up for the last time Ray took a short holiday with my parents and brought Velma with him. I had already noticed during my Glasgow trip how attached the two had become and his bringing her to meet my parents seemed to confirm this.

From the way my mother welcomed Velma I knew she was hoping the relationship would develop and bring more stability into his life. Moreover, Velma seemed like a good match because, like so many Americans, she was generous and warm-hearted, as well as being easy on the eye.

With our house so tiny, I can't imagine how we all squeezed into it, but we did, and in spite of the war news, we somehow managed a happy time together. It was not easy because by this time Russia had invaded Finland which seemed like the beginning of a war with that huge country too. Today we know it was Stalin's ploy to secure the Russian northern flank against a possible German attack but at the time, with Russia and Germany still giving lip service to their unholy pact, it seemed more evidence of the impossible task facing us.

For my part I was now seeing Becky Davidson once a week. She had gone into nursing after leaving school and was now a fully qualified SRN. Although I enjoyed my weekly dates I did not let them go to my head because at that time I was only one of her many boy friends. Being extremely attractive, and having a vivacious and outgoing personality, she was popular and I hardly had a friend who did not want to date her. Even so, I had one advantage over the others. I could play the guitar well by this time and had not a bad singing voice into the bargain. As Becky loved music and singing vocals, we shared interests denied to my rivals. She began visiting our house weekly and, with mother playing the piano, we had some happy evenings together.

We also enjoyed dancing and the Victoria Children's Hospital where she now worked held a number of these during the winter. Whether Becky wanted me for my own self or because of my dancing, I never asked but I was invited to all of them that year.

The New Year came but brought no further news of my enlistment. Enjoying my burgeoning friendship with Becky, I now realised my absence in the Forces might see its end. This brought an ambivalence of feelings that I found unsettling.

The progress of the war was another factor that played on our nerves. We had been geared up to expect heavy air raids and massive casualties, as well as fierce battles on land, sea, and in the air. As our heavy loss of ships from submarines and our even heavier losses of aircraft during this period were kept from us, the war began to seem like a sick joke. The armies in Europe that had been expected to clash in a titanic battle seemed to be doing nothing more than sipping tea and staring at one another.

It was a strange, unreal time. At one moment there would be a sultry tension in the air, a sensation that massive electrical charges must soon discharge in a cataclysmic storm. At others there was a sense of anti-climax, with people muttering about a phoney war. Neither one nor the other was good for nerves or morale.

As Easter approached my long-awaited brown envelope came, ordering me to report to the RAF Reception Centre in Padgate where I would have a further medical and an interview before a selection committee. As these examinations could be lengthy, I should be prepared to stay at the camp for three days.

I caught the 9.20 train the following morning, brightening up somewhat when I found Stan Cook and Des Matthews in the same train and destined for the same camp. We arrived in Warrington around 2 p.m. and caught a bus to Padgate. It was our first glimpse of an RAF Reception Centre and I know my heart sank at the sight of rows of wooden huts separated by muddy, unfinished paths and with groups of half-frozen recruits struggling to keep in step to the yells of NCOs. In fact, with a bitter wind sweeping all before it, it looked like a prison camp on some desolate island. Nor could I imagine was it that different. Told by a Warrant Officer to wait near the guardroom for further orders and so fully exposed to a scything wind, we waited for two hours before a sergeant arrived and marched us to a store where we were issued with a knife, fork, spoon, mug and a couple of damp sheets.

After a quick meal we were taken to a hut where we were shown how to make our beds from the 'biscuits' (mattresses) and blankets already there. At the same time we were told not to believe the letter telling us our stay would be for three nights only. We were here for the duration.

Although later this proved a false alarm, we went through the cock-ups, the incorrect orders, and the bullying yells of illiterate

NCOs that seem the lot of any recruit in the Armed Forces. They were too numerous to be recorded here but they came to a climax when we were assembled for an aircrew selection board.

There were sixty-six to face this board. Those who passed it would be sent for another aircrew medical. Those who failed would be relegated for ground staff duties. As I was the very last of sixty-six to be interviewed, I had a long and depressing wait because not only did many come out of the room with long faces but even those who passed were only offered observer or air gunner courses.

My diary records some of the questions I was asked by the Board. 'What sports do you play?'

'Tennis, soccer, rugby, swimming and athletics.'

'What have you done the 100 yards in?'

'10.2 seconds.'

'Can you shoot? Could you hit a running rabbit with a.22 rifle?'

Here I was stupid and made mention of the games my father and I used to play. Seeing everyone on the panel sitting up and looking at me, I could have kicked myself.

'Do you know anything about wireless?' came the next question.

Acutely aware I was now being considered as a wireless operator/air gunner, I was very,

very careful now. 'No,' I said. 'Absolutely nothing. In fact wireless is a mystery to me.'

'Can you drive a car?'

This was better, I thought, and lied. 'Yes, I've driven my father's.'

'Can you ride a motor cycle?'

Better and better, I thought, and lied again. 'Yes. Of course I can.'

It was all to no avail. After conferring with his panel, the Chairman turned back to me. 'Providing you pass the final medical, we are going to give you the chance of becoming a wireless operator/air gunner.'

'But I want to be a pilot,' I protested. 'That why I volunteered for the RAF.'

His reply was that if I passed my final medical and then my initial training I would be allowed to make a transfer. Having no idea I was being fobbed off I made no mention of the flying I had done during my school days, thinking that could be more effective when I applied for a transfer.

The medical came next and it was even more severe than our first. We were told that the seven specialists who examined us were all from Harley Street. One of them fired a blank cartridge behind me when I was talking to his assistant and I jumped and swung round like a scalded cat. Fearing I had disqualified myself, I was relieved when the doctor shook his head. 'No, that's what your nerves are for. If you hadn't jumped, then we would have been worried about you.'

In all, the specialists spent six hours on each of us and, because the tests were so severe, only ten of us were considered fit enough for air crew, although later, when the air war took its toll, the standard was considerably lowered. In our case Stan Cook did not qualify but Des Matthews was successful and also marked down for wireless operator/air gunner training. This meant he and I and six others had now to be attested.

So there were more muddles and more delays until we finally signed papers and were led into a Wing Commander's office. He welcomed us as trainee aircrews, wished us good luck, and presented us with an RAF Volunteer Reserve badge. We then surrendered our equipment, were given a four shilling travel allowance, and finally allowed to return home. With the war causing appalling train journeys it was 6.30 am the following morning before Des and I arrived back in Hull.

I returned to the Guildhall with mixed feelings. Although our first sight of the RAF had not been auspicious, I was geared to go and it was difficult to put my mind to local government affairs again. It was the time Hitler made his next move by invading and capturing Norway. With Nazi U boat bases now facing our entire eastern seaboard, it seemed to me we were losing the war by default.

I was still seeing Becky as often as our duties would permit and when our twin birthdays arrived we celebrated them by going to a dance at the Victoria Hospital. What happened that night came as a surprise to us both. After all, we had been seeing one another for some time and happy as our meetings had been, they had no relation to what happened that night. Quite suddenly we no longer belonged to a country at war. Instead we were in Arcadia, dancing to the pipes of Pan. We had fallen in love.

As it must be for all young lovers, it was a kind of magic. But for us at that time it had a debit as well as a credit side. Until then I had been geared up to play my part in the war. Now my call-up was the last thing I wanted. My wish now was to go on seeing the girl who had won my heart.

But wishes are one thing: reality is another. Because children were still being evacuated, Becky was often detailed on Sundays to take them to their foster parents. For my part I was still working compulsory overtime, so it was more than difficult to find Sundays or even evenings when we could be together.

And how precious time proved to be a month later when Germany, breaking every promise and treaty she had made, invaded the neutral countries of Holland and Belgium. The phoney war was over: the real war had begun at last. And my calling up papers wasted no time on their arrival. Only two days later, with no possibility of seeing Becky before leaving, I found myself saying goodbye to my parents on the railway station. I don't remember what we said – who ever can – but then the guard blew a whistle, there was a hiss of steam, a final wave, and then, with millions of other young men I went off to war.

TWENTY-TWO

It is not my intention to write in depth about my military training. As it began in the early days of the war, it will hopefully reveal the general chaos we all encountered when the country was trying to train a citizen's army at a time when the enemy was already fully equipped and, so to speak, ready to break down the front door. So it will only mention the absurd situations and the personal incidents that for one reason or another can never be forgotten.

Des Matthews was on the same train as myself the day I was called up. Our destination was Padgate again. Although it was now May and not March as on our last visit, Padgate hardly looked any more hospitable. As we only arrived in the late afternoon, we were given no duties that day but instead were put into one of the huts and told we would receive our kit and medical precautions on the morrow.

We were called at 6 a.m. and after breakfast were given tasks that had to be completed by 08.15 when we would receive our uniforms and be inoculated. Instead we were marched hither and thither and finally brought back to our hut to be told the earlier orders were rescinded and we now had to report to the equipment store at 13.30.

This we duly did, to have equipment thrown at us from all directions. I think most of us were surprised at the kit we received. There were boots, socks, braces, shirts, underpants, vests, a tie, a forage cap, a tin helmet, a gas cape, a water bottle, a greatcoat, an all-purpose knife, three haversacks, webbing, Brasso for polishing buttons, brushes for polishing boots, a huge service gas mask, a 'housewife' for sewing and darning, a first aid dressing ... the list seemed endless. Even when we climbed into our uniforms, which we were now told to do, there was still enough equipment left over to fill the large kit bag given us. I remember my tunic being too tight round the shoulders and too loose round the waist but being told the tailor would take care of it, an assurance that seemed oddly out of place in the surroundings.

To carry the load, we were forced to don our bulky greatcoats. As it was an extremely hot day and we had over a mile to walk to our hut, we must have soon looked like Fred Karnos's army with our gas masks and kit bags slipping off unaccustomed shoulders, and our discarded civilian clothes draped round our necks or tucked into our belts. To complete the ludicrous picture, at least half a dozen men fainted in the heat, which must have made the day for the grinning onlookers.

For the second time our inoculations were postponed and we were set the task of sorting out our equipment and numbering it all in indelible ink. Off duty after our evening meal Des and I listened to the news. To put it mildly it was depressing. Amiens and Cambrai had fallen and the general French situation was becoming critical.

The following day, after being marched round the camp a couple of times, we were lined up to receive our first pay packet which was ten shillings. Afterwards we joined another group to be vaccinated and given our two inoculation jabs.

I remember my surprise in seeing husky men fainting at the sight of the needles entering their arms. At the same time, the effects were not pleasant. Within minutes of receiving mine I developed a headache and my right arm began to swell at an alarming rate.

None of us were in bed early that evening. My diary records somewhat sentimentally that the hut radio was playing many of the tunes Becky, mother and I had often played together. To make matters worse, a radio play of Vanity Fair followed and almost the first name I heard was Becky. With my headache raging and my resistance low, I was full of gloom and self-pity that night.

The next morning my arm was twice its size – in fact the flesh sagged over my hand when I lowered it – and I was irritated to discover that I appeared to be the only one of the group affected.

Noticing my arm, our hut corporal gave me the task of scrubbing the floor of his billet. Unless he was a sadist, I can only assume the medics had issued orders that this was the right treatment for such afflictions. Perhaps, therefore, my comments on that corporal were unjustified. They were certainly unprintable when, after I finished, he ordered me to join the others in scrubbing the entire floor of the hut in anticipation of the Commanding Officer's inspection the following morning.

We had two more days of orders, counter orders and general chaos which allowed me to collect my tunic which now fitted me reasonably well. Then we were ordered to parade in full kit ready to move out. This order was given and rescinded three times before we finally marched to the railway station.

Our next camp was Wilmslow and if we had found Padgate inhospitable, it was a leafy oasis beside Wilmslow, which appeared to be built entirely on sand. We learned it had only been completed a month earlier and that completion referred only to men's basic needs. Apart from the NAAFI canteen, there was no other entertainment whatever. Even radios were not installed in the huts. It was, in effect, a military establishment whose only function was to drill and discipline men until they were considered docile enough to obey any order given them.

As trainee aircrews we had not expected this, and our grumbles came thick and fast. Not that they could be expressed loudly because the Flight Sergeant put in charge of us would have found the greatest joy in drilling them out. Called Hogg, no man could have been more aptly named. In short, we soon hated him, which perhaps he wanted.

For the first few days at Wilmslow we seemed to do little else but hard physical training. Perhaps spotting this was something I enjoyed, our instructor made me the 'senior' man of our group, which was something of a joke because, apart from Des, I believe I was the youngest man present.

This same instructor embarrassed me one day by exhibiting me like a prize animal in front of a full parade of men and telling them

I had the finest physique he had ever seen in his recruits. Why he did this, God knows, but although the comment must have pleased me when reflected on it later, my diary only records my intense embarrassment and my fear that I would have my leg pulled mercilessly afterwards. This did not happen – in general there was not the tendency in those days to see homosexuals behind every tree and lamp post – but one shudders to think what taunts and accusations I would have suffered in today's climate.

Although our only contact with the world was the radio in the NAAFI, by Tuesday alarming news about the war was heard everywhere. Belgium had surrendered and with the way to the Channel ports now open, the British and French armies were in acute danger of being surrounded. Knowing Stewart was with the BEF in France, I had personal reasons to be upset at this news.

We heard this just before a kit inspection and I remember how useless the task seemed and how helpless one felt. To make matters worse, the tempo of our training changed. Until then, despite the news and the chaos, the military machine had displayed no haste or alarm. In fact it had seemed almost phlegmatic in its behaviour. Now we noticed an urgency taking over. We were told to have our kit packed and be ready to march off at a moment's notice. Where we were supposed to go, no one told us, but for forty-eight hours we stood by until finally the order was cancelled. I shall always remember the comment of one wit after standing with us for two hours in the heat without apparent purpose. 'Smithy, if we win this war it will mean only one thing. That the Jerries were even more bloody inefficient than us.' It is a thought that deserves some consideration.

Our training began again but with this new urgency. Drills and lectures were packed in from dawn to dusk. My diary records one day of that month. Called at 6 am. Cleaned buttons and equipment. Made bed. Breakfast at seven. Physical training from seven-thirty to eight thirty. Unarmed combat training eight-thirty to nine thirty. Three separate hours of foot drill until lunch. Two more hours of foot drill after lunch. A second hour of PT before dinner. Stench of sweat in billet unbearable. Everyone in bed by eight-thirty 'totally knackered'.

All this was hard on the older men who made up over half of our hutment, and the billet at nights was filled with their complaints. One should have felt sorry for them but I began to find it irritating. Privacy had always meant a great deal to me, and to have to lie on one's bed every night with nothing to listen to but moans and grumbles, was becoming an ordeal.

By this time we were all impatient to receive mail. Knowing my mother would write me the same day that I left, and hoping that Becky would do the same, I was hungry for news but my first letter only arrived towards the end of the week and it was from my parents.

My pleasure at receiving it was short-lived. Mother had written the letter and I had to read it again before her news sank in. Ray had been taken ill and it was discovered he had tuberculosis!

I went cold with shock. Tuberculosis! With no drug available to contain or cure it, no illness was more feared at that time. Not only was it highly infectious but few deaths were more distressing and painful.

Yet he had seemed so cheerful that Christmas. And so happy in Glasgow. Then I remembered the dry cough I had sometimes heard when I stayed with him and knew the signs had already been there.

From the tone of the letter, my mother was distraught. She made no mention of my grandmother, but I could imagine the state Alice would be in. At the time of the letter Ray was now in a sanatorium on the outskirts of Hull.

Knowing how shattered he would be at the loss of his career I tried to get a short leave but my application was turned down flat. So I could do nothing but write him and no letter was harder to pen.

During this time I had no news at all from Becky. I guessed she was being overworked at the hospital, but my longing to hear from her did nothing to improve my state of mind.

We began gas lectures at this time. As a supplement to them, we had to don our masks and run a prescribed distance under the threat of being put on report if we paused to lift up the rubber seals for air. Although we felt half-asphyxiated at the end, Des and I managed to cover the course without this need, but few of the others did. With so many defaulters, punishment became impractical and the threat was not kept.

We were all inoculated a second time the following day. This was a 75% dose, whatever that meant, and after my earlier experience, I was apprehensive of its effects.

I was not disappointed. The consequences were even worse this time and with two days of rifle drill to come, even my tough hut corporal advised me to go sick. But remembering the flattering comments of our PT instructor on my physique, pride could not allow this and so foolishly I endured two days of rifle drill. With almost every move in the military manual putting the stress on the afflicted arm, I ended the two days feeling the Marquis de Sade had been working me over.

However, Des and I managed a few hours of freedom in Manchester and the reaction of the public surprised and embarrassed us. One old man let out a cheer as we walked past and shouted: 'Here are a couple of the lads in blue. God bless 'em!' At that everyone around us began cheering and clapping. Believing my afflicted arm was the reason and feeling shame at the undeserved acclaim, we dived into a café to escape.

We all had a proficiency test the following day under the eye of Flight Sergeant Hogg. We marched, counter-marched, juggled about with our rifles, and did all the other absurd drills demanded by our yelling NCO, and to our amazement Hogg passed us. I wonder if he were as surprised as we were!

I had still heard nothing from Becky but by this time Ray had replied to my letter. Although he had tried to be cheerful he was clearly devastated by the loss of his career. To make matters worse he had just received news from the States that Velma had also been taken ill with the same disease and there were fears for her life. Indeed, she was to die only a few months later.

We who were budding aircrews moved out of Wilmslow two days later. By this time Des and I had become the closest of friends. Although wartime brings men together out of mutual need, in our case it had been a fight that laid the foundation of our friendship. It had occurred during our first days at Wilmslow. We had been arguing over something or other, and as we both tended to be impetuous the argument had suddenly become physical.

It wasn't an affair of bare fists. It was more a test of strength that young men tend to have, rather like the way two stags fight over a doe. Not that it was less vigorous for that. Neither of us liked defeat and each had personal pride. We fought without thought of injury and it drew spectators from all the huts around us.

I think we were both surprised by one another. I had not met anyone since leaving school who had been my match in this kind of combat and I learned later that Des had not either. We were both so confident of our strength that neither doubted the outcome.

But our confidence was not to last. As the fight continued we began to realise we had both met our match and although we called on every ounce of energy we finally reached a point when we dropped on the ground and stared at one another. Then one of us laughed, followed by the other. We ended up by throwing our arms around the other. We had each met his match and knew it. From that moment on we were as close as brothers.

Our move from Wilmslow coincided with the news that Italy had also declared war on Britain and France. I can't say anyone in our unit showed undue dismay. Perhaps we were too numbed by the previous news or perhaps we did not feel the Italians made the threat any worse than it already was.

Our personal concern was our next station. It turned out to be Prestwick in Scotland and to our surprise and delight we learned we would be billeted for a time in private houses. By sheer luck Des and I were given the same one, a neat bungalow owned by a warm-hearted Scots couple named Grierson.

After our barren and noisy huts in Padgate and Wilmslow we could not have been more surprised or pleased. Nor did our new station disappoint us either. It was a large Scottish manor house set in seventy-five acres of parkland. Rhododendrons were in full bloom on our arrival and flower beds everywhere. After Wilmslow it was like another world.

A gaunt-faced warrant officer called us on parade on our arrival and filled us in with the facts. We were at Adampton House where we would stay for the next sixteen weeks while we studied the wireless part of our WO/AG course. The lessons would take part in the converted stables of the estate and we would lunch in the house itself.

I think we were all surprised as we listened. The news from France was horrendous now and the losses of our aircraft so heavy that estimates gave us air gunners an average of only six weeks survival once on active service. Such losses made us believe the wireless side of our course would be cancelled and we would be rushed onto intensive gunnery training. To learn we had four months of relative security ahead gave us mixed emotions. One was a feeling of reprieve; the other shame to have it so relatively easy when friends and others were engaged in bloody fighting.

Not that the ointment had no flies in it. To Des and I, the greatest one was being told that no pilot transfers would be entertained during the course, and after the earlier promises made to us, we took this badly. Another blow was to learn that no leave would be granted during the course.

However I did at last receive two letters from Becky. One had been addressed to Padgate and the other to Wilmslow. They were full of affection, which came as a relief because I was beginning to wonder if her feelings for me had changed since our last meeting. With confidence restored I was able to concentrate again on my training.

The routine of our days was soon established. We caught a bus in the mornings from Prestwick which enabled us to be on parade at Adampton at 8.30. After a roll call we had a route march and then into the adapted stables for lectures of wireless theory and Morse application. Lunch followed at 12.00, followed by more lessons at 13.00 hours. At 17.00 hours the bus returned us to our billets in Prestwick.

In spite of all the catastrophic news, my abiding memory of those days are the route marches we made every morning. We were led by our commanding officer Flight Lieutenant Bryant, a middle-aged genial man who had been seconded from Scottish Aviation for the duration. He must have had some American connections because he would burst into song during those marches and the songs were always those of the American Civil War. In no time we learned the words and so every morning the Scottish lanes around Adampton would resound to the stirring songs of Dixie, John Brown's Body, and the Battle Hymn of the Republic.

It was all exhilarating stuff. We were all supremely fit young men chosen to help our country in its hour of need and the effect of those songs was electric. Many years later when I wrote my novel Waterloo I introduced those feelings into a description of Wellington's young men marching towards the bloody battle on Mont St. Jean. 'Streams glistened in the morning sunlight, birds sang in the tall trees, and a kestrel soared in the blue vault of heaven. How could death exist in a world as gold and green and beautiful as this? Men felt the strength of their arms and legs, the deep vigorous beat of their young hearts, and knew that whatever else might happen to others, they at least were immortal'

So we felt on those mornings in Scotland. No one, not even those carrying the burden of imagination, noticed the sudden plunge of the kestrel or saw the torn and bleeding thing it carried away in its claws. We were all too intoxicated by our youth.

TWENTY-THREE

As if the news from France was not bad enough, we learned shortly after our arrival at Adampton that Italy had now declared war on Britain and France. It was obvious that Mussolini had decided we were beaten and, like a jackal, intended to have a share of the spoils. I can't remember anyone in our unit showed undue dismay. Perhaps we were numbed by bad news by this time, or perhaps we did not feel the Italians were much of a threat. Whatever the reason, my diary doesn't record the news as being the subject of much discussion.

No doubt we were all too occupied in finding out what the RAF had in store for us. In the case of Des and I we could hardly have been more lucky because the Griersons were like parents to us. Mrs Grierson proved to be a superb cook and insisted that we ate our evening meals with them. After the Wilmslow cookhouse it was difficult to believe we were still in the RAF.

Another memory of the Griersons was the humour we all exchanged. I remember once Mr Grierson telling us what the Scots used to do with captured Englishmen in the days when the countries were at war. 'We'd put 'em inside barrels spiked with nails and roll 'em down the braes,' he would tell us, his old eyes glinting ferociously. 'They'd no come back after that, I'll tell y'.'

Knowing by this time he couldn't harm a fly, we used to pull his leg mercilessly and Mrs Grierson would join in with us. 'Stop your prattlin', you stupid old man. Are y' forgettin' these lads are Englishmen? An' where would you find a nicer pair of lads?'

Regarding our wireless training, I think we were all surprised that it continued. With the news from France horrendous now, and the lives of aircrews, particularly air gunners, so short, we were expecting the wireless side of our course to be cancelled and for concentrated gunnery training to take its place. To discover it was to continue in spite of all else surprised us all.

It was, in fact, a time of mental confusion in so many ways. With the daily news making it abundantly clear that the battle was being lost in France, it was hard to reconcile the seeming lack of urgency at Adampton.

Living in comfortable billets, allowed off duty at five o'clock every afternoon, and with Sundays off, we might have been college students on a training course if one took no account of the military system that ran the establishment. And even that was nothing beside the regimentation we had experienced at Wilmslow.

In one sense, of course, being trainee air-crew, we were students. Once we had passed through the reception centres that took in all trades, a subtle difference had begun to show in our treatment. We were actually addressed as 'Gentlemen' by our Warrant Officer, and we learned that our NCOs were to be drawn from our own ranks and not thrust upon us. As we had all been bawled at, sworn at, and suffered humiliation from illiterate NCOs at both Padgate and Wilms-low, this was a huge relief even although we were warned there must be no favouritism or relaxation of standards. From the grins and winks we exchanged, this was hardly a warning that anyone took seriously.

In service terms, we had landed a cushy billet but inevitably there were flies in the ointment. One, to Des and me at least, was the news that no pilot transfers would be entertained during the course. As Des and I had been told by the Selection Board that this was the time we could make our transfer, we both took this badly. Another blow was the news that no leave would be given us during our four month course. Sixteen more weeks without seeing Becky seemed like an eternity stretching out in front of me.

Soon after our course began we were told a corporal had to be picked to lead our flight, as our unit was now called. The man chosen was a good-looking Australian called Barry Mason. Although throughout the war many British servicemen thought there was a tendency to favour Colonials (as we called them), I don't think any of us begrudged Barry his promotion. To get into the war he had taken a job as a stoker on a merchant ship destined for Britain, and on arrival had immediately volunteered for the RAF. We all liked him and he became a popular NCO, although, as our flight had a very high percentage of odd as well as high-spirited characters, his task was not an easy one.

So our wireless theory lessons progressed. The stables were not as horsey as we feared, being refurbished and divided into twenty classrooms. We were given two technical books on wireless theory and application, but had to buy our own notebooks. Our instructor was a lad no older than ourselves. Rumour had it that he had been a wireless operator in the Merchant Navy and had taken this job to escape the war. How true it was I never knew but I can't say I felt any malice towards him. He was a thin, highly-strung young man, and probably more useful to the war effort in his present role than on a ship. Certainly I did not envy him his job, because our flight sometimes pulled his leg mercilessly.

At the same time, we were all showing strain one way or the other. We had not been there three days before news came through that the Germans were only twenty miles from Paris. No one knew what this signified. It surely could not mean that France would surrender, not after the sacred pledge she had made us not to make a separate peace. And yet the French Army was crumbling on all fronts. What would Britain do if the unthinkable happened and France did surrender? Life had never seemed so uncertain or so fraught with danger at that time.

TWENTY-FOUR

We were soon to find out what would happen. It was only the Friday of our first week at Adampton that we heard in horror that the French had surrendered Paris without a fight. We had all expected a city of that size to present a massive military obstacle and now it had been surrendered it seemed nothing could stop the German Army. I remember how upset our Scots family were when we went home that night.

But the real blow fell on Sunday. Because of the seriousness of the situation, we had been ordered to parade at Adampton House in the morning, and when Flight Lieutenant Bryant emerged and stood before us in the courtyard, we knew we were to hear something momentous.

We were not disappointed. Clearing his throat, he told us that France had agreed to make terms with both Germany and Italy.

I remember the gasp that ran through our ranks. Although fears about France's resolution had been in the air for weeks, I think most of us felt it unlikely she would break her pledge. What we were hearing meant we were now facing alone the combined might of both Germany and Italy. It meant, if numerical figures count in war, that to continue the fight meant committing national suicide.

As if it were yesterday, I remember hearing a skylark singing in the silence that followed. Looking uncertain at what the silence meant, the C.O. appeared almost lost for words when Hanson, the warrant officer, ran out of the house and whispered something in his ear. Looking immensely relieved, Bryant straightened and told us that Churchill had just spoken on the radio. His message was brief but fateful. Regardless of the news from France, Britain would continue the fight against Germany and Italy to the end.

What followed then was astonishing. There was a yell of approval that sent birds all over the grounds shooting into the air. Men cheered and clapped one another on the back as if some great victory had been announced. Bryant's face broke into a relieved smile. He had his answer from his men.

It is unfashionable today to talk of pride of country and as the disillusioning years have swept on I myself have concluded the world would be a far better place if internationalism took its place instead. But I was still young and in spite of all that had happened to my parents I felt that day that I belonged to a great nation and a great people. I also knew that, however small my contribution might be, I was lucky to be alive and young on that grim but glorious Sunday.

But such emotions, however inspiring, are difficult to sustain during the daily grind of worry, work and study. After our initial impression that we were on a 'doddle' at Prestwick, it took us only one week to realise we were on a highly concentrated and difficult course instead.

As promised, I will not go into details but apart from wireless theory which I found interesting, the endless Morse code with its shrill dots and dashes blipping into one's ears became more than tiring. By the time

17.00 hours came each day, we resembled glassy-eyed zombies as we stumbled out of the stables.

Yet although we grumbled, we were only too aware how lucky we were alongside the poor devils in France who were now fighting for their survival. Not that we heard much about them at this time. A massive blanket of security came down when hundreds of small ships were sent to France to bring them back to England and we could only hope for the best. When news broke that most of the Army had been saved, relief showed on all faces, particularly on mine when I heard some time later that Stewart had escaped.

However, there was little or no relaxation of tension. Everyone was waiting to hear what terms France would make with her old enemy. When we heard she had surrendered her navy without a fight I am afraid we all saw it as pure treachery.

On the Sunday of that momentous week I had the first of my eventual lucky escapes. I was put on guard duty on the main gate of Adampton House, a four-hour spell in the morning and another four hours in the afternoon. However a colleague who was down for duty the next day asked if I would exchange dates and as it was Sunday I was only too glad to agree. Des and I took the opportunity of a walk along the Carrie Hills and did not return to the Griersons' until dinner time.

It was then to my surprise that Mrs Grierson burst into tears and threw her arms around me. She had known I was supposed to be on guard duty that day and news had reached her that a fully laden Anson aircraft had crashed into the main gate while coming in to land at the nearby airfield and killed the sentry.

We had no way of getting back to Adampton, so had to wait until the morning to find out exactly what had happened. It was not a pleasant sight, although by that time the bodies had been removed. But it had been a much worse sight for those who had run from the house and tried to save the victims from the flames. The heat had beaten them back but they had heard a man screaming long after he ought to be dead. A further horror had been seen after the flames had died down. A man was visible sitting in the cockpit and from one side of the wreckage he was charred to a crisp. Yet from the other side he was practically unmarked and looked still alive.

It was a freak accident that lay like a shadow over us for a couple of days. Death by fire was the thing all aircrews feared and we had encountered it early. Certainly it did serve to remind us that we were not, after all, students at some country college.

The news from Hull was little better either. Although not as bad as those to follow, Hull was receiving raids almost weekly. Situated as it was on the sharp bend in the river Humber, it was an easy target for enemy bombers to find, and when we heard on the news that 'a large North East town' had been raided the night before, Des and I knew the chances were high the city had been Hull. With the Dunkirk evacuation completed and the BEF driven out of France, it was felt a German invasion was now imminent and like all military establishments Adampton was put on red alert and all of us given invasion duties whose purpose was to watch out for invasion barges and/or paratroopers.

I had one of these night duties with Gabriel, a member of our flight. Gabby as we nicknamed him was one of the larger-than-life characters who comprised our flight. A few years older than the rest of us, with prior flying experience, Gabby had volunteered to fly for the government in the Spanish Civil War and during the next few months had shot down five of Franco's planes before being shot down himself.

Surviving the crash with only minor injuries, he had been sentenced to death until he volunteered to fight for Franco. Incredibly they had fallen for his blather and he was inducted into Franco's Air Force. He flew a couple of missions with them and then, as soon as the opportunity arose, flew straight out of Spain into France, whence he made his way back to England.

It all sounded the most improbable of stories until one of our flight said he had seen Gabby's log book which endorsed all we had heard. With his record Gabby had fully expected the RAF to accept him as a fighter pilot but to his disbelief the best he could get was WO/AG training with the same promise as Des and I had been given that he would be allowed to re-muster later.

One can imagine the effect this story had on us. If a pilot with combat experience was refused pilot training, what chance did we have? Then the cynicism of the serviceman came to our rescue. With its arse-over elbow way of doing things, wasn't the RAF far more likely to turn to us than to choose a seasoned combat flier?

I had the pleasure or otherwise of spending a night duty with Gabby. Our sentry site was the top of a church tower, a high, square structure with a flat top enclosed by a low wall of ornamental bevelled stones.

It was a cold night, with a blustery wind driving clouds across a sickle moon. As we had only our greatcoats for protection, we were soon chilled and around 2 a.m. Gabby muttered something and began taking off his greatcoat. I stared at him. 'What are you doing that for?'

He grinned at me. He was a small man with a sharp pinched face that made him look like a gnome. 'I'm going to get warm, Smithy.'

I thought he meant he was going back into the church. 'That's all right,' I said. 'We'll take it in turns.'

His grin widened. 'Do you mean it?'

'Yes, why not? No one's going to know.'

'They will if you fall.'

I stared at him again. 'Why should I fall?'

He grinned again and then handed his greatcoat to me. 'Hang on to that and I'll show you why.' Before I could say more, he caught hold of one of the bevelled stones and began pulling himself up on it. I grabbed hold of him. 'What the hell are you doing? Have you gone crazy?'

He glanced back at me, his eyes shining with excitement. 'I'm going to get warm, Smithy. Let go.'

'Get down, you fool. It's a seventy foot drop down there.'

'Shut up and keep still,' he told me.

At that I let go of him and stood back. Hard although it is to believe, he began to walk round the square of bevelled stones. As a gust of wind struck the tower I closed my eyes, expecting to hear the thud of his body on the flagstones below. Instead, I heard him give an excited laugh and my thoughts turned from his safety to mine. If he fell what would I tell the police?

Surely they'd never believe any man would be such a fool to risk his life this way. They would believe we had quarrelled and I had thrown him over the wall. My God, yes. I might be accused of murder!

To cut the story short he circled the tower twice before telling me how warm the excitement had made him and how better I would feel if I did the same. I won't repeat what I said to him but the incident does epitomise the kind of men found among aircrews in those early days of the war. Although modern psychology might state they had a death wish, it made them highly suited to the role they were given. As our flight had more than its fair share of them and although we of more cautious genes eyed them with disbelief at first, such devil-may-care temperaments are infectious, and before long we all found ourselves doing things that once we would have thought crazy. Nor do I think anyone will now be surprised why I used Gabby as one of my characters in my 633 Squadron novels in later years. Nor do I think he would have minded either.

TWENTY-FIVE

It is fascinating to look back and realise that the clock of one's life runs on a different time scale when one is young. Although after our first month at Prestwick we had only been in the RAF for a total of eight weeks, it seemed like years at the time and made us feel we were veterans.

Perhaps for that reason Des and I became impatient with the wireless course. If we could have by-passed it and made purely air gunners, we would both have settled for that. Although I for one had no burning desire to kill my enemies, with the country bracing itself for a massive invasion, the prospect of being relatively untrained appealed to neither of us.

But it seemed there was no escape. The RAF had enrolled us as WO/AGs and wireless operators the RAF would make us. So we could only knuckle down to it and hope for the best.

By this time we had sampled most of the entertainments the district had to offer. In Prestwick there was the local cinema and the bathing pool on the sea front. In Ayr there were more cinemas, a dance hall called Bobby Jones, and a large ice rink. In the surrounding district there was Bellister Park and Manor, and lying to the west of Ayr the memorabilia of Robbie Burns with his old cottage and the Banks o' Doone.

I was shown the Burns' monuments by Margaret, a girl of the same family name who claimed to be a direct descendent of the poet. How I met her I can't remember but she knew everything there was to know about Burns and his life. As I was never keen on drinking, I would sometimes meet her when the boys were spending a night in the local pub.

It was nothing more than a platonic friendship. She was engaged to a boy in the navy and I had my infatuation with Becky. But we enjoyed one another's company and it was she who introduced me to the Carrie Hills, from which one had a superb view of the coastline as far as the Clyde. As we were now living under double summer time, there were hours in the evenings to walk the entire length of the hills before taking the bus back to Prestwick.

Another month passed without invasion although scares and rumours were heard almost daily. The air war was growing even fiercer, particularly over the south of England. It was, of course, the beginning of the Battle of Britain, although it was not given that name at the time. We all knew that if the battle was lost, a massive invasion was inevitable. The effect was to heighten our feeling of impotence.

We began having gas drills at this time, which made us believe the war was soon to take an even uglier turn, and it was a grotesque sight to see a hundred odd men, looking like elephantine creatures from another planet in their gas masks and capes, running about those spacious lawns with their gazebos and flower beds. I could never escape the feeling that we were defiling them.

Because our hosts, the Griersons, had relatives coming to stay with them that month, Des and I had to move our billets. Our new quarters was a house set among rockeries and flower beds and owned by a man named Taylor who was a director of the Johnny Walker whisky firm. After being given refreshments by him and his wife, we were shown our room, which was an observatory sitting room that overlooked the Prestwick golf course. Beyond it was the sea and then the Isle of Arran, a spectacular view on a clear day. When the Taylors withdrew, we sank down into our chairs and looked at one another. Was it possible we had fallen on our feet again? When after a week our hosts invited us to dine with them on Sundays and bought us two new chairs because they felt the originals were not comfortable enough, it was all too much to believe. Or it could mean only one thing. Fate was fattening us up for the slaughter.

To add to our incredulity and against all we had been told earlier, we were given four days leave shortly afterwards. My father, as dependable as ever, met me at the station. I remember thinking how tired he looked, the result of working all day and fire-watching at night. On our way home he told me it was the first Friday for weeks there had been no air raid alarm.

But perhaps it is better not to dwell too much on those four days because there is no doubt they were emotionally charged. Like all leaves it was a balancing act. You knew your parents wanted you to spend as much time with them as possible and yet you had your girl friend to see too. So no matter how you tried you knew someone would be hurt and nine times out of ten the losers were those who deserved it least.

It was such a leave. Becky managed to visit the house one afternoon and we persuaded mother to play the piano, which my father said she had not played since I was called up. We played and sang for hours, indeed we must have gone through our entire repertoire. It was a sentimental occasion for us and one I remembered often in the days ahead.

I tried to see as many friends as I could although a number had already been called up. Johnnie Gemmell was still in the Guildhall, however, and he came round one evening and took photographs of us all. He seemed very fond of Becky and she of him, but with them both close friends of mine I thought nothing of it. My mother's state of mind was worrying me however. Since seeing a German plane shot down in flames, she had developed a paranoia about flying, and I found her pleading for me to request a transfer very distressing.

The second debit side of that leave came when Becky told me she had completed her course at the Victoria Hospital and in seven weeks time would taking further training in a large London hospital.

I was more than upset. Not only would it be far more difficult to see her but everyone felt London would soon be the target for massive air raids. With selfish thoughts mixed with concern for her safety, I did all I could to dissuade her. I even brought up the matter of our engagement which she had earlier felt should wait until our futures were more defined. Although she still wanted to wait, to soften my disappointment she handed me one of her own rings which I then put on her finger. Although we both laughed, I don't think either of us were certain how to take the moment.

So the leave ended and my father drove me in his firm's van to the station. To my relief mother decided to stay at home but her expression as we said goodbye made me realise as never before the hell war is for parents.

To my relief Des was also on the station with his parents and his girl friend. As I chatted to them I heard my name called and saw Becky running towards us. She had risked the wrath of her matron to be there and she pressed a packet of cigarettes into my hand as she kissed me. Then a last handshake with my father and the train was pulling away. As their two figures grew smaller on the platform and I dropped back into my seat I found my feelings impossible to analyse. Had the leave been a success or a failure? There was only one thing I could be sure about at that moment. Welcome as leaves were they drained one emotionally.

TWENTY-SIX

The journey Des and I took back to Prestwick was as uncomfortable as all train journeys were at this time, but my feelings about Becky were greatly eased when I received a letter from her two days later. Her work, she explained, did not come before me, and it was only because of the war and the fact that she and I were likely to be separated for a long time that she had decided to take the London course. A State Registered Certificate would not only allow her to be more useful during the war but it might also be a financial asset to us both after we were married.

It was a well written letter with some moving passages, and although it did nothing to lessen my fears for her safety, it eased any doubts about her affection for me. With her London plans my only reservation, I wrote back to tell her so.

September came and with it the first anniversary of the war. During this time Des and I had met a Lancastrian named Bob Roberts, and when we discovered he was also sending in weekly applications to re-muster for pilot training our friendship grew until the three of us became known as the Three Musketeers. It was also the time when London suffered its first mass air raid. It came on a Sunday when at least 400 people were killed and over 1400 seriously injured. Heavy damage was done to the docks and hundreds of homes were now only piles of rubble. On Monday a second raid there killed over two hundred civilians with 1300 injured.

It was, of course, the end of the Battle of Britain and the beginning of the blitz on our cities. We knew now if we had not known it before that this was to be a fight to the death with no mercy shown to soldier or civilian alike.

Needless to say our personal feeling of impotence grew but the only change in our circumstances came when we were ordered to leave our billets and move into Rosemount, another Prestwick wireless school. Rosemount was a Scottish manor house similar to Adampton, and we were transferred there because the four wireless flights it had been training were moving south.

So Des and I had to leave our kindly Mr and Mrs Taylor and billet with the other twenty-four men of our flight. It was a huge contrast but considering what others were going through at this time I hope we kept our grumbles to ourselves.

I had more news about Ray at this time. After an operation on his infected lung, another cavity had been found which suggested the disease might be spreading. Being told officially his dancing days were over and believing he had not long to live, he expressed a wish to see me but by this time there was no chance whatever of compassionate leave. On the radio Churchill told us that the Germans were massing barges all the way from Norway to Southern France and that we must be ready for invasion at any time.

Naturally enough, my objections to Becky going to London were increased tenfold by all this news and my letters expressed it. While she made no mention of her forthcoming move she did tell me that my mother had lent her one of her own dress rings to wear until we had the chance to look for an engagement ring ourselves. I remember wondering if this meant we were now formally engaged.

The one bright spot in the general gloom came when Becky wrote to say she was being given a fortnight's leave before going to London and would I like her to spend a week with me in Prestwick. If I did, she could come on the following Wednesday.

Coming as a total surprise it would have been a delight had I not just heard that our entire unit was shortly moving out and unless she could come quickly we might have only a couple of days together. So I phoned her hospital and to my relief she obtained permission to leave the following Monday. Excited again I buzzed about Prestwick trying to find accommodation we could afford. Eventually I was put in touch with a kindly spinster, Miss Kerr, who offered us bed and breakfast for four shillings a night.

We had begun flying that week, going up in an old four-engined Fokker after our daily lectures. Our route took us over the Carrie Hills, down to the Southern Highlands, then east to Edinburgh, over the Solway Firth, then across to the Clyde, and south again to Prestwick. There was a certain tension when we flew along the east coast because only a week before an Anson carrying four pupils from another flight, had been attacked and shot down by a Messerschmitt 110.

Monday came, only for me to find I was down for guard duty. To help me out, one of our flight, a Canadian Starkey-Benz, did my duty for me, so allowing me to meet Becky at the station.

It was a reunion made even happier because only a few weeks before nothing had seemed more unlikely, and it was not until the evening that Becky gave me her news about Johnnie Gemmell. Only a few days after I had returned to Prestwick he had paid her a visit and confessed that he had fallen in love with her.

In a way I think it had surprised her more than it did me. After all, she was a vivacious, attractive girl and Johnnie, for all his intelligence, had always given the impression of being a lonely man. Perhaps I should have shown some indignation at his confession, which could be construed as an attempt to win her from me, but I felt I could hardly blame him for emotions that I had myself. Moreover jealousy has always seemed to me the most sterile of emotions, so I cannot say my friendship towards him was in any way affected.

The week that followed was idyllic in many ways, perhaps because we knew it must be our last for a long time. Each day I would make for Miss Kerr's house the moment our lessons broke up and spend the sunlit evenings showing Becky the beauty spots I had learned to love. After dark we might spend an hour or two in Green's Café in Ayr, in the Kettledrum, or the Dutch tea rooms, although how we afforded to have even a cup of tea in such places I can't imagine because money was a perpetual problem in those times. While I don't remember accepting any from my friends, I have no doubt they would give it because by this time there was a camaraderie between us that knew no limits of generosity.

Most nights, however, we spent in Miss Kerr's old-world sitting room. She, dear understanding soul, would retire to bed by ten o' clock, leaving us alone until I had to leave for camp. This was usually between 2 a.m. and 3 a.m., and as the last transport to Rosemount left at 10.45, it meant I had a long walk ahead of me. In fact, I seldom sank into my bunk before 4.30 a.m. With our passes expiring at midnight, it was the 'blindness' of the guards, all drawn from our own unit, that made it possible. Most of them knew my girl friend was in Prestwick and I wasn't challenged once during her entire stay there.

When our last day together arrived, I decided to break out of camp. Aware of the risk I was taking, Des and Bob decided they had to share the risks with me and did the same. (By this time we were so inseparable that we were known by officers and men alike as The Three Musketeers). While the other two headed for Glasgow, I spent the day with Becky. By this time we were down to our last few pennies, and I remember we laughed a great deal over what we could and could not afford. It all helped us to forget the morrow.

Sad day although the morrow was, it was eased for me by Becky agreeing to postpone her move to London, a thing I had been nagging since it had come to my notice. At the same time it was of little help when I left her in the early hours of that day. She was due to catch the 9.45 a.m. train, and as it seemed certain I would be slapped into the guardroom on my return, I had no hopes of seeing her off at the station.

Until then I had walked the three miles back to Rosemount every night since her arrival and it had seemed little more than a stroll. Nor had I missed my sleep, although I can't have had more than two to three hours a night. This night, however, the miles seemed endless, and with a drizzle coming down and a mist clothing the flanking trees, I realised for the first time that autumn was here and winter not far away.

TWENTY-SEVEN

Even if the word were only used figuratively, winter was most certainly the right word when we were told our next station would be Cranwell. Known as the home of the RAF, Cranwell was said to have the toughest NCOs in the country and a malicious MP behind every lamp post. After our easy time in Scotland it was not a posting any of us relished.

It also meant saying goodbye to the many Scottish friends we had made. Among mine was Margaret Burns whom I had not seen before my leave home. I was shocked at her appearance when she stepped off the bus. She was dressed in black, her face was pale, and her eyes swollen with grief. At first she would not tell me what had happened, only saying she would like us to go out to Burns monument and to the river.

Barely a word passed between us on the bus, but when we walked down to the river she told me she had heard the previous day that her fiancé had been killed and lost at sea.

I didn't know what words to say although I remember telling her she should not have made the effort to see me that day. As she would not let me take her home we spent the rest of the evening visiting the places she loved. Before we parted she took my hand, and said very quietly: 'Will you promise me something, F.E?'

'Yes,' I managed. 'If I can.'

'Don't get yourself killed, F.E. It hurts one's family and friends so much.'

Before I could say anything, she reached forward and kissed me. Then her bus pulled away and I never saw her again.

I remember very well my thoughts that night. The world was now so full of sorrow that one's very body ached in sympathy. Already there was a tidal wave of it and yet the war was only in its early stages and the full hell was yet to come. The thought was so awe-inspiring, so overwhelming, that it numbed the mind.

We moved out two days later and said goodbye to our friends, in particular Miss Kerr, the Griersons, and the Taylors. All gave us presents and the women shed a tear or two. All came to the station to see us off and they were not alone. There must have been over two hundred other townsfolk paying us farewell too. They were warm-hearted people in Prestwick and Ayr and I know we all left them with deep regret.

Nor did our foreboding about Cranwell seem misplaced when our train reached

Lincolnshire and began chugging over its flat, mist-enveloped fields that were such a contrast to the heather covered hills of Scotland. I think every man of us knew that our salad days were over, and to be fair to our better selves, we did not regret it. We knew we had been on a relative picnic for over three months and it was high time we played a more active part in the war before it was won or lost. We little knew at that time that there was no urgency: that it was to last for another five endless years.

Cranwell did not disappoint our forebodings. With its huge expanse surrounded by fences and guards, it seemed designed specifically to bring down to earth airmen who, by some administrative bungle, had been allowed to escape the discipline designed to deflate all men who take the King's Shilling.

If that was its purpose, it went about its task with awesome gusto. It had some of the foulest mouthed NCOs I had ever encountered. After having a clash with one I remember one of those fantasy thoughts that invade the mind on such occasions. Perhaps our geologists have got it all wrong. Perhaps beneath the surface of the earth there is a second breed of humankind who are only able to break out and mix with us in wartime. If this is so, Cranwell was their Mecca where they could take revenge on us for their previous incarceration.

And take revenge they did. They bawled at us, yelled at us, screamed and swore at us and after our treatment in Scotland we hated it. To make things worse our Cranwell course consisted entirely of Morse. Every morning and every afternoon dot-dot-dot, dash-dash-dash was fed into our protesting ears.

With Des and Bob wanting a pilot transfer as much as I and also sharing something of my own paranoia about bullies, it was not long before we decided to fight back. After all we were now relatively close to Hull and if some weekend we broke out of Cranwell's high security net and went home, would this not represent some kind of personal victory?

We did this on the weekends when not on duty. Our method was to latch ourselves onto a squad that was being marched out of camp. We would secrete ourselves near one of the main gates and when a squad was marching past, attach ourselves to its rear rank. Then, head high and arms swinging, we would march out past the guards, wait until the right moment came, and then escape to a few hours freedom. This bold-as-brass tactic proved highly successful although our hairy-faced NCOs might well have decided we were cutting off our noses to spite our faces. This was because our illicit excursions only allowed us a few hours at home, and with winter coming early that year most of those hours were spent in dense blackouts, drenching rain, endless delays on draughty railway stations and the risk of being caught on our arrival back to Cranwell. Nevertheless, apart from being psychologically beneficial, the visits allowed us to see that our parents were safe because, with the bombing of Hull and other cities now almost a nightly occurrence, we lived in constant fear they might be the next victims.

Disappointingly however I saw nothing of Becky at this time. She had been transferred to a hospital in Scunthorpe on the other side of the Humber, and it proved impossible to fit in her off duty hours with my unpredictable excursions.

Of course our luck had to end eventually. We were spotted marching out one weekend and given cookhouse duties. On the surface it might be seen as a mild punishment but that was only when one forgot that the population of Cranwell in those days was greater than many a small town and men passed in their thousands through its cookhouses. I was paired with a little Cockney who had a permanent dewdrop at the end of his pointed nose. We stood in front of an enormous sink filled with steaming greasy water. Beside us were fifty-one piles of dirty plates, with approximately forty plates in each pile. (The numbers are exact because they are burned on my brain). These we would lower into the water and sinking our arms up to their elbows in the noxious grease, we would wash them with a rubber cloth provided for the purpose.

This took hours because we had to dry them afterwards. The mountains of dishes would no sooner be finished when the next meal would commence and the ghastly cycle would begin again.

Only God knows how many dishes I washed in that fortnight. By the second week I was desperate. Had some operations officer come to me and said without preamble: 'Smith, we need you for a mission of great danger. Will you volunteer?' I would have sunk on my knees and kissed his polished boots. 'Yes, yes, sir. I'm your man. Just send me. Please!'

I can think of no better way of turning cowards into heroes than a day or two at that steaming sink. Imagination must have been in short supply among our military leaders not to have recognised its potential. The threat alone would have produced Kamikaze pilots by the thousand.

But there are always exceptions. My little Cockney was one. He loved that sink and those dishes. When he heard what my ambition was the dewdrop fell off his nose into the dish water. I wanted to be a pilot! Was I mad? Didn't I know I might get killed? And wasn't I being selfish? Didn't I fink about my parents and my girl friend? If I put in a proper application, I could have this job for the duration. No worries, no danger, just three meals a day and money at the end of it. 'It's a doddle, mate. You've lost yer marbles if yer pass it up.'

I lost my marbles and after a fortnight returned to my flight with red forearms and a deflated ego. It was then we somehow met the officer whose advice was to totally change the direction of our service lives. How it came about I cannot remember unless it was due to the weekly applications that Des, Bob and I had been putting in since our arrival. Whatever the reason this officer called the three of us in to ask why we were being so persistent in our applications for pilot training. What was this talk about the promise we had been made?

Seeing he was a man prepared to listen, we poured out our hearts and told him everything. Could he not help us? With all we had learned so far, we would pass the pilots' course in double quick time.

When we had said it all, we made our last desperate plea. If what we asked was totally impossible, then could we not be made into straightforward air gunners? We were total misfits as wireless operators.

Our fervour seemed to impress him and to our amazement he said he would try to help us. But in turn we would firstly have to re-muster to another trade. If we did that, and passed the course, there was then every chance our applications for pilot's training would be accepted.

We believed him, although none of us wanted to waste time learning a trade we wouldn't need. So we asked his advice and he suggested the trade of gun armourer. It was only a short course of eight weeks and the knowledge we would acquire of guns and their ancillary equipment would be of great use to us when we went on the pilot's course.

Seeing our hesitation, our friendly officer must have been something of a psychiatrist because he added that armourer was a man's trade and full of danger. In addition gun armourers were still being used as air gunners in some squadrons, a thing we all knew to be true.

I think that final sentence clinched it for us. We took his word that the course would prove a passport to our ambition, and from my point of view, having handled guns since a child, I felt it was a course I could pass quickly. So we filled in the necessary applications and waited for our posting. How little I guessed at the time the effect it was to have on my personal life.

TWENTY-EIGHT

During our vicissitudes at Cranwell my brother Ray had been moved to a London hospital to undergo more surgery and had again asked to see me. As we heard it would be at least a couple of weeks before our gun armourer posting would come through, I was allowed a short compassionate leave to visit him. I remember thinking Cranwell had its good side after all.

There was no way I could afford to take the train down to London, so I had to hitch hike my way there. My diary says I needed fifteen lifts before arriving. As it was now dark and my first visit to London, I was a long while finding the best way to the South Mimms Sanatorium. By the time I did, the sirens had gone and there was no possibility of finding transport. Searchlights were criss-crossing the sky, anti-aircraft guns firing, and soon bombs began to fall. Yelled at by wardens to take cover, I tramped down pitch-black, deserted streets looking for a shelter. Eventually I found a police station and sought advice there. They suggested a large boarding house further down the road and I ran for it.

I found its shelter full of beds: the common practice in those hectic days. I received no welcome from the woman who ran the boarding house. If bombs hadn't been falling she would without doubt have told me to look elsewhere. As it was, she said the shelter was too full but there was a spare bed on the top floor of the house if I wanted to take the chance of sleeping there.

As things stood I had little option. The room was tiny with a boarded-up window so one could not see what was happening outside. Perhaps it was as well because by this time the explosion of bombs was deafening and shards of shrapnel from the ack-ack guns were raining on the roof. Deciding it was better not to get undressed, I lay on the bed and tried to sleep.

I was not that hard-boiled. Plaster kept falling from the roof and every now and then the house would rock to some massive explosion. However, I must have drifted off for a few hours because I was suddenly aware that there was a chink of daylight in the blacked out window and the hellish din had ceased.

I paid the woman grudgingly and began hitch hiking towards the sanatorium. As it was north of London, I didn't arrive there until noon but Ray's expression on seeing me made everything worthwhile. During our conversation I learned that a week or two ago, while undergoing surgery, bombs had damaged the hospital emergency generators and his operation had been carried out in candlelight. No place, it seemed, was safe now that total war had begun.

Although he made no complaints, I thought at first how wan and ill he looked. But as we talked colour began to come back into his cheeks and his conversation became more cheerful. Later he was to tell mother and father in a letter that our meeting had done him a power of good. I found that very gratifying.

We had most of the afternoon together before I had to leave. By this time darkness was falling and well before I reached London another raid had started. With all traffic except emergency vehicles cleared from the roads, there was no chance of my hitch hiking back to Cranwell so I spent the night in a public shelter, full of crying babies and distraught mothers.

When the all-clear sounded towards daylight, I started off again. My route took me by the large house in which I had stayed the previous night. At least it had been large then. All that was left of it now were a few shattered walls and a huge smoking hole in the ground. I think that was the moment when I realised the war was making us nothing but playthings of fate and our destiny was almost totally out of our hands.

Back again at Cranwell I found our posting

had not arrived and so somehow managed a day in Scunthorpe to see Becky in her new hospital. We had a meal in a café near the river and for some reason the view from its window stands out in my mind. Everything was very clear and very distinct. The sky was a winter blue, the river calm and still, and the barrage balloons poised over Hull were standing out as if seen through a three-dimensional lens. It was one of those days that England seems to have as her own. To prolong our time together I saw her back to the hospital and we said our goodbyes at its gates.

Our posting arrived a few days later. It was to Creden Hill, a camp near Hereford. Congratulating ourselves that the Three Musketeers were still one unit we set off with high hopes that our posting was our first real step towards pilot training.

It took less than a day at Creden Hill to make us wonder if we had been misled again. If we had thought Cranwell was a tough camp, Creden Hill taught us how much we still had to learn. Rumour had it that its CO had once been in charge of the 'glasshouse' (slang for the RAF Punishment Centre) and no one had any reason to doubt it. Our first inkling of it came when we were issuing blankets so damp that one could squeeze water from them. Then came news of our course. Before it even began we would have an examination that would grade us. Only then would our armourer training begin. As for out of camp permits, they would be granted for only three evenings a week and even then we had to report back by 9.30pm.

To be fair to all three of us I don't think we complained about these rules and regulations. If they had to be obeyed to get us pilot training, so be it. It would all be worth it for the reward at the end.

We had our grading examination two days later. As we all passed into the 'A' class of the course we were told we would begin our gun training right away.

During this time we had been moved from billet to billet until we finally ended up in one of the two huts that housed our course. I mention this because of what happened shortly after our move into it. Taken there while the others were out on a parade, we found a few empty beds and deposited our kit alongside three of them. Then, while Des and Bob went off to the NAAFI, I waited for the rest of the course to return.

At this point in time we had not met them and I viewed them with interest as they filed in. Unlike the aircrews we had known in Prestwick, their ages varied from young men of our age up to men of thirty-five. Their background, as we were to learn later, was equally varied. Many had not progressed beyond elementary school and had been manual workers, yet some of the older ones were professional men and one or two owned their own businesses.

So democracy was in evidence among them and, just as I was reflecting that they seemed a reasonable bunch of men, one character came to my bedside and nudged my arm. Burly in build, he had a flattened nose with scarred eyebrows and a thin, vicious mouth. Without preamble, he told me he wanted the bed and I had to 'fuck off out of it'.

I stared up at him. 'Why? Don't you have a bed?'

'Yeh, I've got a bed,' he said. 'But I want that one?'

'Why?' I asked again.

'What the fuck's that to do with you? I want it, so fuck off.'

Since my entry into the Armed Forces I had never failed to be amazed how this one word could be used as so many parts of speech. But this character brought a new dimension to its use. I sat up and swung my feet to the floor. 'I still don't understand why you want this bed if you've got one already.'

Another leer, this time a threatening one, and a tobacco-stained finger jabbed at the coke stove nearby. 'See that, sonny. That's fucking why. Now are you movin' or do I make you.'

I still kept my temper, although more out of astonishment at his behaviour than from self-control. 'Go away,' I said, or something to that effect. 'The bed was empty and I'm staying in it.'

At that his language went from bad to worse. Words of filth I had never heard poured from him. Then he made his big mistake. He grabbed my arm to drag me from the bed.

That was it. I jumped up and hit him with all my strength in his stomach. As he folded up like a punctured tyre, I brought my knee up into his face with such force that he cart-wheeled over the neighbouring bed before collapsing in a heap on the floor. As I sank back on my bed, someone in the hut let out his breath and muttered 'Jesus Christ'. Then shouts of approval came from all sides. It seemed Flat Nose was not the most popular man on the course.

Nevertheless there was some concern because the brute was a couple of minutes before he recovered consciousness. When he stumbled from the hut I thought he had gone to the M.O. and expected the arrival of MPs to take me away for assault. Instead I heard nothing further from him and found out later he had arranged to move into another hut. As he was on a different course to ours I saw next to nothing of him after that.

In spite of this, the encounter had an effect on me. Had my reaction been due to my paranoia about bullies? If Flat Nose could trigger off such a violent response, what would the war do to my temperament in the days ahead? It was not a thought I welcomed.

My other thoughts were purely Pickwickian. Perhaps that underground world which such characters came from was only a large sewer. It would certainly account for their language and so made it even more likely why they resented our open air existence. But to breed and multiply they must have women down there and what kind of woman could mingle with, much less have sex with such depraved animals? It will be noted from these thoughts that I still had a high opinion of the weaker sex.

Having received Grade A marks from our examination Des, Bob and I were introduced to our corporal instructor. He was a small man who was endlessly complaining about his indigestion and his enforced separation from his wife, and he seemed to take a perverse delight in following me around and complaining about the quality of my practical work. Initially this was cutting and shaping pieces of metal to prescribed shapes and sizes, and although I freely admit that 'metal bashing' was not my forte, I soon grew tired of his complaining and told him that when all this nonsense was over and we got to the nitty gritty of the course, he would find that I could handle guns as well or better than he.

Although later this was proven true, it made no difference to our corporal. Foolishly, I had made an enemy whose spite was to hurt me severely in the weeks ahead.

We moved over to guns after eight days in the workshop. Our brief was to learn about every weapon and every projectile launcher used in the Air Force. These were many and included Very pistols, the 3" signal cannon, .38 Smith and Wesson and Webley revolvers, Lee Enfield Rifles, Brownings, Lewis and Vickers machine guns, and so on all the way up to the huge 20mm Hispano cannon. As we had to know the name of every part and to assemble every weapon blindfold, it was a course that in peacetime took several months. As it was, we had eight weeks to either pass or fail.

I don't think any of the three of us found this a problem. We had set our hearts on the pilot's course and if this was to be the stepping stone to that ambition, we would make quite certain we passed it. We even enrolled in an evening night class, not because we needed the simple mathematics that were taught but because we felt the mention of it on our documents might further our case.

Yet in spite of its seamy side Creden Hill had its compensations. Its greatest was its countryside. With my need to be alone at times, I'd put up with the problems of obtaining evening passes to escape into it. Snow had fallen recently and the Herefordshire hills were looking quite beautiful. I remember one evening just before Christmas leaning against a gate and gazing down at a village below. Because of the snow the silence had a breathless quality and as I listened I heard the faint sound of carols as the faithful in the village confirmed their allegiance to the Prince of Peace. I was only too aware of the irony and yet the gentle rise and fall of those voices seemed to give hope that one day the world'd recover its senses and peace would take the place of barbarism. When I finally broke the spell and returned to camp, I felt rested and at peace with myself again.

TWENTY-NINE

Christmas Eve arrived and half the hut, including Des, Bob and myself were put on duty. Because of the bitter cold Des was detailed as a 'bog orderly', which meant he had to pull every WC chain in our wing of the camp to prevent the cisterns freezing up. Thus he would appear every fifteen minutes to warm his hands before continuing on his vital task. Each visit would be greeted with cheers and ribald comments, and I can still see his face as he received them, for, without his saying a word, Des could produce in his expression the most wonderful mixture of wry humour and disgust.

Not that he could have gained much warmth from popping into our hut because the national fuel shortage meant we seldom had more than half a dozen cinders of coke glowing at one time in our stove. It'd be no exaggeration to say that we were cold twenty-four hours a day that Christmas and most of us were driven to sleeping in our uniforms.

Bleak and cold the camp undoubtedly was but we in our hut had noticed there was a tempting pile of coke at the back of the NAAFI building. For days we had racked our brains how to reach it but it was protected by a high, chain-link mesh fence topped by barbed wire. Then John Denton, a member of our course, came up to me with what he called a great idea.

Denton was a member of The Three Apostles, a trio so named because of their forenames, Mark, Luke and John. Denton was in his mid-thirties, one of the better-educated men I have mentioned. Luke, the second member of the holy trinity, was a man of much the same age and background. The only blue-collared member of the trio was Mark, an ex-miner, and as rivalry between the Three Musketeers and the Three Apostles was always likely to end in a physical if friendly confrontation, we suspected he had been drafted into holy orders less for the sanctity of his name than for the muscle he provided.

John's conversation to me went something like this. 'There is a way round this fuel problem, Smithy. Only it's something you have to do.'

'I? What?'

'Arrange it from the inside. Get the girls to give us a bag or two.'

'How can I do that?'

'C'mon, Smithy. You're smooth with women. You tell them how cold we are.'

'You think that's going to make any difference? There are a thousand men here just as cold. So why should they help us?'

At that John put a forefinger alongside his nose. 'It'll be payment, Smithy.'

I stared at him. 'Payment for what?'

'For services rendered. I'm thinking of Betty, the one Des says took a shine to you on your first night here. She'll be putty in your hands, lad.'

By this time half the hut had gathered around us and were listening. My yelp was one of indignation. Although Betty was a worthy enough girl, fate had not gone to extremes over her appearance. Indeed one wit had likened her to Olive Oyl, Popeye's flat-chested and spindly girl friend in the popular cartoon series. 'You think I'm going to seduce her? So you can get a bag of coke for Christmas?'

John was nothing if not Machiavellian. His look reproved me and then moved round the circle of grinning men. 'I'm not thinking of myself, Smithy. Nor should you. This is for your comrades in arms. An act of self-sacrifice. A Christmas gift, if you like.'

As a loud murmur of approval came, I knew I was in grave danger. Before I could speak, John gave a raunchy grin and went on: 'It'll be easy, lad. You promise Betty bliss beyond her wildest dreams on condition she opens that coke yard gate for just thirty minutes.'

As loud shouts of approval rang out I knew he was winning and my protests became more hysterical. 'She could get the sack for that. Anyway, the other girls wouldn't let her.'

'Then promise them the same. That'll keep 'em quiet.'

'Who the hell do you think I am? Casanova?'

'C'mon, Smithy. Betty's our only chance for a decent Christmas. You can't throw it away. Not when we all rely on you.' John's gaze moved round the circle of grinning faces. 'Doesn't everyone agree?'

From the back-slapping and encouraging shouts that followed, I knew I was defeated. So on the night before Christmas 1941 I performed one of the most selfless acts of my life. It wasn't the deed of glory I had hoped to perform for my country, but as I watched John and his other two villains gleefully carting off bags of coke to our billet, I reflected that no matter what his ambitions, a man is limited by his opportunities and so can only do his best within those limits. As I sank back in my bed that night in a warm hut, I felt I had done mine in full measure.

Our gun course ended in February and was to be followed by a fitter's course taken somewhere up north. After it was completed we had been assured our re-muster application would be granted and we would commence our pilot's training. Full of hope and confidence, and longing to see the back of Creden Hill, the three of us waited for our postings to arrive.

They came but my name was not among them. Des and Bob were down to go but I was not.

I couldn't believe it. At the end of our training we had taken a final examination and I had found it so easy that I had obtained 100% marks. Then how could my name be omitted when others, who had done far less well, were on the list? Feeling it must be a mistake, I made a violent protest but to no avail. My spiteful little corporal had taken his revenge by insisting a fitter's course would be useless to me.

I was shattered, particularly when I learned that those not going on the fitter's course would be posted abroad. That meant many things and all of them huge disappointments. It meant goodbye to my parents and Becky, it meant goodbye to Des and Bob, and in effect goodbye to my hopes of pilot training. In my state of mind I hardly knew which was the greatest loss.

Because our ambitions had become known to the other men and because they all knew what close friends The Three Musketeers were, a number of them offered to exchange places with me. As a wartime posting abroad meant a minimum of three years for a married man and four years for a single and would almost certainly land one in an active theatre of war, these were astonishing offers although at the time I was too upset to fully appreciate them.

Unable, however, to accept such sacrifices I sought an interview with the C.O. Believing until now he was an unfeeling despot, I was surprised by his reception. He appeared to know all about me and praised me for my course results. As this praise was quite fulsome I used them to support my case. I must have put up quite a reasonable one because he said he would not only recommend me for pilot training (and fighter-pilot training at that) but would also recommend me for a commission.

It all sounded too good to be true and of course it was because before the interview ended he issued his regretful warning. He would do everything in his power for me but I must remember that Records seldom changed their minds about overseas postings and 'he was only an officer'. I should also be warned that Records moved slowly and I might well be on a ship before a decision was made.

I left unsure whether to be hopeful or depressed. In the meantime, Des stepped in. Fully aware that if his application were accepted, he would also lose his chance of pilot training, he tried to get himself off the fitter's course and to be included in my overseas draft. It was typical of him and he would not let me dissuade him. Fortunately his application was turned down flat.

So that was that. After all our postings and times together, the Three Musketeers were to be separated at last. To make certain my cup of misery overflowed, the leave I should have been given at the end of the course was cancelled because of my overseas posting.

I saw them both off at the guardroom. Later I returned to my hut. The boys there wanted to take me to the canteen and get me drunk, but all I wanted to do was crawl into a hole and pull it closed around me. Had it been possible I am sure that is what I would have done.

THIRTY

The next few days at Creden Hill were spent having medicals, dental examinations, and waiting for orders. In all, seven days passed before we were issued with ration cards. Even then we were kept standing in full kit near the guardroom for over three hours before transports came to take us to the nearest rail station.

We were being given twelve days leave, after which we had to report to West Kirby for dispersal overseas. As I would be away for four years, I had not yet told my parents, feeling it was news better given in person. As for Becky, I had wired her and she said she would do her very best to get over from Scunthorpe for a couple of days.

As many other men must have experienced, those overseas leaves were so packed with emotions that it was difficult to handle them. My first one on my arrival was a happy one. Ray was home. He had made such good progress since his last operation that the hospital had felt it safe to release him. With her two sons both home, even if only for a short time, my mother was happier than I had seen her for years.

After that it was a kaleidoscope of events during which one's spirits rose and fell in bewildering sequence. Stewart managed a couple of days with us and I heard the details of his Dunkirk escape. Becky managed her couple of days and this time agreed on our engagement which made me feel that the clouds that had occasionally shadowed our relationship had disappeared at last. I remember her words as I slipped the ring on her finger. 'When you go, I shall miss you quite dreadfully. I shall feel as I did when my mother died. I want you to know that.'

I don't know what I replied. I don't know there is a reply to such a comment. But although that was a credit, the debits came just as quickly too. My mother contracted pleurisy and was very ill for a few days, Ray told me in private that in spite of what he had told mother he had given up all hope of a permanent recovery. On top of everything else none of us could forget the long separation soon to come. It hung like a black cloud over everything we thought or did.

It all ended with Dad and Ray seeing me off at the station. Dad had said very little over the weekend but then he never needed to. He understood me better than I knew myself, and a handshake from him was worth a thousand words. Even in those days I was aware what a sensitive and understanding intelligence he had and nothing that happened in the years ahead ever changed this opinion. I was more than lucky with my parents.

My journey to Liverpool was not as difficult as journeys could be in those days and I arrived at my transit camp on time. The camp had the cheerless appearance that all such places had, and the welcome awaiting new arrivals was the standard one: we were kept waiting hours in the bitter cold before a hut was found us for the night. The one bright spot in a depressing day was the appearance of some of the lads who had been at Creden Hill with me. Huddled together round stoves that seemed to give out no heat, we did our best to cheer one another up.

It was not always easy. One man, Les Osborne, I felt particularly sorry for. He had a son that he had only seen once and the thought of going abroad for three years was crushing him. Like the rest of us, he was afraid the country might be invaded while he was away, in which case it was unlikely he would see his boy again and the fear of this was his nightmare.

Our stay at the camp was remarkable only for its discomfort and disorder. Over four thousand of us had now arrived and the food situation alone suggested the expedition was an urgent one. It was nothing for us to queue two hours for our meals and even then they were totally inadequate for grown men.

Queuing, indeed, was our lot at that camp. We queued for everything, and if we were not queuing, we were standing shivering on parades, waiting for orders that never seemed to come. If an enemy spy had mixed with us for information he would have ended up more confused than we were. Not only had we no idea when our convoy was sailing, we did not know its destination.

I spent most of these evenings with Les Osborne, and although I did my best to cheer him up, I can't have been the best of company myself. I had caught a severe cold and I must have infected half the citizens of Hoylake and West Kirby with my sneezing and snuffling.

However, all things come to an end and on our sixth day we were told our destination. It was to be Greece. Until now, since the Italians had invaded that country, the Greek Army had proved more than a match for them and driven them back. But now, with the Germans pushing aside the Italians to do the job themselves, the situation had drastically changed. Although my diary expresses satisfaction that Britain was keeping her promise, general opinion was that our relief force was too late and would prove too costly in lives and ships. Sadly this was to prove only too true.

On the sixth day we were called out on parade to receive our orders and our boat tickets. As we stood there in our thousands, one of those extraordinary things I mentioned earlier happened to me. We had been standing there about an hour when an orderly hurried through the massed assembly and passed a chit to the officer in charge. He read it then lifted his megaphone and called out one name and number. They were mine. My overseas posting was cancelled and I had to fall out of the parade.

I could not believe it. Of all the thousands of men I was the only one dismissed. My first thought was that some clerk at Records had confused one Smith for another. Than I wondered if the recommendation of my C.O. at Hereford had worked the oracle and I was being sent at last on my pilot course. What I had no way of knowing at the time was that my dismissal might not only be saving my life but also changing its entire future in ways I could not even imagine.

On reporting to the Orderly Room I discovered I was being posted to an airfield in Norfolk. Although the posting made no sense to me I was now realising how lucky I was. Not only was I not leaving Becky and my parents for four years but should my pilot training recommendation be accepted, I would be here to receive it. In this happier frame of mind, I took the train to the airfield and reported in to its Orderly Room.

Not altogether to my surprise I discovered no one had received any warning of my arrival. In other words I was a surplus airman with no given role to play. It ended in the most ludicrous way possible. Some administrative officer asked me what I would like to do! Finding I was now at the sharper end of the war I told him about my gunnery training and so a machine gunner I was made.

Thus for the first time in my nine months of service life I had a task of some use and merit, particularly as the air war was now white hot. Finding their losses in direct combat with the RAF were too high, the Germans were now attacking our airfields in an attempt to thin us on the ground. In turn we were defending our cities and airfields with all we had and at the same time still trying to make their losses untenable.

It was a time when I learned more about myself than any other period of my life. I discovered I was a divided personality. By that I mean there was one part of me that detested all that war stood for, its call to meretricious patriotism, its suppression of truth, and its denigration and ruthlessness towards life itself. I detested the fascism of service life with its regimentation and its crudity. Moreover, I discovered that I was a natural rebel who could not help questioning many of the orders I was given (and, by doing so, often finding they were suspect).

And yet I could not escape from the part of me that found pride in my unit, the RAF, that had so far resisted the seemingly invincible Luftwaffe. Nor could I contain my aggression when under attack. I had never thought myself a brave man, but the hatred that rose in me when confronted by a bully or an aggressor seemed to more than compensate for fears of personal safety. At such times I believed that I was worse than the men I despised. All in all, I was discovering a dichotomy in myself that I had not known existed.

It was while I was in Norfolk that we'd news about my one time convoy. Not only had it suffered heavy losses in the Mediterranean but most of the survivors were later either killed or captured in Greece and Crete. Like my experience at Adampton, it seemed a quirk of fate might have saved my life.

THIRTY-ONE

The roller coaster ride that was my service life continued in my following days at the Norfolk Airfield. Astonishingly another overseas posting arrived for me, only again to be cancelled at the last moment. During such unpredictable times, with Scunthorpe not that far away, I was able to see Becky on a few of my off duty days and noticed a strange change in her. She looked the same, she acted the same, her gestures were the same, and yet at times I had the feeling I was talking to another girl.

I was soon to learn why. It seemed she no longer cared for the things she had previously enjoyed, such as the cinema, the theatre, and dancing. Of late such amusements had lost their attraction and her wish now was to become a true Christian and live a life with meaning.

I hardly knew what to make of it. I had always known that she had religious tendencies but they had never disturbed me, perhaps because I had felt the world might be a better place with a little more Christianity. But this sudden shift of priorities did cause me some concern because I wondered if the war victims she was attending daily were affecting her mind.

At the same time I was not such a fool as to quarrel with her. After all, I argued, this world we were enduring was changing us all and if she emerged from it with stronger Christian principles than before it might be no bad thing for either of us.

My suspicion the war was changing her was reinforced graphically when our CO gave me a weekend to visit my parents. The date, which was to prove infamous in Hull's history was the 8th May. As I approached it in the train, two old people in my carriage told me they had left Plymouth because of the bombing there and were going to stay with relations in Hull where they hoped life would be quieter. I hadn't the heart to tell them they were going from the frying man into the fire. Nor did I need to tell them because, when the train was within fifteen miles of the city, all its normal lights were extinguished, leaving only a cold blue light in each carriage. As the old lady gave a whimper of terror and the old man put his arm protectingly around her, I had to turn my head away. War was bad enough for the young. For the old it was the final obscenity.

The night that followed was one to remember. By the time we pulled into Hull's Paragon Station the night sky was ablaze. There were flares, searchlights, the long flashes of guns, the twinkle of bursting anti-aircraft shells, and the immense shuddering flashes of bursting bombs. I helped the old people to reach their relatives, who were pluckily waiting at the barrier for them, then ran back to collect my kit which I had left in the Signals Office. I was just picking it up when there was a scream and a loud whoosh and we all dived to the floor. The entire station shuddered and a large piece of ceiling fell down on us but there was no explosion. We were just congratulating ourselves when half a dozen policemen and wardens rushed in to tell us we must evacuate immediately as the bomb was buried under the pavement outside and, if it were a time-delay, it might cause the entire station to collapse. We pretended to obey but returned after they had gone.

The Germans dropped both time bombs and bombs with screamers that night. The aim of the latter was to terrify and demoralise. One would hear the oom-oom of unsynchronised engines and then a faint scream that would grow louder until it seemed one's eardrums would split. The explosion that followed and the heave of the ground beneath one's feet came almost as a relief after the hellish banshee wail proceeding it.

It was 06.30 am before the raid ended. Some idea of its ferocity can be gauged from the Signals Office. The previous evening it had had twenty-six communication 'tic-tac' machines operating. When we left in the morning, with lines blown up everywhere, only four were still serviceable.

Outside the station the city was unrecognisable. Roads were strewn with broken glass and bomb craters everywhere, many containing Zus 40 bombs designed to kill anyone attempting to remove them. At first glance it looked as if the entire heart of the city had been destroyed and I was full of fear for my family when I started my walk home.

To make walking easier I left my kit in a YMCA hostel, saying I would pick it up later. Even so, the walk of four miles took me over two hours because of the detours caused by exploded or time delayed bombs. The damage was so great that by the time I reached the corner of my parent's road, I hardly dared look down for what I might see.

To my great relief, the house was still standing, although the field behind it was pitted with smoking bomb craters. At the same time my mother's appearance shocked me. Although Dad said she had been very brave for the first few hours, towards dawn the strain had taken a heavy toll. Ironically, her one comfort was that neither Ray nor I were present. Ray had gone to stay with his aunt and uncle in Bridlington for a few days, and she hadn't known that I was on the train that evening.

I was fascinated to hear the news of the raid on the radio later that day. The very words are in my diary. 'Last night there was a short, sharp raid on a north-eastern town. Some damage was done and a number of people were killed.' Beside this entry, there is a number I was given years later. It states that over five hundred people had been killed, with God knows how many injured and maimed. Such were the understatements and lies that war was now forcing upon us. That night I remembered something Quinton Reynolds, the American commentator, had said when making his famous 'London can take it' speech. 'Hatred' he had said in that deep sonorous voice of his: 'Hatred is an honest emotion – as honest as love'. Seeing my mother huddled in the damp shelter and seeing my father's weariness after days and nights of toil I knew only too well what Reynolds meant.

I managed to see Becky a couple of times before my leave ended and although she still showed affection for me her new interest in religion occupied so much of our time that I began to resent it. Foolishly and selfishly I began arguing that the enjoyment of life was not a sin in itself and the kind of self-denial she favoured was neither virtuous nor desirable.

It was not the right approach. When she stressed the selfishness of people dancing and drinking in a world torn by war, my touchy and over-sensitive self began to wonder if she were including me in her condemnations and soon we were skirting the brink of a quarrel.

Naturally I said nothing about it to my parents the next day but my father was too perceptive not to notice my preoccupation. In a pub that evening he startled me by asking what was the problem between myself and Becky.

He showed no surprise when I told him: In some way I never understood, he had foreseen the problem coming and it worried him. In turn I assured him that our relationship was nowhere near breaking point but even if the worst happened, I had no intention of going to pieces. I could only hope my words comforted him.

My last day of leave arrived and as I had arranged to see Becky on my way back to camp, I took the ferry across the Humber. I had the usual problems when trying to see her and because she was only off duty at noon I decided to take a later train back to camp. To my relief she was full of affection that afternoon and so when we said our goodbyes I felt that after all our misunderstandings, at the eleventh hour we had come to terms with them.

While I cannot say my mood was joyous on the journey that followed, at least I felt better than I had hoped. Not that there was much opportunity for reflection because the train was strafed by two enemy aircraft before we reached Peterborough. In a way the attack was not unwelcome for there were no casualties and it did take my mind off the long separation that I believed must come soon.

It was a belief that was short lived. I had no sooner arrived back in camp, where I was forgiven for being eight hours late, when I was told there was a delay in my overseas posting and in the meantime I would co-tinue with my duties in Norfolk as before.

For all the reasons stated, nothing could have suited me more. At the same time I was beginning to see myself as a piece of flot-sam, being tossed hither and thither by a Records Department who, for reasons I could not fathom, just could not decide what to do with me.

THIRTY-TWO

If I had believed my roller coaster had at last entered a level stretch of line on my return to my airfield I was soon disillusioned. In fact I was to experience a series of events that would change my life not merely for the present but for the entire future. Nor did East Anglia offer any clues because by this time it was at its best. Apart from its fields of tulips and its daffodils, the orchards kept by cider makers were coming into bloom, and white and pink buds were everywhere. With the air war as fierce as when I left, the contrast between beauty and death had never seemed so poignant or dramatic. As blossom broke out white and pure against blue skies, as bombs fell and bullets ripped through flesh, it seemed in that glorious spring of 1941 that both heaven and hell were sharing the land together.

One memory remains very vivid. A Hurricane from one of our squadrons had power-dived from 15,000 feet into an orchard. Volunteers were called for and as I was off duty at the time, I felt obliged to put down my name.

A 15 cwt truck took us to the orchard. At first there was little to see except for a few bits and pieces scattered over the site. The high speed of contact had driven the nose and engine deep into the loamy soil and it took us a half hour of digging to find them.

It fell on me to reach the body which by some freak of collision was now underneath the engine. I passed up over twelve pieces of it before reaching the torso proper. As this was welded to the engine, it took three of us to tear it loose and bring it to the surface. Finally the remains were put into a sack and lowered into the back of the transport. The arms and legs we never did find.

The boy had been nineteen years old. And all around us the sun was shining, the buds showing pink and white, and the birds singing their hearts out. As I walked towards the transport I knew that however long I lived I would never be able to make sense of a world that could present both beauty and death with such indifference.

It was yet another heavy raid on Hull that began the series of outrageous events. The raid came only two weeks after my return to the airfield and as always I sent a cable to check all was well. Usually I had a quick reply but this time I heard nothing. I cabled again but once again no reply. Anxious but feeling I could not expect another leave in such a short time I wondered what other actions I could take.

With my need for privacy as urgent as ever I took a walk in the country one day when I had a few hours off duty. If it was an attempt to occupy my mind or solve my problem it was successful in a way no one could have imagined. I was walking down a country lane a few miles from my airfield when I heard the snarl of engines and saw a German Heinkel flying in my direction. He was no more than a thousand feet high and waggling his wings so violently that at first I thought he was signalling to me. Then I saw there was a trail of smoke pluming out of his port engine and a bomb dangling from his bomb bay. With a shot-up engine the pilot was struggling to shake the bomb loose before starting his perilous journey home.

I had no sooner recognised the situation when I saw the bomb shake free and fall in my direction. I flung myself down on the grassy roadside and tried to protect my head. I remember a blinding flash and that was all.

I awoke in a first aid station, very dazed and sorry for myself. A St. John's Ambulance man who attended me said that a motorist had found me lying unconscious near a tree on the roadside. As there was a smoking bomb crater nearby, it was thought the explosion must have thrown me against the tree because bark had been found in my hair. As it was feared that my skull might be damaged I was told I must go into hospital for an X- ray.

What happened after that can only have been due to my muddled condition. Knowing I was due on duty in a few hours I refused to go to hospital and said instead I must get back to the airfield. When my First Aid man protested, I told him that on my arrival I would report sick to the airfield's medical officer. This seemed to satisfy him and he organised a lift to take me to the station.

I am telling this from disjointed memories because at the time I was too dazed to know all that was happening. I did not know what village I was in, nor did I understand fully the extent of my injuries. All I remember was a compelling desire to return to duty and to find out if my parents were still alive.

Groggy or not, I must have put up a convincing argument because I was back at the airfield an hour later where I learned all flying had been cancelled that day because of weather conditions. Immensely relieved because of the pain in my head and neck, I managed to reach my billet unaided where I dropped on my bed and tried to put my thoughts in order. Although it meant another break from duty in less than three weeks, I had to know if my parents were safe and so in the morning I would ask the CO for a short compassionate leave.

I don't think I slept at all that night for the pain in my neck and when I went in to see the CO in the morning I used my forage cap to hide the part of my head that had been shaved and taped. To my relief he seemed not to notice the deception. Instead he was very sympathetic to my request and rang the duty pilot with orders to fly me up to Kirton Lindsay, an airfield near the Humber. So less than an hour later I found myself in a Miles Master being flown north by a Flight Sergeant Craig, DFM, who, sadly, was to be killed only a few weeks later in a mid-air collision.

The flight took only forty minutes. As I was so near to Scunthorpe, I decided to try to see Becky on my way to Hull. Because of my concern for my parents, it was a decision I was not proud of in later years and my only excuse is that the pain in my head and neck prevented me from thinking clearly.

I had my usual difficulty in seeing Becky, and even then she was only granted an hour off duty. I thought she looked worried and apprehensive as we met but her expression changed on seeing my appearance. 'What's happened? You look so ill!'

Before giving her the reason I took her to a local café we had used before. When I told her what had happened and then assured her my injury was nothing serious, she sighed and then said very quietly: 'I've something to tell you. I'm just praying that it won't make you too unhappy.'

With that she laid her left hand on the table and I saw the engagement ring was no longer on her finger.

I don't think I felt anything at that moment and can only assume my injury had a numbing effect on my emotions. I sat and listened, and although I don't remember everything she said, the gist was simple enough. She could fight her religious yearnings no longer. Her intention was to become a nursing missionary and as soon as she was fully qualified, she would go abroad and fulfil God's will. This meant that any intimate human relationships had to end.

A few words I do remember. 'You must believe this, FE. It is God I am leaving you for, not another man. There is nobody else. I swear it.'

In her religious conversion she meant it as a comfort to me. To the heretic that I was, it seemed as if the door to any hope of winning her back was not only slammed but tightly bolted as well.

Of course I said all the wrong things. Perhaps the worst was my accusation that she was the victim of pride. Not content to be a simple nurse ministering to the sick and the wounded in beleaguered England, she had to be another Florence Nightingale carrying her shining lamp into Darkest Africa.

It was all hurtful and pointless and made her cry. During her tears she admitted that she was worried about her friends in Hull. No doubt clinging to a straw that if I saw her again she might change her mind, I promised to look them up and would return to bring her what news I could.

So our hour ended and I took her back to the hospital. She reached the main entrance, glanced back, and gave me a small, wistful wave of her hand. I did not know as I turned away that it was the last time I would see her.

What followed are impressions more than memories by the time I reached Hull. The damage was horrendous but my senses seemed unable to take it in until I walked past 579, the house in which I was born. It was almost totally destroyed, as, I learned later, was every home we had lived in since my birth. Such was the extent of the devastation. As I kept seeing ruins that had once been buildings of happy memories, the feeling grew that the world we had known was nearing its end. The barbarians had broken through the barricades and civilisation was being put to the sword.

To my immense relief my parents' house was still standing although there was heavy damage nearby and many incendiaries had fallen around it. I also learned that neither of my cables had reached them. I believe I did make an effort to find out how Becky's friends had fared but I was only able to contact two of them because of the intense pain in my head and neck.

There was another raid that night, although not a heavy one by recent standards, but in any case I slept right through it. I think I was feverish from the pain because I kept having nightmares in which lofty cathedrals were bursting into flames and dreaming spires collapsing in ruins. Mixed with such dreams was a growing bitterness. Civilisation was being destroyed by barbarians and when I awoke in the morning I knew the extent of the evil was not confined to bricks and mortar. A cry for retaliation was growing in the land. I could feel it myself and knew that of all the crimes the Nazis were committing, this was the greatest of them all.

The remaining memories of that short leave are once more disjointed. After saying goodbye to my parents I somehow reached Scunthorpe, only to discover Becky had been on night duty and was now sleeping. If I wished to see her, I would need to see the matron. In turn the matron told me I must wait until Nurse Davidson was off duty which would be at least six more hours.

In vain I pleaded my case and reasons for seeing her. In return I received a shrug. I was only one of millions with similar problems. Now would I please leave as she had a hospital to run.

What happened then can only have been due to my injury. I remember running down a corridor, throwing open dormitory doors, and then being set upon by orderlies who told me I must leave at once or the police would be called.

My next clear memory was talking to a middle-aged man in a pub somewhere in Scunthorpe. My diary records he was the manager of the locale Labour Exchange and had told me that should my parents ever lose their home, he would do his best to help them. He also told me he had been a pilot in the First World War and then asked if I would like another drink.

I must have said yes because I remember taking a glass from him and lifting it to my lips. Then, like a film sequence suddenly cut out and another substituted, the pub disappeared and I found myself walking down a country lane with high hedges on either side.

The transformation was so sudden that I found myself looking down for the glass in my hand. It was not there, nor was the man from the pub or the pub itself. I was entirely alone, with the sky above me and the sun on my back.

As I stood there, utterly bewildered, an old man came cycling round a bend in the road. Signalling him to stop, I asked him where I was and stared at him in disbelief when he told me I was south of Peterborough and barely thirty miles from my airfield! Not believing him at first, I asked what day it was and he told me that it was Thursday. With that he cycled hastily away, no doubt thinking that I was either mad or suffering from the granddaddy of all hangovers.

I soon discovered he was right. I was many miles from Scunthorpe. And it *was* Thursday. Somehow I had lost a whole three days of my life.

Yet where had I been? I was washed and clean shaven and my uniform gave no indication that I had been sleeping rough. Moreover, if I had suffered amnesia, a compulsive instinct to reach my airfield must have run through it because of the distance I had travelled since my blackout.

Afraid the C.O. would think I had abused my privilege, I wasted no time reaching the airfield. Although I was told by the Provost staff that my lateness would be reported to the C.O., he took no action against me, nor, I believe, was a report logged in my records. This was just as well because the truth would have sounded so far fetched that I would have been thought either a highly imaginative liar or put into hospital for psychological treatment.

Since discovering many years later how severely injured I had been (my neck had been fractured), it seems something of a miracle that I had survived those few days hitch-hiking when it seemed a severe jolt would have killed me. It certainly explains my bout of amnesia. But where I went and what I did during those lost three days has remained a mystery to me ever since.

THIRTY-THREE

It was another month before my next posting abroad came through. As I still had severe pain in my head and neck it is a mystery why I did not report sick. I suppose I had some high-minded idea that after the easy time I had previously had it was time I did something worthwhile, and to go sick would turn me into a liability again.

For the war was still going badly for us.

Germany had now successfully invaded Crete and our naval position in the Mediterranean became even more precarious when the island fell. It was beginning to look that if we were to survive the war, even children would have to be called into service.

So I managed to keep going and gradually the pain and the loss of Becky began to ease although I doubt if I were cheerful company. Nevertheless during the next month a Wisbech girl I shall call Joyce Chambers befriended me. I cannot think why because of the peculiarity of our relationship. I was unwell and undoubtedly embittered, and she was in love with a young sailor in the Navy. To those who do not understand the nature of love, her behaviour and generosity towards me would have seemed fickle and faithless. Yet how wrong they would be. When the motive is compassion, there is no guilt in loving. Young though we were, I think we both understood that. While I could not know the comfort I gave her, for me she restored some faith I had lost, and our brief meetings outside the airfield also made the war more bearable. When the time came to say goodbye, I knew that I would always be in her debt.

There were half a dozen men from my airfield posted overseas with me and I was given the task of seeing they all reached West Kirby safely. This we did and unlike my previous visit things moved swiftly and with purpose. In no time we were issued with tropical kit, which convinced us that our destination was the eastern Mediterranean where things were going from bad to worse.

It was while I was at West Kirby that the sensational news broke of Germany's invasion of Russia. I can't say it had a great effect on the men around me. I had already discovered that servicemen seemed immune to headline news, treating disaster or success as equal impostors. Whether it is the de-humanising effect of military discipline or the self-protective mechanism that shields us from shock, I do not know, but it was something I noticed throughout my service life.

To me, however, the news was momentous. At last we were no longer fighting the Nazi giant alone. One hundred and fifty divisions that might have invaded Britain were instead going east and crashing through the Russian steppes. One ought, of course, to have felt sympathy for the Russian people, but after Russia's cynical pact with Germany, that was perhaps asking too much of a young mind. All I could think of was that the long feared invasion of Britain might be ended at last.

We boarded ship on Friday the 13th July, not the best of omens, particularly after someone leaked the news that the convoy before ours had been savagely mauled by U boats and survivors were still being brought in. Nor did the reception of the public give us any encouragement as, loaded like camels with our 120lbs of kit, we tramped through the streets of Liverpool. I can't remember one voice wishing us luck. When one remembered Manchester only a few months earlier it showed how quickly public sentiment could change.

Our ship was the Rangitata, a 10,000 ton New Zealand ex-meat boat. As we numbered over 3,000 men, it took hours for us to file up her gangplanks. On board, we were herded down into the holds which had been adapted for troop accommodation.

Because it was wartime, one hesitates to make too much of the conditions that faced us. Yet to anyone who has never experienced a wartime troop ship, they might prove of interest. The holds were divided into sections, each one consisting of a long table flanked by bench seats. As there were hooks for hammocks in beams above the table, each section was intended to be both the mess and sleeping quarters. As we were packed in like sardines, a man at night had to crawl beneath the hammocks to find his own, and even after he climbed into it he would find himself pressed tightly against the men on either side.

But this discomfort was nothing beside the rest. Little if any attempt had been made to clean the holds from their meat voyages and the stench was nauseating, particularly when men, drenched in sweat from their long march, poured down the companion ways. As their numbers grew and grew and the bedlam of voices and curses became louder, the thought of spending weeks under such conditions was intimidating.

We moved out into midstream at 7 p.m. and were fed shortly afterwards. This seemed to attract the cockroaches which infested the ship. Every now and then a man would curse as an insect fell from the timbers above to his plate. As darkness approached, we were ordered to close the portholes to preserve the blackout. This locked in the heat and the stench became worse. Nor was it possible to escape the conditions by sleep. As one lay squashed in one's hammock, the cockroaches kept falling down on one and then going God knows where. To someone who had always been queasy over insects, I found this a nightmare.

We sailed at 1 p.m. the following day. Men crowded the rails and climbed on every vantage point for their last glimpse of England. Those who obtained a view saw only deserted wharves. There was no *God speed and come safely back* as in American films. I think we all felt expendable as the skyline shrank and then faded away.

There was a call that afternoon for volunteers to man the ship's automatic weapons. Being qualified, I saw it as a way of avoiding the cockroaches and so hastily put my name down. A naval officer interviewed us and gave us our duties. Two hours on and two off and if any aircraft, other than a Sunderland, approached within 1500 yards of the convoy, we were to open fire. Each gunner would be given a loader and we would man the gun posts until the ship was out of range of enemy aircraft.

At this interview I was introduced to my loader. He was a small North Countryman with the inevitable nickname of Lofty, and one of the most unprepossessing characters I had yet encountered. He reeked of B.O. and halitosis, had a face full of blackheads, and a line of conversation that would have fascinated any glottologist by its astonishing variety of Anglo-Saxon swear words. They garnished every statement he made, although as these statements were always concerned with his sex life, he could have argued with justification they were not out of context. The thought of spending days and perhaps weeks with him in the tiny confines of a gun post almost made me wish I had stayed with the cockroaches.

After receiving our orders, we were led up a steel ladder to our gun posts. These must have been designed by civilians because they consisted of platforms and side plates bolted on metal stays high up in the ship's superstructure. The guns rotated on a tripod in the centre of the metal plates. These plates, while meant as a protection, were barely waist high, which meant they might give some protection against ship to ship fire, but were worse than useless against aircraft high angle fire which would ricochet inside them and in all likelihood cut down the defending gunners.

After being allotted a gun post each we were told we would begin our duties the following day, whence I beat a hasty retreat from Lofty's B.O. and halitosis.

As we steamed due west – tactics designed to put us out of the 1,200 mile range of German Focke Wulf Condors – more and more ships began to enter the convoy. Two of the largest were the Athlone Castle and the Monarch of Bermuda, of which I still have photographs from a camera I smuggled on board. Because of their importance, these were stationed in the centre of the convoy. We, of lesser importance, took station on its right flank.

Along with many other men, I carried my blankets up to the deck that night. After laying them down in the middle of the deck, just aft of the rear funnel, I joined a party of my own draft. As we were talking, a sailor who was hosing the decks suddenly turned his hose and quite deliberately drenched our bedding.

It was an act of pure malice, for had he needed to wash that part of the deck, a request for us to remove our blankets would have been sufficient. It was my first taste of the extraordinary dislike that existed at that time between naval personnel and the RAF.

We covered ourselves as best we could with dry items from our kit and then settled down, under the strictest orders not to smoke because of the submarine peril. It was our first night at sea and one I shall always remember. Above us there was that strange rushing noise that comes from the funnels of large ships; in the distance there was the eerie cry of destroyers as they herded and shepherded the motley convoy; and beneath us the swell and rush of the waves. Knowing we would not see England again for many years and with no knowledge of our destiny I think we were all glad when darkness came to hide our thoughts and our misgivings.

Lofty and I did our first spell of duty at 6 a.m. the following morning. Our gun post was the mid-starboard one high up near a funnel, which gave us almost a bird's eye view of the convoy. My diary states it had grown during the night and now had fourteen ex-passenger liners along with sundry merchantmen. Our escort was four destroyers and four light cruisers who periodically weaved in and out of the convoy. We were also told that two capital ships, the Renown and The Furious guarded our front and rear but as we never saw them I cannot vouch for this.

Although the size of the escort hinted that trouble was expected, I can't say I went into the gun post with much trepidation. With a gun in my hand I was always optimistic. What was a disgrace, however, was our total lack of protective clothing. We received no duffel coats, no heavy duty sweaters, and no scarves or gloves. Nor were we issued with tin helmets. Our only protection against the North Atlantic weather and any German attacks were our greatcoats and our forage caps. It is no exaggeration to say we were permanently cold in our gunpost until we turned south and neared the tropics. Lofty's four letter words as he berated the inefficiency and amateurism of that ship were for once fully appreciated.

My optimism as a gunner, however, did not extend to my head and neck, which were still extremely painful, nor to my stomach either. With the gun post high in the superstructure, it swung in a wide arc in the Atlantic swell and when the glare of the sea was added, conditions were ideal for sea sickness.

And sea sick I was. In Lofty's words I puked all over the effin' gunpost and all over the effin' ship. He barely exaggerated. I had never known sickness like it. It lasted for almost the entire time we manned the guns.

Nor did it cease when we came off duty, so I must attribute it to some extent to my injured head and neck.

Thus Lofty had to put up with my retching for many a day. Perhaps, in retrospect, it was his punishment for his B.O. and halitosis. At the same time it had its compensations. If prior to it I had ever felt concern about a submarine attack, my sickness took good care of it. After a week of vomiting I was willing every submarine in Hitler's wolf packs to make straight for the Rangitata. A watery grave would have been blessed relief after that infernal sickness.

We did sight one or two enemy aircraft during the first few days but none of them made an attack on our ship. I also believe we had one or two submarine attacks. I say believe because in general war is a hopeless muddle and the serviceman is often the last to know what is happening. More than once a destroyer or small merchant ship would come between us and the open sea, which usually meant submarines were closing in, and we would see depth charges exploding. We also often heard dull explosions at night and saw fires on the horizon; and a rumour circulated that a troopship had gone down and four hundred men were lost.

But nothing was ever certain. After nearly three weeks at sea we turned south and began heading for the tropics. As helpless as a load of cattle, we were now smelling like one too.

We crossed the tropic of Cancer at 11.00 hours on Sunday, the 6th, when we were ordered into tropical gear. This meant we had already been at sea for 23 days. My diary records thatI took off my tunic and my boots for the first time in nine days. On the 7th we were told a convoy ahead of us had suffered a submarine attack and we in the gun posts must keep a sharp lookout for wreckage and survivors. We zig-zagged a great deal, no doubt more because of enemy submarines than in hope of finding survivors, of which we saw none. By this time our convoy was down to only eleven ships and one cruiser, and we could only guess what had happened to the others.

For us in the gun crew, the day to remember was the day it was reckoned that the convoy was now beyond the range of enemy aircraft and we could stand down once our current spell of duty was over. Duly celebrating, we were counting the minutes to our stand down when booted feet sounded on the quarterdeck below. A moment later Lofty nudged my arm. 'Smithy! What the fuckin' hell's going on down there?'

I glanced down and saw a helmeted sergeant, all square jaw and bulging muscles, leading a squad of marines across the quarterdeck. All were wearing tin helmets and battle dress and two men in the rear were carrying what appeared to be a gas cylinder. The sergeant halted his men and strode to the foot of our ladder. 'You up there! Come down.'

I was puzzled. 'You mean us?'

'Who bloody else? Come on down. You're relieved.'

I was lost. 'What do you mean – we're relieved?'

'What's the matter with you, lad? Can't you understand King's English? Get your arse down here. We're taking over.'

'Taking over what?'

'The bloody defence of the ship of course. What else?'

Behind him two of his men were bending over the cylinder. A moment later a rotund shape began swelling up. Beside me I heard Lofty's bewildered voice. 'It's a balloon, Smithy. They're blowing up bloody balloons.'

The sergeant heard him and gave a smirk. 'Target practice, lad. That's how my lads keep their eyes in.'

The truth came to me like a thunderclap. 'You're the ship's gun crew, aren't you?'

I received a wink of pride. 'Professionals, lad. Been on this old tub for over a year and she's never had a scratch.'

Lofty's yelp said it better than I could ever have done. 'You mean that while we've been manning these fuckin' guns, you've been hiding below decks? And now we're safe, you're takin' over? What sort of a bloody outfit do you call yourself? The Rangitata girl guides?'

The sergeant's face darkened. 'Don't get cheeky with me, my lad. I don't have much time for you Brylcreem boys. Another word and you'll be in the brig.'

We had no alternative but to climb down. As we stood on the quarterdeck, one of the marines took the filled balloon and held it ready at arm's length. Above him, now settled in our gun post, the sergeant cocked the guns and gave him a nod. As the balloon leapt upwards and then swerved sharply astern, the sergeant began firing. A moment later Lofty gave a malicious chortle. 'He's missed it, Smithy! He can't even hit a sodding balloon.'

Seeing the dark glances of the marines and the sergeant, I took Lofty's arm and led him to the nearest companionway. Reaching it, I allowed him one last yell of malice. 'It must be hell fighting those balloons. What do they give you poor bastards? Danger pay?'

With that I hurried him down to the main deck. There we met other members of the RAF gun crews, all with the same story to tell. With a fully trained gun crew on board, we had been given the task of guarding the ship until all chances of air attacks were over. I think that was the moment when I realised that war was not only an obscenity but an ultimate in absurdity too.

THIRTY-FOUR

A tannoy system which we hadn't known existed came into life at this time, giving us a chance at last to hear the news. It also allowed us at nights to listen to the songs of the day, usually sung by Vera Lynn; 'All the things you are', 'There'll come another Day', 'White Cliffs of Dover'. By this time I had become friendly with a Jewish lad called Micky Serchuk and like the rest of us he had memories linked with some of the songs and I remember how every time he heard Vera Lynn singing 'I'll be seeing you' he would rise from his blankets and walk away.

By this time we knew our destination was not the eastern Mediterranean. In our ignorance this left two other possibilities, either the Middle East or Singapore. Before we had left Britain, the newspapers had been dwelling more and more on Japanese aggression and suggesting our Far Eastern bases should be reinforced. So Singapore seemed a reasonable bet. Lofty smacked his lips at the possibility. 'Gawd, I hope so, Smithy. They say the women out there are bloody marvellous. All tits and arses. I had an oppo once who's been to one of their shows. He says one of the bints took a penny and...'

It was not the first time I had heard the grisly details, nor was it the last as the convoy headed south. Because of the heat most men were sleeping on the decks at night. This created a problem because deck space was limited. An answer would have been to use the top A deck but this was the domain of the officers, and in spite of repeated requests from the ship's padre, they would not relinquish it even although most of them had comfortable cabins in which to retire. Because of the British class structure one might have expected this but there were as many Dominion officers as British on the ship. I remember thinking it was just one more illusion destroyed.

From this point onwards I doubt if our journey was very different from that of any troopship at that time, although one hopes other ships had more democratic officers and braver gun crews! We were hot, crowded, uncomfortable, and remained curious about our destination as no doubt were all troops on similar long voyages. We docked in Freetown to re-fuel, counted over sixty ships lying there because of the Mediterranean closure, watched the 'bum' boats and their divers, and cursed the mosquitoes that forced us to keep wearing our shirts with sleeves buttoned up. We also showed relief when there was a tropical storm on the second day. Men packed the deck, lifted their faces to the lashing rain, and let it run into their thirsty mouths.

In all, because an engine overhaul had to be carried out, we remained in Freetown for three more days. When our anchor was at last lifted I doubt if any of us felt regret as the coast of Sierra Leone faded behind us.

Because of submarines the ban on lights and smoking was still enforced but apart from a minor deck fire for which we were warned by a destroyer that we would have to leave the convoy unless it were quickly extinguished, we had no other alarms at this time.

In fact monotony was our main discomfort now. The short tropical evenings were making the nights seem endless, particularly with the tannoy system no longer working and entertaining with its Vera Lynn records. With no wish to play cards in candlelight below decks, Micky Serchuk and I would sit sucking on our empty pipes and listening to the distant cries of destroyers and the chatter of men around us.

I found it interesting to note the effect of this monotony. When in constant danger men had found comfort in their numbers and proximity. Now the danger had lessened they were finding that proximity a burden and wanted to escape it.

Even so, the nights were becoming cooler as we sailed further south. An interesting footnote in my diary records that the convoy was averaging 12½ knots per hour which should have given us around 300 nautical miles a day. But the need to take evasive action by zig-zagging cut down our daily mileage considerably, and no doubt explained the length of the voyage.

Since crossing the Equator we had been told our next port of call would be Durban, which convinced us we were bound for the Middle East. Now for the first time we heard it was to be Cape Town which fostered the belief that because of the increased belligerency of Japan we were being sent to Singapore. It was a belief that made every blackhead on Lofty's face stand out in anticipation.

It proved as false as so many other rumours did in those days. Instead we were finally told that South Africa was our destination. We were to be a part of the Empire Training Scheme for aircrews, and on landing would be shipping to various parts of the Union according to the needs of the airfields.

My feelings were mixed on hearing this. Being no hero I wasn't sorry to receive a relatively safe posting. On the other hand I felt cheated that I was once again being taken from an active role to one that seemed more fitting for a civilian.

Even so, I shall always remember my first sight of Cape Town. We approached it at early dusk and for me, who had never been abroad, it was a thrill to see that huge, beautiful grey-green mountain with myriads of lights twinkling around its feet. None of us had seen city lights for years and so even they were a thrill. But the mountain looked magnificent. Although rain was falling and its upper heights were wearing its famous south-easter, I was one of those who stood for hours watching it growing nearer and nearer.

At that moment I had no idea what Africa had in store for me: the complex mixture of joy and happiness to be followed by the separation and the pain. In other words I was totally unaware of the massive change to my life that South Africa was soon to bring.

THIRTY-FIVE

Although we learned our destination was Benoni, a town a thousand odd miles up country, we were kept on board the ship for three days because of heavy floods that had damaged the railway tracks. No general shore leave was granted during this time, which caused considerable frustration to men who had been penned on board that ship for so long. But eventually 'my' draft, comprised of about three hundred men, was marched off the ship and embarked on the train that was to take us to Benoni.

We left at night and I think all of us feasted our eyes on the lights that swept past the carriage windows until we finally left Cape Town behind and the only lights came from the tiny hamlets strung along the railway track.

When dawn came we found ourselves in the Karro, a vast area of scrub and stunted mountains. Our interest revived when, thirty-six hours later, we approached Johannesburg. Although it was night when we passed through it, the sea of lights told us it was a large city and we began hoping Benoni was not too far away.

We need not have worried. The lights of the gold-bearing Reef followed us until the train halted at a station twenty-five miles further east. This was Benoni and it was then our bewilderment began. The station was flooded with arc lights and packed with people both inside and outside who gave us a great cheer as we began filing from the train. Totally at sea, we were called to attention while the mayor of the town gave us a speech of welcome and then invited us to be his guests in the Town Hall.

What followed then was out of this world. Bedraggled from our long journey, we were marched through the town to its Town Hall which we were invited to enter.

I think everyone, from the C.O. downwards, was amazed at the sight that greeted us. Trestle tables, covered by white tablecloths, were lined up along the hall, and behind them more substantial tables groaned under the weight of food and drink. None of us had seen so much food for years and men looked dazed as women took our arms and led us forward.

A toast to the King was made and then the buzz of astonishment quietened while we gorged ourselves on all that food. When at last we were replete, speeches were made and a toast given to the RAF. Afterwards, every man was given fruit and cigarettes to take to camp with him. Later we discovered the welcome had been laid on by the South African Womens' Auxiliary Service, better known as the SAWAS.

Needless to say it was a gesture fully undeserved. From the speeches we heard we were being given the credit for the Battle of Britain victory. One felt a complete charlatan but at the same time it was impossible not to feel pride that one wore the same RAF uniform.

My diary tells me the banquet broke up around 9.30 when we were marched to our camp. It was about four miles from the small town and situated on a bare plateau on the veldt. Apart from aircraft hangars that were still under construction, it consisted entirely of tents, but this we had expected and they caused us little hardship. It was August, which is winter in the Transvaal, and rainfall is almost nil in that season. It was true that there was sometimes frost during the nights, but with the sun rising like clockwork every morning and shining down all day, we found the conditions ideal and astonished the locals by wearing sleeveless shirts and shorts during daylight hours.

The only discomfort came from the occasional dust storms that filled the tents with grit. Also, because of the altitude – the entire Transvaal is a six thousand foot plateau – it took us five to six weeks to acclimatise. But these were such trivial things that we hardly considered them alongside our good fortune.

To add to our belief that we were dreaming, the uncompleted hangars meant that in the early days we had little to do except parade in the mornings, keep our kit in order, and get to know our men. At this time I became friendly with two of the instructors who would eventually teach pupils the theory and skills of navigation and bombing, and I made a point of learning all I could in case my requests for a pilot's course should ever be granted.

We soon discovered our undeserved reception had not ended in the Town Hall. Around 6pm the next day huge American cars began massing on the dirt road outside the camp. Driven by townsfolk their purpose was to take us to their owners' homes and give us further hospitality.

And this they did in full measure. The great majority of South Africans could not do enough to show their friendship to us and to Britain. To illustrate this, my diary records I was given thirty-five addresses to visit in my first ten days at the camp. We were given sumptuous meals, taken on excursions, and in many cases virtually offered foster homes when off duty. It all seemed too good to be true.

Naturally enough, as we were mostly young and virile, girls were foremost in our minds and here we could hardly have been better served. Perhaps because of the climate and the sport available, white South African women tend to be nubile and attractive, and because of the false glamour surrounding us, they flocked to the camp. As many had their own cars, it is no exaggeration to say that in the early evenings one had only to walk down the lines of cars to receive half a dozen invitations from both married and single women.

It would be hypocritical to make excuses for our willingness to accept these offers. Although I've no doubt there were many like myself who often felt guilt at our sybaritic life, it was not difficult to thrust it away. After all Benoni had not been our choice. Faceless men in Records had sent us here as they might have sent us to the Middle or Far East and we would be fools to wear a hair shirt because of it. Those faceless men could just as arbitrarily shuffle the deck and hand out new cards as I for one was eventually to discover.

So, until the intoxication wore off and we came to our senses, we took what fate was offering us. In my own case, although it is not meant as an excuse, I feel my behaviour had a connection with Becky, and there is no doubt that my sexual adventures at this time helped the wound to heal.

I lived this hedonistic life until the day I was given a lift by an elderly and wealthy couple from Johannesburg who insisted on taking me to their beautiful home in Parkwood where I met their two daughters, Peggy and Ann. Peggy, the younger girl, who in spite of her parents' wealth worked as a volunteer nurse in an African hospital, was a girl I admired and it was my relationship with her that brought me back to my senses. I visited the house as often as I could and was invited to stay there whenever I could obtain a weekend pass.

It was a month before our hangars were ready and we had enough equipment to begin training the pupils who were brought in. Next came our aircraft: tiny Tiger Moths which were used in South Africa at that time for *ab initio* training.

It all began disastrously. The first pilot to fly one must have forgotten the 6000 foot altitude of the airfield because he crashed and killed himself when trying to land. Less than three weeks later another of our pilots and one of the men who had served with me in East Anglia, spun in from three thousand feet and were both killed.

My job now was teaching armament and the theory of air gunnery to the pupils. It must be said here that the quality of the South African trainees that I encountered was first class. They were all keen, eager, and trustworthy, and I can't remember having the slightest trouble with any of them. It was an assessment I never had cause to retract throughout my entire stay in the country.

In later years such men tended to lose the recognition they deserved when their government introduced the odious political system of apartheid. This was unfair. It should always be remembered that they had no need to volunteer for combat. It was possible for them to gain the glamour of uniform without having to face the enemy because two categories of volunteers existed in South Africa at that time. If a man did not take the 'blue oath', he could not be sent out of the Union on active service but only needed to serve within the country.

All our pupils had taken this oath and were eager to fly alongside our own men in North Africa. Only men who have served in wartime know the warmth a soldier feels towards men who volunteer to fight at his side. The wrongs of governments should not let debts of this magnitude be forgotten.

Although at the time we could hardly believe our luck, we were soon to learn that wherever there is honey, there are wasps. Our wasps were the Ossewa Brandweg. This was a pro-Nazi organisation set up among some of those Afrikaners who had never forgiven the British for the Boer war. Their main presence was in the Orange Free State and the Transvaal. There was some dispute over their numbers: some had it as low as 10,000 and others as high as 30,000 or more. Whatever their number they greatly resented our presence, and as it was rumoured that two German ammunition ships had berthed in South Africa just before the war and their contents secretly distributed to the Ossewa Brandweg, they were not a threat to be discounted.

In this context I was given an interesting theory by a senior South African officer. He believed our presence in the Union was due to these OBs, as they were nicknamed. With Smuts, the prime minister, suspecting they were planning a coup d'etat to overthrow him when the cream of his army was away in the Middle East, Smuts had suggested to the British Government that an Empire Training Scheme be introduced on the lines of those already existing in Canada and Australia. On the surface its personnel would fulfil its role and train aircrews. But with the threat of the Ossewa Brandweg in mind, that same personnel was a trained and armed reserve that could help resist any attempt to overthrow the legitimate government. How true this is I have never been able to discover although it would certainly explain the exceptional military training we had received. But later that year, on the eve of Christmas, something was to happen that made me believe Jannie Smuts was every bit the canny old fox that both his admirers and detractors believed him to be.

THIRTY-SIX

Although warned by both our officers and Union officers of the dangers of the 'OBs', the great hospitality of the South Africans around us made us feel the danger was exaggerated. However my diary records that two weeks after our arrival three airmen who had been hitch-hiking to Jo'burg had been found on the roadside by the police. One was 'maimed for life' (whatever that meant), a second badly beaten up, and the third had had an eye kicked out of his face. It was suddenly clear that the threat was real after all and a number of us began carrying rubber tubes full of lead shot in our tunic pockets.

Even so it seemed a puny threat beside the ones faced by our countrymen elsewhere and few of us changed our habits because Jo'burg was a wonderful city for servicemen in those days. One seemed to pay for nothing. The trams and buses were free, the theatres and cinemas were free, and quite often the shop-keepers would wave us away without accepting our money. Goodwill towards us seemed inexhaustible. Another reason was our youth. In some ways we were trained to accept danger and so the risks were a challenge that added spice to our nights. So we continued to thumb lifts on the Reef Road in order to savour the delights of Jo'burg. I remember the jacaranda trees were in full flower at the time and their delightful blue blossoms remain my most abiding memory of the city.

Not that I was long in discovering the OB threat was real. One Sunday I met a beautiful Afrikaner girl called Zelda. We spent the afternoon swimming at Randfontein and in the evening drove in her car to the Zoo Lake where we listened to the band that played there. By this time it was 10.30 and because I was due back in camp at midnight she offered to drive me there. But at the same time she let me know, in the most demure way possible, that she lived alone in East Boxburg and if I had an all night pass, she felt certain the hotel proprietor would let me have a room alongside hers.

I could recognise an invitation when I heard one and if I hesitated at all, it was only for a moment. After all, I had broken camp for less propitious reasons than this. So we drove to Boxburg and for the next two hours I had no reason to regret my decision. It was only when she whispered that she must get some sleep if she were to do any work on the morrow that the problems of the world began to come back to me.

It was a clear night with a huge veldt moon turning the night into day as I left the hotel and started down the street. My plan was to get back to the main Reef Road and hope there would be a late traveller making his way towards Benoni. But I had barely cleared the frontage of the hotel when there was a clatter of boots and half a dozen men brandishing clubs came rushing out from a side passage.

There was no time to run. All I could do was snatch the rubber tubing from my pocket and hope for the best. By luck more than intent I caught the first man between the legs and he gave a yell and doubled up. The second thug I hit somewhere around the ear and he dropped as if pole-axed. For a moment this brought the other four to a halt and I ran like a hare down the road that led to the Reef highway.

I blessed my ability to run fast but at the same time I knew my knee was not appreciating the effort and might rebel at any moment. To make matters worse, I had not noticed how far the Reef highway was. So, having established a reasonable lead on the pursuers, I had to slow down and pace myself.

Once again I was lucky. The Reef Road was little more than a mile further away and I reached it a good two hundred yards ahead of the OBs. However, I still had to keep running along the road until a car came into sight.

Headlights appeared only a minute or two later. I thumbed the driver who braked immediately and asked where I was making for. When I explained my problem he told me to jump in and he drove me right to the gates of the camp before resuming his journey.

My luck held to the end. I'd once done a favour for the NCO on guardroom duty and on hearing my story he roared with laughter and booked me in as at midnight.

So ended my first clash with the Ossewa Brandweg. To this day I've never known if Zelda set me up or not. If she did I bear her no ill will. For however one looks at it, it does seem that I got much the better of the bargain.

On looking back, those sybaritic days at Benoni seemed to last a long time but that is only because of the elongated time scale of one's youth. In reality it was less than two months before the first postings were pinned on the notice board and my name was among them.

I was to go to Baragwanath, a one time civil airfield which was now No. 1 E.F.T.S. (Elementary Flight Training School). At first I was disappointed, believing I would lose contact with my new South African friends, but then I discovered the airfield was only four miles east of Jo'burg. Unlike Benoni, which was staffed entirely by the RAF, there were only thirty of us at Baragwanath, the rest being South African ground personnel. My section was a small one with only two young South Africans and an RAF character called Ken Addey. Addey was a 23-year old Londoner, a pipe smoker with a graveyard sense of humour. He was also a self-styled Communist, although with lugubrious features and a somewhat heavy body, he was the antithesis of the rabble-rouser. His own words described his attitude to the war effort better than I ever could. 'Why should I be an eager beaver and get myself killed so we can have another touch of the Lord Salisburys and the Lord Norfolks? What have the bastards ever done for me? I'm playing it cool, mate, and if you've any sense, you'll stop trying to get that pilot's course and do the same.'

There's no denying we had different views on many things but war has a way of bringing disparate characters together and we were soon the best of friends. Our task was to teach trainee pilots the mysteries of armaments, gun sights, cine cameras, and the theory of air gunnery. As the South Africans had had little access to the latest equipment, much of the work fell on Addey and myself, he handling the armament side of the course and I the air gunnery side.

I had my first confrontation with a snake at Baragwanath. Approaching the armoury one morning at 5 am, I saw a large coir mat in front of the entrance shifting from side to side. As the world never behaved rationally for me at that time in the morning, I thought nothing of it until I put my foot on the mat. A second later I let out a yell and froze.

The mat had fallen aside and a huge ringhaus was rearing up. For those who know little about snakes the ringhaus has a nasty habit of uncoiling itself to the level of its victim's eyes and then spitting venom into them. With its prey effectively blinded, it then takes its time in administering the coup de grace.

It was now a race whether its diamond-shaped head could reach my face before I could break the spell and run away. Fortunately for me the cold veldt morning was slowing down its movements, which gave me time to let out another howl and flee. My yells brought one of our black workers to the scene. Grinning broadly, he fetched a stick and dispatched the huge creature in seconds. The Aryan super race, I remember thinking. What a sick joke that was!

By this time my wilder days were over and I was visiting Peggy's home whenever I could get into Jo'burg. We would drive off with her sister Ann in one of the family cars, pick up Ann's boy friend, Oscar, and sometimes drive to the Zoo Lake and listen to the orchestra that played there. On other, rarer times, we might visit one of the girls' favourite clubs, such as the Orange or Coconut Grove. With such exclusive venues out of reach of my service pay, I would spend my cash first and then leave the rest to the girls and Oscar. As that meant we could only visit such places on my pay days, I remember how amused they were at my Yorkshire Puritanism.

It was during this time I met King George of Greece. It came about because the girls' influential father seemed to like me and very occasionally invited me to lunch with him and his Jo'burg business friends. Although my diary records nothing of the conversation we had, it does say the king was recuperating in Jo'burg before travelling down to Cape Town where a house had been provided for him and his family. My diary also adds that 'he was a charming, patriarchal old man with a long white beard.'

Needless to say I kept up my letters to home all this time. We could buy air mail letters at sixpence each – single sheets of blue paper – and they usually got through in three to four days. Mother wrote me regularly and it was a great relief to hear the heavy air raids had ceased at last.

I contracted a fever around this time and spent over a week in hospital. On my discharge the MO gave me sick leave and Peggy managed a leave at the same time. We had a few days in Durban together where she and her friends took me on trips around Natal. We visited Unkomaas, Umsholte, the Valley of a Thousand Hills, and on our last full day went to Isipingo.

Here I thoroughly disgraced myself. Isipingo is at the mouth of the river of the same name and in those days it was a popular place for picnics. But it is not the best place for swimming because of the powerful tide and Mozambique current that runs down the coast. In addition, because of the food and refuse swept down the river, Zambesi sharks tend to congregate on its estuary. A swimmer was safe enough if he kept within prescribed boundaries but beyond them it was dangerous.

It was raining when we arrived and so the other three decided to forego their swim. But my blood had not yet thinned in the heat and as the day was sultry I said I would like a quick swim before we ate. No one objected but Peggy warned me to stay close to the shore because of the swift river tide.

I don't know exactly what happened after that. I'm not usually stupid enough to ignore such warnings but this day I was careless because, after swimming about for ten minutes, I turned to make my way back to the bank only to find I was being swept to the coastal estuary. Minutes later I was in the sea and then in the Mozambique current.

I put everything I had into the effort but although I was a strong swimmer over short distances I could make no headway whatever. I also remembered what I had been told about sharks. Forcing myself to keep calm I realised my best chance was to turn and swim with the current and try to edge my way towards the beach. This I did and, knowing I might have a long swim ahead of me, tried to conserve my strength as much as possible.

Then I saw my first shark. A fin rose from the water fifteen or twenty yards from me. It was followed by others a few seconds later. I was never more scared in my life as they came nearer and appeared to circle around me. Knowing that Peggy and her friends would have called for help, I could only hope a rescue boat would arrive in time. Until then I could do no more than swim with the current and try to edge my way ashore.

It seemed hours, although I doubt if it was more than thirty minutes, before I was among the breakers and felt sand under my feet. I was far along the coast by this time but Peggy and friends had followed my progress and helped me up on the beach.

I felt the world's biggest fool when I recovered and saw the rescue boat had arrived and was lying out just beyond the breakers. Somehow we managed to convey to its crew that I was safe and they, no doubt expressing graphically their opinion of idiot airmen who wasted their time, returned to their base. For myself I could only assume I was alive because the sharks hadn't considered me a tasty enough meal. Chastened, I climbed into my uniform and made my apologies to Peggy and friends. Then I was driven to the nearest cafe where I was given coffee and brandy. These worked wonders and in no time I was well enough to enjoy the rest of that short holiday.

On my return to Baragwaneth I had another confrontation with the Ossewa Brandweg. Unlike the Reef highway the road to Baragwaneth was considered unsafe and motorists would not stop to pick up hitch hikers. As a consequence I used to take the bus back to the airfield until one night when I missed the last one and had to walk. This particular night I was perhaps halfway to the airfield when I saw headlights slowing down as a car approached me. Thinking the driver was going to give me a lift, I stepped out on the road, only to jump for my life as the headlights swerved towards me. As I recovered the car skidded to a halt and then began to reverse. Thinking again its driver intended to pick me up, I began to walk forward, only to see a car window being lowered. With some sixth sense warning me, I turned and dived for the roadside and at the same moment heard the report of a revolver.

Fortunately for me I can't have been an easy target with the dark veldt my background. Even so I was not armed and had the man or men in the car given me chase my chances would have been poor. So I was lucky when more headlights appeared down the road. One final shot was fired at me and then the hostile car drove off.

A few days later I was posted again. My section officer, D'Aubrey, had recommended that I be sent on a training course in Cape Town which would officially make me an instructor. As I had been doing nothing else but instruct since I arrived in the Union, the move seemed a trifle late but by this time one took such absurdities in one's stride. It meant promotion if I passed the course but it also meant leaving my new friends of whom I had become very fond.

They all saw me off at the station and

Peggy and Oscar gave me presents, Peggy a new suitcase and Oscar, perhaps feeling I might need it in the future, a tiny derringer pistol that had belonged to his grandfather. I remember Peggy looking upset when my train finally pulled away and I wasn't feeling too happy myself. What I did not know and did not find out for a few weeks yet was that life was moving me ever closer to the person who would change my life forever.

THIRTY-SEVEN

I ran into a problem almost as soon as I arrived at my new airfield outside Cape Town, which was built on flea-infested sand. The fleas were serious enough for me, who seemed to have a blood group they smacked their lips over, but even worse someone had blundered at Records. The course I was due to take was for men conversant with the entire range of bombing equipment as well as guns, and because of my training I was conversant only with the latter.

Thus at first it seemed I might not be allowed to take the course but not wanting to lose the chance of promotion I pretended I had taken the same bomb course as the others.

It was an ambitious as well as a deceitful decision because not only had Records sent me three days late but there was also to be an examination on bomb equipment at the end of the week, which meant I had only three days to learn about a subject that took three months back in England.

So I had to rely on my memory and my ability to go without sleep for long periods. Arming myself with the necessary APs on bombs and their ancillaries, I spent the three nights memorising their contents. With virtually no sleep that week I felt rather proud of myself when the test marks were read out and I had obtained the top marks of the class, 89%. In fact, of course, the credit was due to my memory rather than my diligence but even then it had its drawbacks. Believing I was a real 'gen man' on bombs, our instructors in the days ahead would often call on me to illuminate certain aspects of their teaching and this did cause me problems. Nevertheless, I managed and no one ever discovered my deceit. I like to think that if anyone reading these memoirs should think I spent my South African days doing little else but enjoying hedonistic pleasures this small incident will illustrate that I did always put my service duties first. Detesting bullies as I did, doing my small part in the war was always my major concern.

It was at this time that my desire to write

began to surface again. I bought myself an old, second-hand typewriter and began writing poems in off duty hours. After completing a dozen or so I posted them to my parents and then forgot all about them

The course we were taking was extensive but off duty passes were generous and I spent mine roaming round Cape Town's beauty spots of which there were many. On one evening I found myself in the suburb of Clifton. Lying at the other side of Table Mountain to my flea-ridden airfield, Clifton was a beautiful place. Facing the blue Atlantic, it consisted of four beaches of pure white sand fringed by coves of granite boulders, semi-tropical vegetation, and small wooden bungalows. Table mountain, with its dramatic slopes covered in protea, aloes, and silver trees rose behind them. In turn as the mountain swept past Clifton it became the twelve peaks known as the Twelve Apostles. No place I had ever seen is so dramatic and yet so beautiful and no place has ever had such an effect on my life as did Clifton in the weeks ahead.

But all I knew that evening was the beauty of the place. Reaching a promontory with a small café at its entrance I treated myself to a bun and a cup of tea. As I paid the café proprietor, he asked if I were going to the dance that was being held in the Scout Hall. When I showed my ignorance, he took me outside and pointed to a large wooden hut opposite. As we stood there I heard music and he told me that dances were held there every Saturday evening by the SAWAS and as a serviceman I would be welcome.

Remembering the hospitality of the SAWAS at Benoni, I crossed the promontory to take a closer look. Because the evening was warm a door had been left open and I saw a dozen or so couples dancing inside. As I stood in the doorway an attractive, middle-aged woman approached me. She insisted that I joined the dance and during it introduced herself. She was Mrs Eileen McGrath and after the dance she took me down the promontory to her bungalow where I met her husband, Roderick McGrath.

Over supper, which they insisted I shared with them, I learned that they had three children, a married son who lived and worked at the other side of town, and two daughters, one an actress called Monica who at that time was over in the United States, and a younger daughter Shelagh who was married to a South African airman and living in Durban. I listened to all this without the slightest idea of what it would mean to me in the months and years ahead.

Before I left the couple invited me to visit them again and to stay overnight if I could obtain permission. I accepted their offer not only for their kindness and the exquisite beauty of Clifton but also because the camp fleas were driving me crazy and making my body look as if I had virulent smallpox.

Thus during the rest of my course when I could obtain an all-night pass, I would spend the evening with them, rise at 5.30 a.m., catch an early bus to town, where another bus would take me within a few miles of my airfield.

It was during this time that I met a girl I shall call Synevva. She was not the person who was to change my life but there is no doubt she had a profound effect on my beliefs and my Yorkshire puritanism. She was perhaps three years older than I but in the arts of life and living a hundred years my senior. She was an artist, a painter of some renown, and because of her sophistication and good looks she seemed to attract every officer in Cape Town. Why she chose me, a mere NCO, I could never fathom unless she found pleasure in teaching a naive young man the arts of living and exoticism that she practised so well. For reasons of brevity I will not say more about my affair with her but this I can suggest with total sincerity. Every young man ought to have one Synevva in his life to teach him a woman's wishes and needs. It could well be the answer to the many domestic breakdowns that occur today.

If this mention of an affair seems to contradict what I said at the beginning of this chapter I should perhaps stress that my applications for pilot transfer were still been sent in every week. I was only too aware that the war was still going badly for us. Since Japan had attacked Pearl Harbour and so entered the war she had invaded and captured Indo-China, Thailand, Burma, the Malay Peninsula, and the Dutch East Indies. Then Singapore fell, our campaign in Libya failed, and even the Russian's new offensive to relieve Leningrad was not the success that had been hoped.

Indeed disaster seemed to be coming in from every point of the compass and a man felt compelled to give his best no matter what his role. Hopefully this was shown in my case by the 90% marks I received on my final examination.

The question was now where I would be posted. I had hoped it would be back to Baragwaneth but instead it was an airfield in Queenstown, a town six hundred miles from Cape Town and four hundred miles from Johannesburg. While it did not sound promising, I was told that because of my high marks I would be recalled to take the senior course once I had done some field work to gain experience. With this promise I had to be content.

THIRTY-EIGHT

Although none too pleased at a posting so far from my friends, my feelings recovered when I learned I might soon be flying again. I was told this during my interview with Queenstown's chief flying officer, one Squadron Leader Short.

Short was a large plump Englishman with a fearsome temper. He was an old RFC airman with an astonishing serial number of only three figures. Although he had a second in command called Hathaway who handled the practical side of the training, it was Short who doled out the duties. In giving me the purpose of the airfield he told me to my surprise that Queenstown, officially known as No. 47 Air School, was in reality Prestwick transported overseas. Even so, few of the original personnel had moved with it and I recognised only a few faces in the days that followed.

The pupils, I discovered, were observers who, after completing their navigation training elsewhere, were sent to Queenstown to learn all about bombs and how to drop them with precision. For this purpose we had simulators in which pupils could initially practice without the expense of using real aircraft. Afterwards they progressed to the real thing by dropping practice bombs on a range near the village of Waverley, some thirty miles away. For this purpose we were provided with twin-engined Airspeed Oxfords and Ansons.

At first I was unable to lecture on the theory of bombing because this was the task of Senior Armament Instructors. This did not satisfy me. As a junior instructor I did not get as much flying as the SAIs and so between tapping their brains and studying in my own time, I was able take a course of pupils of my own within three weeks

During this time I had received a letter from Synevva saying that she was thinking of coming to Queenstown to be with me. Missing her as I did, I had enough sense to know it could never work. Synevva moving from her sophisticated environs in Cape Town would be like an exotic plant taken from its ornamental greenhouse and planted in a garden of weeds. Although it was painful, I finally wrote and explained to her there was no future in me. My pay would not cover her weekly hair expenses and I could be posted anywhere in the world at a moment's notice. She wrote me a few more times but eventually her letters ceased and I knew the affair was over.

Although hardly any of the personnel had been at Prestwick, nearly all were British and because most had lived in cities over there they found the town lacking in entertainment and the surrounding veld barren and lonely. This I did not find. After a few days I took a walk into the veld, climbed a few hundred feet up a kopie, and sat down on a ledge there. As I watched the sun go down and the distant kopies turning blue and mysterious as mountains do in the evenings, I had the same feelings when as a child I had sat on the warehouse steps and watched the evening sun tinting the smoke from chimneys. I learned to like the veld and its loneliness and returned to my kopie whenever I could.

Back at the airfield my affairs were greatly helped by the arrival of 'Taffy' Williams. Taffy, an observer with the rank of warrant officer, had flown 52 sorties in Blenheims until a shell, bursting under the bomb aimer's bay, had sent a splinter through his left eyebrow and affected his sight. Sent to Queenstown to replace Hathaway, who was posted away to receive a commission, he recognised me the moment we met. 'You were trained as a wireless operator/air gunner at Prestwick early in 1940, weren't you, Smithy?' When I said yes, he told me he had been on an observer course at Prestwick and been billeted only a few houses away from me. He wanted to know the whys and wherefores of my presence in Queenstown and, after hearing them told me that from then on I would work with him. Moreover he promised to see that all my weekly applications would be passed to the right channels.

Looking back, I think he favoured me because of my willingness to fly in all weathers. Taffy was an 'eager beaver' who was fiercely keen to win the war at any price, and he tended to despise any pilot or instructor who objected to taking unnecessary risks because of inclement weather. So, one way and another, although I received no promotion for it, I was given the same work as Senior Armament Instructors.

Without question this was heresy in RAF terms but Short was a realist and once Taffy convinced him I knew my subject as well or better than anyone, he turned a blind eye and allowed Taffy to use me however he liked.

Use me Taffy certainly did. My diary records that at one period he worked me between twelve and sixteen hours a day, with fifteen minutes for lunch and dinner. Nevertheless it was a relief to work under a man who was taking the war seriously and doing his utmost to turn out fully trained aircrews. It all made one feel a little more useful to the war effort and for that reason alone I liked Taffy Williams.

At the same time I did take risks that other men tried to avoid. One was flying with young pilot officers who had only just received their wings and yet believed they were God Almighty. I had an experience with one of these when Taffy asked me to take a single pupil over the Waverley range and try to find out why his bombing results were so poor. We arrived at the pre-arranged time of 14.30 and circled round until the range gave us permission to commence bombing. I signalled the pupil to crawl into the nose hatch and I opened the camera hatch to check where his bombs fell.

The exercise took a long time because we had to drop bombs from four different bearings and the pupil was painfully slow. Seeing his bombs were missing by hundreds of yards, I called him out and checked his bomb sight settings. Finding they were correct, I told him to try again.

He dropped two more bombs and over the intercom I heard the pilot swearing at him. Knowing this would hardly help his concentration and seeing the time was now 15.30, I told the pupil we would finish for the day and asked the pilot to return us to base.

He refused point blank. We still had four bombs left and he wouldn't leave until they were dropped. After that our conversation went like this: 'We must leave now, sir. There are three Ansons due over the range at 15.30 and as we're all flying at 6,000 feet there's a danger of a collision.'

He laughed at my timidity. What a load of

bull. Did I think he was blind and couldn't see three bloody big Ansons in the sky? We were going to drop those four bombs and that was the end of it.

'But my orders are to return at 15.30 and it's already 15.33.'

'I don't give a damn about your orders. My orders say we're going to drop those bombs.' With that the pilot glanced at the hesitant pupil. 'Get back to your bombsight and let's get on with it.'

At that I became bloody-minded myself and told him who was in charge of the exercise. All that did was make him even more determined to drop the bombs. Damning the fool under my breath, I told him he must take full responsibility and that I'd have to put in a report on our return. Then I sat back and left him to it.

By this time I could see the distant Ansons circling as they waited for clearance from the range. Although this can't have been given I saw one Anson break from its orbit and become a stationery speck. This meant it was either flying away or towards us, and as the speck grew bigger I knew it was the latter. Although I couldn't imagine my pilot not noticing it, I tapped his shoulder and pointed forward. His impatient mutter suggested he had seen it but still intended to complete his bombing run. As there was only one target and both aircraft were at

6000 feet as they tracked towards it, it meant in effect that we were on a collision course.

I watched the Anson through the windshield and as it grew bigger could only assume its pilot had not seen us or was playing the same fool game as mine. All this time my pupil, lying in the hatch over his bombsight and giving his bombing instructions, was oblivious of his danger. Hating the thought of chickening out I gritted my teeth and waited until the Anson seemed to fill the entire windshield. Then, deciding enough was enough, I let out a shout and hit my pilot on the shoulder.

I saw him give a start and realised that in his tantrum he hadn't seen the Anson. In shock, he heaved back on the wheel and the Oxford reared up like a startled horse, throwing me back into my seat. At the same moment the aircraft shuddered from nose to tail, then reeled to one side and began spinning down.

Startled cries came in the intercom from the pupil who had not seen what was happening. Certain that we had struck the Anson and were badly damaged, I tried to drag him out of the bomb hatch but, as always happens on such occasions, the hooks of his parachute harness became snagged on a cable or strut and the more we struggled the worse the entanglement became.

While all this was happening, the pilot was

fighting to gain control of the Oxford, but with the sky and landscape still spinning round us and our altitude falling by the second, there seemed no hope of avoiding a crash. I remember my feelings very distinctly when it became obvious there was no way of getting the pupil out and no hope of reaching our parachutes which were stored towards the rear of the Oxford. They were pure rage that we should die so pointlessly because of this stupid puffed-up brat of a pilot.

I can't say what our altitude was when the Oxford finally came out of her spin but as we skimmed over a mountaintop I could see frightened baboons running for shelter. Nor can I remember what I said to the pilot. He was searching the ground as we circled and I knew he was convinced as I was that we had struck the Anson and her wreck was lying somewhere below us.

To everyone's relief the Anson was waiting for us at Queenstown when we landed. Although her pilot confirmed he had also felt a shock when the near miss occurred, I never discovered if she had suffered any damage. Luckily for me, my pupil had heard everything that had passed between my pilot and myself and so I was cleared of any responsibility. What happened to both pilots I never found out but mine disappeared from the station and was not seen again. In my case I drew out my caul from my wallet and gave it a kiss before returning it. By this time I was certain it was protecting me.

It was my willingness to take the odd risk now and then that made Taffy use me so much. Yet there was no question of bravery involved. In truth I had been behaving in similar fashion even before I left England and it has taken hindsight to offer an explanation. My head and neck injuries, which I learned later were far more serious than I had believed, allied to my loss of Becky to God (as she had put it), had perhaps affected me so much that I no longer put a high value on my life

There was one side to Queenstown that we all hated. The courses we trained usually went up to the Middle East and were soon in action. Periodically and somewhat sadistically, we were sent details of their casualties. These were often very high, and as we had made friends with many of the men, these lists would throw a gloom over us.

One course, number 16, stands out vividly in my mind. It was comprised almost entirely of ex-London policemen who frankly admitted they had joined up as aircrew to escape the bombing. Although it seemed to us they had jumped from the frying pan into the fire, they were as fine a bunch of men as I ever hoped to meet, and I used to enjoy my hours with them.

Like all the courses, they held a party at the end of their training, and I was their guest of honour. I tell this because I was closer to those men than any other course I took. So when their casualty sheet arrived it was harrowing to read that over fifty percent had been lost in two months. The war was like a meat grinder, devouring men at a fearful rate, and I found it disturbing that we were training men to die while we lived in comparative safety.

An interesting although less harrowing feature of these courses was the farcical way promotions were handed out. When each course ended we were told to recommend one third of their number for commissions. Naturally we picked the men we had found to be the brightest and the best, but these were seldom the ones who received commissions. They were given to those who had gone to the right schools and colleges, no matter how low their marks with us had been. I feel it ought to be mentioned to dispel the notion that the curse of Britain, its class system, disappeared in the carnage of the Second World War.

By contrast, I had an amusing experience a couple of weeks later. The Powers That Be, deciding we needed a refresher course in infantry training, sent us a young Army captain, a tall, supercilious character whose name I forgot to note but who obviously saw us as a bunch of Brylcreem playboys. Nothing could have gotten under Short's skin more than that, and after the captain (whom I shall call Carruthers) had been with us a week, he called me to his office.

'You know what this chap's doing, don't you, Smithy?' When I shook my head: 'He's taking our lads on the rifle range and getting 'em to put bets on the winner.'

'So?' I asked, puzzled.

Short scowled. 'The bastard's fiddling them. He uses his own rifle and they draw theirs from the armoury. Then he only allows 'em one sighting shot. So he can't lose. But the bugger's going to when he gets to my section.'

'How?' I asked.

Short gave me his wicked grin. 'Don't act the bloody innocent with me, Smithy. You've probably thought of it already. Get down to the armoury beforehand and fix him.'

With my devious mind alerted, I had no need to ask how. Five days later I visited the armoury and had a few words with a friend of mine. Two hours later ten of us, issued with 303 rifles, were lined up on rifle range. Carruthers, neat and tidy in his battle dress, was at his supercilious best. 'I know you chaps aren't used to this kind of thing but wars are about guns and bullets, y' know. At the same time there's no reason why we shouldn't get a bit of sport out of it, is there? How about a three quid bet apiece on the winner?'

With my section alerted, the dubious glances he received were phoney. 'I thought you chaps in the RAF liked to play games. At least that's the impression my lads have of you. I'll tell you what. You can all have one sighting shot and I'll forego mine. That's fair, isn't it?'

At that our bets were laid and the shooting began. His face was a sight to behold after he fired his first shot. 'Who's been tampering with my rifle sights?'

I looked as innocent as possible. 'Who would do that, sir?'

He glared at me. 'Someone has. It's firing at eleven o'clock.'

'Perhaps yours got a knock in the armoury,' I suggested. I held out my rifle. 'Why don't we start again and you use mine and I'll use yours. If you have a sighting shot too, it'll be the same for us both, won't it?'

I had him and he knew it. We fired another ten rounds apiece and in army language I shot the pants off him. Afterwards, as arranged, I paid back the three quid bets my section had contributed. Short loved it when he heard the story and insisted on buying the entire section a drink that night.

Be all that as it may it seemed only a short

time before Short called me to his office and told me he was sending me back to Cape Town to take the Senior Armament Course. It would not teach me anything I had not already learned, he told me, but should earn me the promotion I deserved. When I thanked him he told me with a twinkle in his eye that he would need to apply for two men to take my place while I was away. When I accused him of flattery he grinned and held out his hand. 'Why not, lad. A bit of flattery is good for us all. Come back and we'll throw a party for you.'

Fully aware the Services are not replete with officers like Short and Taffy, I left Queenstown with considerable regret when my posting came through a week or two later.

THIRTY-NINE

My personal fairy must have been in something of a tizzy when I arrived back in Cape Town, unable to decide whether to give me grapes or gallwood. Arriving too late to reach the airfield that night, I booked a bed in the Soldiers' Club and was shown to a large dormitory where a couple of South Africans were cleaning their kit. When I asked which beds were free, one glanced at the other, then pointed to an empty one near the door. 'You'll be O.K. there, man. It's been free for a couple of nights.'

As I thanked him and began lowering my kit, I thought I heard a suppressed titter but when I glanced round both men were straight faced. I cleaned up and then went out to phone Mrs McGrath, only to hear she had let her bungalow for a couple of months and was staying with a cousin in the suburb of Rondebosch. Gaining her address but not her phone number, I decided to visit her at my first opportunity. After that I wandered around the city for a couple of hours and then decided to have an early night.

I slept peacefully enough until just after midnight when I felt something pushing and trying to burrow under my back. Waking with a start, I turned and in the dim light of the dormitory saw a huge animal poised over me. Shocked and still half asleep, believing it was some wild animal that had gained entry, I rolled out of bed. At the same moment the lights were switched on and roars of laughter broke out all around me.

It was then I saw my assailant was a Great Dane. Massively built and indifferent to my humiliation, he jumped into my bed and as I watched with disbelief, he laid his huge head on the pillow, gave a grunt of contentment, and closed his eyes.

It was my first introduction to Cape

Town's wonder dog, 'Just Nuisance' or Nuisance as he was generally called. Without question he was a wonder dog. Made a rating in the South African Navy based at Simonstown, he spent his working days in Cape Town where his duties lay in finding drunken airmen or sailors and 'escorting' them to the Soldiers' Club. These duties were carried out by gripping the sleeves or tunics of drunks and, regardless of their protests, tugging them without ceremony to the club where SAWAS ladies resuscitated them.

Soldiers he ignored. Why I never discovered unless it was due to the different colour of their uniforms. But to sailors and airmen he was both a guardian angel and a military policeman.

Indeed it was said that nothing happened of military significance without Nuisance being aware of it. Stories of his exploits were being heard everywhere, in hotels, in bars, in private homes. He was, as I was soon to find out, the great character of Cape Town and eventually his fame was to spread the length and breadth of the land.

Nor has time dimmed his memory. Only recently I read that a statue of him, paid by public subscription, had been raised in Cape Town. I consider myself privileged to have shared his bed and to have been involved in one of his exploits which was to occur later.

However, apart from my introduction to Nuisance, my arrival at Youngsfield was hardly auspicious. Checking in at the guard-room the following morning I learned there had been many changes in the personnel since my last term there and I would need to make enquiries about my section from its present staff. Accepting this, I started down the path that lay alongside the parade ground and saw ahead of me two young flying officers talking to a South African warrant officer. As I walked towards them with my kit, the warrant officer drew my attention. With a body resembling a 500 bomb, he was wearing summer military uniform: brown boots, khaki shorts, bush jacket, and a circular topee. Black hair sprouted from his bush shirt and his legs looked like the pillars of Hercules. I remember wondering how a gorilla had managed to reach the rank of warrant officer as I reached the trio and asked where I could find my section.

The two young officers were friendly enough and after pointing out my section offices, one asked me the reason for my posting. As I was telling them, the gorilla suddenly turned on me. 'What the hell do you think this is, corporal? A bloody tea party? Get over there and report to your section. At the double!'

The lack of protest from the two officers had its message for me. Giving them a salute, I started towards the block of buildings at the far side of the parade ground. But I hadn't gone more than ten paces before I heard the gorilla's voice again. 'Man, you can't get away from these damned bluebottles these days. I had a dust up with one in Cape Town last night. He made a pass at my girl and I knocked the bastard down. I wanted him to get up because he had more coming but these bloody roineks are all the same. Once they're down, they stay down.'

I should have ignored it. Of course I should. But my Mr Hyde never failed to leave his cave when bullies insulted him. So I walked back. 'I heard that – sir. And there's only one way to prove you're right, isn't there? Knock me down and see what I do.'

I'll swear his eyes filled with unholy lights. 'I thought I told you to report to your section officer.'

'You did and then you insulted me. Why?'

The gorilla glanced at the two officers, saw their disapproval, and shutters closed over his eyes. 'Eavesdroppers get what they deserve, corporal. Like everyone else, I've got my opinions.'

I should have left it there but couldn't. 'And I've got mine too – sir. Want to hear them?'

The look he gave me was almost thoughtful before he snapped up a salute to the two officers and marched away with stiff, jerky strides. After a dozen yards or so, he halted and turned. 'What did you say your name was?'

I told him and he marched on. It was then I heard one of the young officers release his breath. I turned to him. 'What else could I have done?'

Both men were looking embarrassed. After glancing at his colleague, the younger gave his reply. 'Just the same, corporal, if I were you I'd tell your section officer, Flight Lieutenant Price, what happened. He'll be able to advise you.'

I stared at him. 'Advise me on what?'

He lowered his voice 'The WO's watching you so we'd better not keep you any longer. I'm sure Mr Price will explain everything.'

I discovered my Flight Lieutenant Price five minutes later. No more than five feet two inches in height, wearing an RAF shirt with sleeves rolled up over thin arms, there was something about his movements that made me think of a perky house sparrow. 'Are you the SAT course Officer, sir?' I asked.

His friendliness could not have been less military. 'I am, lad. Have you been sent on a course?'

I said yes and gave him my name and number. He glanced into a book and then, to my surprise, walked round his desk and shook hands. 'I've got good reports about you, Smithy. I think you'll enjoy the course.'

I noticed now that he was wearing a pair of shorts that came well below his bony knees. This was no sparrow, I decided. It was the world's first commissioned gremlin. At the same time, after Short's behaviour in Queenstown and now this, I was beginning to revise my view of RAF officers.

Price told me I would be in charge of a billet of u/t armourers for a while, gave me the hut number, and then details of my course. As I picked up my kit to leave, I remembered the incident on the parade ground and made mention of it. His expression suddenly changed. 'You've been in a fracas with Kruger? Just after you arrived?'

'Yes, sir. I'm afraid I couldn't help it. It was the things he said about the RAF.'

Price wasn't listening. 'What star were you born under, Smithy?'

I stared at him. 'Star, sir? Why?'

'It must have been Mars, lad. No question about it.'

At this point I decided there was a ghost here that had to be laid. 'What's so special about Kruger, sir? Why were those two officers so wary of him?'

Price shifted and scratched his backside. 'Let's put it this way, Smithy. I like to look after my lads, so if at any time you get into trouble, don't say a word until you've seen me. I was a solicitor once, so know a thing or two about getting men off charges. All right?'

I was lost. 'But why should I be put on a charge?'

Price scratched his backside again. 'These things happen for all kind of reasons. Sometimes because a man's born back to front. And sometimes because a man hates the British.'

I was with him now. 'And both apply to Kruger?'

'I didn't say that, lad. Just watch yourself, read DROs every day, and come and see me if you get into trouble. Now let's go and meet the rest of your course.'

In going the rounds I met Ken Addey again who had been retained there and it was good to hear his dead pan humour again. Later on we caught up with our news. When I mentioned my fracas with Kruger his opinion was more graphic than Price's. 'Kruger! He's an out and out bastard. He's only been here a few weeks and even the station's cat hates his guts. But why the hell had you to clash with him? Can't you stay out of trouble for five minutes?'

Remembering Addey had always seen me as a jonah who brought trouble to his friends as well as himself, I told him the affair was over and finished. He laughed at my optimism. 'You called Kruger's cards and you think he'll forget? You'll be in red ink on his hate list.'

I discovered how right he was that very evening when just after 23.00 hours my billet of twenty odd men was raided by one of Kruger's disciplinary sergeants and I was put on a charge for allowing cigarette ends and dead matches to litter the floor.

Remembering Price's offer, I saw him the following morning before being taken in front of the C.O. and his advice was to say that in the RAF men were only liable for the cleanliness of their billets after morning reveille and I had not known it was different in South Africa.

It was enough for my charge to be dismissed but was hardly calculated to improve my relations with Kruger. Taking my escape to heart and no doubt guessing I had Price on my side, he did his very best in the days that followed to outwit us. It became so bad that I felt like a tethered goat being attacked on the one side by a hungry gorilla and on the other saved by a diminutive gremlin. Yet this miniature war – it was nothing less – faded into total insignificance beside the event that was to change my life for ever. But as that was still some weeks away, perhaps its fullness should be told in another chapter.

FORTY

In spite of Kruger I found myself enjoying the course because as its aim was to teach the entire techniques of bombing and gunnery so its pupils could pass on these skills to their own pupils later, it involved plenty of flying. This was meat and drink to me because as I was already fully conversant with the various theories and technicalities involved, I could enjoy the flying for itself alone.

Not that Kruger made life easy for me. He seemed to have taken my stand on the parade ground to heart and he tried every trick in the book to get me on a charge but to date, with Price's help, I had kept my record clean.

In spite of his harassment I still found the flying great fun. When at Queenstown I had discovered a way of dropping bombs without using the standard bombsight. To avoid tedium I won't go into the deeper technicalities but in brief I had calibrated an ordinary school ruler to cover airspeed at a fixed altitude. I would then place the ruler on the perspex hatch and move it around until its angle coincided with the aircraft's drift. Then all I had to do was draw a grease pencil line on the perspex, mark it off with the necessary calibration, and I had a bomb-sight that, including the grease pencil, cost three pence against the thousands of pounds the conventional bombsights cost.

Not that I told anyone about it. With the services as they were, I would probably have been put on a charge for showing contempt of the system. But providing the aircraft tracked in on the right compass bearing, my ruler proved very accurate. So accurate in fact that it put me into even deeper trouble with Kruger. For reasons I never discovered he had been involved in the construction of an illuminated sea target off the coast at Eerste Rivier. I was told it was his pride and joy and so the Mr Hyde in me, resenting his constant persecution, was on full alert when I was sent out to bomb the target.

Not that I really hoped to hit the thing. The safest place to be on a bombing range was on the bulls eye itself but on this day conditions were perfect. The sky was a robin's egg blue, the Oxford rock steady, and I couldn't see a trace of drift as we approached the coast. If ever there was a day to get my own back on Kruger, I knew this was it and making sure the pilot did not see me, I drew the ruler from my flying overalls and began tracing a grease line on the perspex. Then, pretending to use the standard bombsight, I began giving my approach instructions.

Although it looked tiny from 6,000 feet,

the target was a fifteen foot floating platform surrounded by a ring of pontoons with a hundred foot radius. As we droned towards it, my pilot, who was the younger of the officers I'd met on the parade ground, gave a laugh over the intercom. 'You know what Mr Price calls it?'

I was squinting along my grease line. 'No. What?'

'He calls it Kruger's ring.'

I grinned. 'It's a bit small for a gorilla's, isn't it?'

'Maybe, but it cost the earth just the same. It's festooned with bulbs for night bombing and think of the length of cable involved.'

I felt my mouth watering. 'Let's see if we can't bounce it.'

Another laugh came over the intercom. 'You're an optimist, aren't you?'

'Why not? Let's have a go at it anyway.'

The compass swung as we came round on the bearing I wanted. Calling instructions, I waited until the bull's eye reached the sighting mark on my grease line and then squeezed the bomb release. Leaning forward, I watched the bomb falling like a tiny dart. For a moment it vanished altogether, then there was a puff of smoke. 'How's that?' I asked.

The Oxford banked steeply as the pilot tried to look. 'How close?'

'Inside the pontoons,' I said.

He sounded sceptical. 'You're sure?'

'Certain. Let's try another.'

We dropped another eight bombs before I let out an excited yelp. 'That's it! I got it! Right on the button!'

The pilot sounded sceptical again. 'You mean another one inside the pontoons?'

'No. On the target. On Kruger's ring.'

'Come off it, Smithy. No one hits the bullseye.'

'That bomb did. Go round and see if I can do it again.'

My pilot decided enough was enough. 'Not on your life. If you're right, we're going to be the two most unpopular guys on the station when we land.'

I realised he was right. 'What can they do? The target's meant to be bombed, isn't it?'

'You think that's going to appease Kruger? If you're right about that bomb, he's going to want your guts for garters.'

The plotting office verified my claim. I had landed a practice bomb slap on the new target. Price looked like a gloating gremlin on hearing the news. 'Bloody marvellous, Smithy. Bloody super, in fact.' Then his expression changed. 'But it had to be you again, hadn't it?'

Kruger appeared a few minutes later. If looks had been knives I would have been skinned alive. I had hit the gorilla in the tenderest spot possible and although he could take no direct action, the looks I received made me think of a steam boiler ready to explode.

Nor was my situation eased by Addey's reply when I told him the story. 'You stupid clot. The bugger's watching us like a hawk as it is. Why had you to make things worse?'

I was beginning to feel a wronged man. 'What was I supposed to do? Drop bombs all over the South Atlantic?'

All I got from Addey was a snort of disgust. 'He's got the two of us linked together like Tweedledum and Tweedledee. So the next time think about me before you act like Guy Gibson.'

It was then my idea came. It was made feasible because by this time we prospective tutors had been freed of our hut duties and were billeted together. 'You hate Kruger, don't you?' I asked.

Ken stared at me. 'That's a stupid question. Who doesn't?'

'Then let's take the mickey out of him. Let's do something that makes him look an incompetent clown to the rest of the lads.'

'How the hell can we do that?'

'We get a room out of camp and sleep there. It'll free us of ants and when the lads hear about it they'll know we're tweaking Kruger's nose. It'll lose him respect. Let's take a chance and do it.'

With all the risks involved I've no idea how

I persuaded Addey but in the end he reluctantly agreed. So we worked out how it could be done and I like to think our solution was ingenious. At that time the RAF magazine Tee Emm sported a popular character called Pilot Officer Prune whose flying mishaps were meant to illustrate the mistakes aircrew should not make. Also featured was an NCO called Sergeant Bullshit or some such unpoetical name. Aware that the Afrikaners who manned the guardroom were not highly educated and so unlikely to read Tee Emm we decided to use their weakness to our advantage. We would purloin empty pass forms, fill in our names, and then authorise the passes with the signatures of Sergeant Bullshit and P.O. Prune.

It was our use of these fictitious names that gave our plan its Machiavellian undertones. We already knew that Price had an excellent sense of humour, and rumour had it that the C.O. was equally blessed. We had no illusions about Kruger, whose sense of humour resembled that of the Marquis de Sade, but even he could not alter the chain of command and our reasoning went that if Price or the C.O. found us out, our very effrontery might tickle their fancy and minimise our punishment.

Unlikely as that would be, and dangerous too with Kruger breathing fire from his failures to catch me, we were young enough to accept its risks and so we searched for outside accommodation and found a Mrs Mellin in Rondebosch who would let us have a room for ten shillings a week. With her house on the main bus route that led in the direction of the airfield, nothing could have suited us better and we snapped up her offer.

We had one final hurdle to overcome. For the convenience of married men who lived out of camp, transports waited every morning at the end of the bus and train routes to take them to their respective airfields. As our airfield was a considerable distance away, we had no alternative but to brazen it out and climb aboard a transport along with the married men who were all South Africans.

Knowing we could not fool them, we had decided earlier to tell them everything and rely on their good nature. This we did and on our first morning the transport rocked with laughter. Everyone hated Kruger and when we reached the airfield, men shielded us as we disembarked in case he was in the guardroom.

How little I knew at the time what this arrangement would do to my life. The name of the suburb Rondebosch should have been a hint but it only reminded me that Mrs McGrath was staying with a relation there and that I had already been remiss in not contacting her. This, I told myself, I must do soon.

So Ken and I began to live out of camp like married men while at the station the course went on. Kruger continued to make himself hated, Price kept saving me from faked charges, and to balance things Nuisance entered my life again. It was on a day when the entire personnel of the station was ordered out on the parade ground. A number of airmen had been involved in a fracas with sailors in the Del Monica hotel in Cape Town and a Group Captain had arrived to read us the riot act.

Kruger, all hairy bronzed limbs and white gaiters, was in charge of the parade and was in his element as he bawled his orders for the parade to form three sides of a square. When this was achieved he turned to face the approach of the C.O. and the Group Captain. The latter was a big, lantern-jawed man carrying a briefcase under one arm. As two men approached, Kruger lifted up a polished boot, crashed it down alongside the other, and saluted. Then he let out a massive bawl that scattered the pigeons roosting on the top of Number One hangar. 'Parade! Attention!'

There was a roll of thunder as hundreds of boots stamped down. The lantern-jawed officer acknowledged Kruger's salute and then stepped belligerently into the open side of the square. Thrusting out his chin, he began his admonishment with no preamble.

'Some of you might have heard about me. Others might not so I'll put you all in the picture right away. No one gives my group a bad name and gets away with it. No one. So I've told your Commanding Officer that if anything like this Del Monica brawl happens again, the whole lot of you will have your passes stopped for a month. And that's just for starters. The offenders will serve time in the Glasshouse. You're a military unit and by God you'll behave like one. Is all this getting through?'

As men gave dubious nods, my attention was drawn to a huge dog that was moving in purposeful fashion along the road that led towards us. But Lantern-Jaw had his back to it and in any case was in full cry now. 'And it was all over a football match. Don't you know why we encourage you to play games? It's to forge friendships with other units, not to knock the hell out of them.'

Still behind the two officers, Nuisance gave a yawn and peed against a lamp post. As muffled laughs broke out, Kruger let out a yell that made a pigeon discharge in flight. 'Silence! Silence on parade!'

An anticipatory hush followed. Lantern-Jaw, who still had not seen the dog, was breathing heavily now. 'So you think that behaving like hooligans is funny, do you? I wonder how you're going to feel when I confine the lot of you to camp next....'

His voice broke off as Nuisance, deciding the right moment had arrived, padded forward and sat down on his tail about fifteen paces in front of Lantern-Jaw. There, staring straight at him, he made a sound that was halfway between a fart and a raspberry.

Lantern-Jaw swung round on the C.O. 'Whose dog is that?'

'No one here, sir. It's Just Nuisance.'

'I know it's a bloody nuisance. But who does it belong to?'

'It's the Navy's, sir. It's their mascot.'

'Then what's it doing here?'

Some wit on the parade could contain himself no longer. 'He's heard about this circus! He always knows when one's on.'

It brought a scream from Kruger. 'Silence! Silence on parade!'

Lantern-Jaw turned to him. 'Get rid of the bloody thing, Warrant Officer. Right away.'

Kruger gave a start. 'Me, sir? Yes, sir. Of course, sir.'

Hundreds of gloating eyes watched as Kruger approached the sitting dog. As he held out a cautious hand and made encouraging sounds, there was a shout from a hopeful airman. 'Go on, Nuisance! Bite the bugger.'

By this time Kruger's cheeks were florid. Drawing heart from the dog's tail that was thumping the ground like a carpet beater, he tried to grab its collar. At that Nuisance turned his head and gave a deep, deep growl.

As Kruger jumped back, jeers and delighted laughter rolled over the parade ground.

A loud shout from the Group Captain compounded Kruger's discomfort. 'What's the matter with you, Warrant Officer? Are you afraid of a bloody dog?' Spotting two nearby sergeants, Lantern-Jaw turned on them. 'What're you two grinning at? Go and help him.'

The sergeants fared no better than Kruger, retreating hastily at a series of warning barks. Cursing, Lantern-Jaw started forward himself. As if this was the moment he had waited for, Nuisance rose on all four legs and gave a deep let's-have-you growl. As Lantern-Jaw halted abruptly, Nuisance moved towards him.

Recognising an impossible situation when he saw one and with his dignity in mortal peril, Lantern-Jaw had had enough. Glaring at Kruger, he said something to the C.O. and the two of them began marching back to the Administration offices. In spite of Kruger's hysterical yells, discipline collapsed as men broke ranks and howled with laughter. Kruger, astute enough to know that when leaders retreat, subordinates are wise to follow, bellowed and cursed but in the end gave up and disappeared too. Left the sole victor, Nuisance was surrounded by cheering men who almost dragged him into the canteen. There, along with Addey and myself, men toasted him with beer and sandwiches until his huge frame could take no more. My last sight of him that day was when he was making his way towards the camp entrance. There, lurching along as drunk as a sailor on shore leave, he had a half-eaten meat pie stuffed in his mouth. As he reached the guardroom he seemed to give it a nod and then disappeared down the road. There is no question about it at all. Nuisance was the dog of the century.

FORTY-ONE

This encounter with Nuisance came the day before I made my belated visit to Mrs McGrath and so was perhaps in tune with the event that was to change my life. It happened on only the third evening that Ken and I had ventured out of camp after our lectures and I decided it was high time to pay my visit to the good lady.

I discovered the house in which she was staying was quite near to our room and so after a quick meal with Ken I found myself walking up a road that approached the slopes of Devil's Peak. The house, large and detached, faced a large wood. I knocked on the door and a few seconds later was welcomed by Mrs McGrath and her cousin, a tall, good looking woman in her forties. They took me into the sitting room and as I was chatting to them a girl no older than myself entered the room. She held out her hand to me, our eyes met, and then the world tilted and slid off its axis for me.

There are no other words to describe it because it was not the simple attraction I had felt for other women, not even for Becky. It went far beyond the appeal of sex and beauty even although I had never seen a more lovely girl in my life. It was as if the image of her had been in my mind always but safely secured in a guarded cell. This night the door had been unlocked and its treasure revealed to me at last.

To my astonishment it also seemed she had similar feelings because, although for the rest of the evening we obeyed the social conventions, her eyes kept moving to me as if she were asking herself the same questions. What was this thing that was happening to us? What could the mystery of it be?

To me it was like a symbiosis, a meeting of two lovers from another age. I am only too aware how many will smile at such imagery but there is no other way to describe my feelings that night. The tools of language are too clumsy.

What makes it more difficult to understand is what little affect her mother's introduction had on me. I had been told Shelagh was her younger daughter, that she was married, I might even have been told she was in the early stages of pregnancy, but none of it had an effect on my spellbound mind. This alone was odd because in fairness to myself I usually took notice of such restrictions. But not this night. I was enchanted – there is no other word for it – and when I finally made my way back to Ken and our room I could think of nothing else but my next meeting with Shelagh.

This was not long because I phoned the house the very next evening. Shelagh came to the phone and when I asked if she would have dinner or a drink with me she agreed in a way that suggested she had already anticipated my invitation. After the evening was over Ken told me I had better keep an eye on myself or my elated persona would warn Kruger we were up to some mischief at his expense.

From that second evening onwards I saw Shelagh whenever my duties allowed it. I make no excuses for this, nor did Shelagh. It was as if the affair was not in our control and we were obeying the orders of a guiding hand. To me she was everything I desired in a woman; beautiful, warm, generous, truthful and, as I was soon to discover, immensely brave. What she saw in me I cannot imagine although she did once tell me that I was the only person she had ever been able to open her heart to.

Whatever the reasons, we were so deeply in love that we could not conceal it from Mrs McGrath who by this time had moved back to her Clifton bungalow. One would have expected her, a mother, to frown on our relationship and do her best to terminate it but she did not. This made me wonder if she did not like Vincent, Shelagh's husband. Shelagh, never one to complain or make excuses, had never said a word against him to me, but one day Mrs McGrath admitted she had always found him a hard and uncompromising man. Having never met him, I had no way of knowing whether this was true or false.

But if my mention of it sounds like an excuse, it is not intended. I had no right or need for excuses, such was my enchantment. Nor did Shelagh resort to them either. We knew we were in the wrong and although we reproached ourselves time and again it made no difference to our relationship. As I have already suggested, it was almost as if we had no control over ourselves. I remember her once saying this to me when we were sitting together on Table Mountain with the city spread out beneath us. 'Why are we like this, darling? Why aren't we ashamed of ourselves? What is it that makes us forget the entire world when we are together?'

I had no answer nor have I one today. We were like two asteroids who had been drawn together regardless of the planets that had once contained us. If it reads like an excuse I have no other. It was something beyond our control and, as time has proved, it has been that way ever since.

Even so, we did manage to obey the conventions of the time as far as our physical relations went. In today's climate this might seem disingenuous or even hypocritical, but there were reasons for this. There was Shelagh's pregnancy, which emphasised the fact she was married, there was the memory of my distress after Becky had broken off our engagement, there was Shelagh's background, for, although she was no longer a practising Catholic, she had received her education at a convent school. To add to all that, we perhaps felt that if and when a crisis came, we could face it better without adultery on our conscience. We were that young and naive.

It was during this time that my attitude to myself and my life subtly changed. I discovered this towards the end of the course when we potential instructors had to fly certain exercises that we would teach to our own pupils later. Such exercises involved flying in Hawker Audax or Hinds, tiny two-seater, open-cockpit biplanes which the South African Air Force had obtained from the RAF between the two wars. They were hopelessly outdated for current military requirements, but with no other aircraft available for training purposes, they gave pupils some practise of aerial gunnery and, in the case of the Audax, some practise at night bombing too.

Flying in these lovely old aircraft presented no problems for me. They reminded me of my first flight in a Tiger Moth when the entire machine shuddered as if it were a living thing and the slipstream tore excitedly at one's goggles. It was real flying for me and I enjoyed it until my turn came to simulate aircraft to aircraft attack. This meant flying over the ocean at medium height and firing at a canvas drogue dragged along by a second aircraft.

My exercise was scheduled at 06.00 hours and because I was never at my best in the early morning I was late in reaching the armoury to collect and fill my magazine drums. With Kruger always waiting like a predatory hawk to catch me for the slightest misdeed, I hurriedly filled up my two drums and then sprinted for the Hind that was already ticking over on the tarmac. Giving me a look, the pilot waved the chocks away and the little biplane was climbing from the airfield before I got my breath back.

It was then I had the feeling I had left something important behind. I checked my parachute and saw it was in its container. I checked my two ammunition drums and saw they were safely on their spigots. I glanced down and then my heart missed a couple of beats. I had forgotten to put on my parachute harness.

This was serious because the harness had another purpose than being an attachment for one's parachute. In those old aircraft there was a chain on the cockpit floor that one attached to an eyelet on the base of the harness. This, nicknamed a monkey chain, served to prevent a gunner falling out of the cockpit if his place rolled sideways or overturned. Without a harness, the chain was useless and yet our exercise, the quarter cross-over and under tail attack, meant we would be banking steeply and even turning upside down to give me full sight of the drogue.

Common sense said I should inform the pilot right away but knowing he would take us straight back to base, I kept thinking about Kruger and how he would enjoy reporting me for such a stupid oversight. So instead I bent down and tied the monkey chain tightly round my left ankle. Then I kicked away the canvas covering of my seat and thrust my other leg through its tubular frame. Knowing I would also have the gun to hold and support me, I somehow convinced myself these precautions would save me from a six thousand foot drop to a watery grave.

By this time I could see the drogue being drawn towards us by another Hind. My pilot swung towards it and as it passed a few hundred feet below, he signalled to me and rolled the Hind over on her left side. As I leaned sideways to sight the drogue I felt a strain on my right leg which warned me I had better not waste time on the exercise. So I fired a long burst more to expend my ammunition than to hit the target. As the drogue flashed beneath us, my pilot threw a puzzled glance at me as he prepared to make a second pass.

Although with my awkward stance in the cockpit making accurate shooting difficult, all went well until I was halfway through my second drum of ammunition. This time, no doubt frustrated by my hurried and hasty firing, the pilot took the bull by the horns and turned the Hind clean over so that I had an uninterrupted view of the target

This was too much for my abused legs. As my right one began slipping out of the seat, I grabbed hold of the VGO gun, but because of all the firing I had done it was now too hot to hold. As my hands involuntarily jerked away from it, my right leg slid from the seat and with a yell I fell clean out of the cockpit.

It was only the monkey chain tied round my left ankle that saved me, but even so the rest of me was outside and dangling in the slipstream. As I swung towards the tail unit, I was certain the chain, which was cutting into my ankle, would give way or slide off my ankle and my end would come.

Needless to say the pilot felt the enormous drag on his plane and turned to see what had happened. When he saw me dangling out there like a fish on a line, his expression was something to remember. As I yelled at him he began to slowly turn the Hind right side up, which allowed me to climb up my legs and eventually grab the cockpit rim. When at last I dropped back on my torn seat and he turned his goggled face to shout something at me, I was in no state to listen or reply. I was too busy vomiting my heart out on the cockpit floor.

Yet my luck held again. On landing, the pilot halted the Hind at the end of the runway and turned to me. In his anger he almost choked himself. 'What the hell was that all about? What in blazes did you think you were doing?'

Unable to find an answer I let him continue. 'You moron! Do you realise the trouble you'd have got me into if you'd fallen loose and killed yourself?'

I found that funny and so did he later when I explained that Kruger had been my reason for not reporting my omission. The name and reason were enough because

Kruger was not loved by the pilots either. And so I escaped a charge for my stupidity.

Nevertheless the day had taught me something about myself. Only a short while ago I would have dismissed it as one of those things that happen to a man in wartime. But I could not dismiss it so easily now. By this time I was only too aware of the problems our relationship was causing Shelagh and so I should no longer value my life so lightly. I had huge responsibilities now and must live up to them for her sake. I think I whispered this to my caul that night before I kissed it and put it safely away.

FORTY-TWO

If only for personal reasons I would not like it to seem I was neglecting my service duties during the time I was seeing Shelagh. My obsessional dislike of bullies made certain of this and between the lectures we attended, Addey and I designed a contraption which we believed would speed up the training of bomb aimers and save the War Office time and money. It was a complicated gadget in both construction and mathematics but it worked so well that a visiting officer insisted on taking it away to give it more detailed tests. When we never heard of it again but heard that the officer had received promotion, we could perhaps be forgiven for our suspicions. Price, who had been away on leave during the officer's visit, told us we had been a couple of fools to tell him about it

Price, of course, was a delightful officer to work under and one wanted to do well for his sake alone, although in my case I needed high course marks to ensure I was retained in Cape Town. Fortunately I did, receiving 83% which under the current ruling made my retention almost a certainty.

It was an immense relief to me because Shelagh had her baby at this time, a boy whom she called Barry. My close attendance during her pregnancy gave me such an interest in the child and such a closeness that my feelings were almost that of a father.

As my high marks might suggest, my wish for active service was no longer my priority. Indeed since meeting Shelagh I had even ceased to apply for pilot training. Some would say, and I would not argue with them for one moment, that with a war raging, my South African posting should not have lasted as long as it did when so many others were suffering elsewhere. Indeed, until I met Shelagh, I had thought of little else myself. But now I feared being sent away in case Shelagh would need me in the days ahead. I knew she had the same thoughts because of her relief when she learned that my high marks ought to keep me in Cape Town.

But then we had news that put everything into perspective. Shelagh had a cable telling her Vincent was due for leave in two week's time. It was something we had known would happen but we were no more prepared for it than we had been earlier. What should we do? We agonised over it for days until Shelagh made the decision I had always felt she would make. Intrinsically a loyal person, she felt a man coming home from war deserved a better homecoming than we were offering him. There was also the possibility the war might have changed him. She would make every effort to live with him throughout his leave so that he would not return with a broken marriage on his mind. If she discovered during that time she could not face a lifetime with him, she would not break the news until his tour of operations was over. If, on the other hand, she discovered a permanent relationship with him was still possible, we would have to say goodbye and forego our dreams of a life together.

My feelings were hopelessly tangled. The thought of the woman I loved living on intimate terms with another man, even if he was her husband, was a form of torture. At the same time, at the risk of sounding a hypocrite, I had long flinched at the thought of Vincent going back into action with his marriage in ruins and there was some relief in knowing he was being spared that trauma.

As we had arranged not to meet during the fortnight he was home, the days seemed endless. I snapped at my trainees, mooched around the camp, drank too much in the Mess, and my nights were filled with the kind of imaginings that give a man no rest. After a week, certain that Shelagh would decide in Vincent's favour, I began fervently wishing that my earlier requests for active service or pilot training would come through before she contacted me again.

Both of us should have known better than to make such a sentimental arrangement. Although Shelagh's wish not to hurt Vincent was sincere enough, the basic honesty in her that I had always admired could not sustain the lie she was living. One night I received a distressed phone call telling me that she had broken down and told him everything. He had refused to see me but before walking out of the bungalow had announced that he would be filing for divorce immediately.

Although immensely relieved that I'd see her again, I mentally braced myself. Nothing was easier for South African servicemen to have RAF personnel posted if they had suspicions their marriages were being compromised. My nightmare now was that I might be posted out of the country at the very moment when Shelagh was giving up her marriage and perhaps her very security for me.

I was soon to learn she was giving up much more. Wanting custody of the child, Vincent had made a promise through his solicitor that he would not petition for my posting if she would allow the child to live with his sister until he was demobilised. Afraid what might happen to me and still believing he was the wronged party, Shelagh had agreed.

Had I known earlier about this harsh condition, I would never have let her agree to it. But to avoid distressing me, she made no mention of it at the time, although her mother told me later that she had never seen a girl suffer such anguish as when the baby was taken from her. Such was the courage, the honesty and the integrity of the girl I had fallen in love with. Believing Vincent was the wronged party and therefore had a right to the custody of the child, she was prepared to accept this punishment for breaking her marriage vows and to save me from a punishment posting. The next two or three weeks passed in a daze for both of us. She was grief-stricken by the loss of Barry and I was wracked with guilt at being the cause. At the same time neither of us could find words to express these emotions. Perhaps we were too young and inexperienced even to understand them.

It took an incident at the station to bring

home the change Shelagh's grief was having on me. Now that I was officially an SAI instructor, one of my tasks was to blood u/t armourers in the art of fusing live bombs. One course I had been given consisted almost entirely of young farmers from up country and they were known to be somewhat raw in technical skills. At the time they moved over to me they had already been shown how to fuse bombs by using dummy detonators and inert exploders. Now they were to experience the real thing and I had to take them out to a deserted site among the coastal sand dunes in case an accident occurred. This was necessary because we were now to use live detonators in real bombs and so risks were present.

Not that the bombs were dangerous in themselves. They only became lethal when they were fused. It was in the detonators that the risk was present. Highly sensitive, they could explode if crimped or dropped and were carried in a special can that I kept in my possession when we were all driven out, bombs and all, to the sand dunes. The task there, when the bombs were unloaded, was for each pupil to choose the right detonator for the bomb he was given and then carefully slide the detonator into the bomb's fusing tube. Needless to say I kept repeating my warning to handle the can of detonators with great care.

All went well until the task fell on a huge man called Van der Merwe. He'd caused me trouble before with his brand of humour and I paid him particular attention when he took the can from me. However, he chose his detonator correctly and after sliding it correctly into the bomb he made some comment that the job was a piece of cake. Relaxing, I was congratulating him when instead of handing the can back to me, he turned to the other pupils and shouted 'Catch'. A second later I saw the can sailing through the air towards the next man in line for the exercise.

It was a moment of pure drama. I saw the pupil was not expecting the throw and moreover it was badly aimed because it was dropping towards a live fused bomb. Terrified what might happen if the can struck the bomb casing or even the ground nearby I hurled myself forward in an attempt to catch it.

I did but only just. In fact I dropped heavily on the bomb as my hands closed round the can and the impact winded me. Even so I managed to roll off the bomb with the can still gripped in my hands and lay there for a full half minute before I recovered.

I won't repeat what I said to Van de Merwe because it would sizzle these pages but that night I gave my caul an extra kiss. If I had learned anything that day it was that when a man falls in love his life gains alarmingly in value. In other words he becomes a hostage to fate.

Shelagh's belief that after her sacrifice I would remain with her until my overseas tour ended was shattered less than two weeks later. Our first intimation came when Price called me into his office and closed the door. A confidential document had reached the C.O. asking for details of my peacetime education and profession. It also wanted an assessment of my work at the airfield and my character. As my Section Officer, Price had been called in to give his opinion. I remember so well his expression as he laid the document back on his desk. 'It doesn't look good, Smithy, does it? I think it's what you feared. I am so sorry.'

Thus Shelagh and I were forewarned but there was nothing whatever we could do, particularly as Price had risked his commission by warning me. Only one decision could be made in the next week of uncertainty. If promises had been broken, then all previous agreements were null and void. Shelagh would be fully justified in fighting for the custody of her child again.

Ten days passed and then it happened. I was posted to 'Overseas Dispersal'. On the 27th October I was to take the train to the overseas transit camp in Durban, the very day before the final court case of Shelagh's divorce. I had wanted above all things to be present to give my support and encouragement and instead I was being shipped away like a criminal. I had never felt more helpless or frustrated in my life.

At the same time I can't remember feeling any bitterness towards Vincent. For myself I had never asked for clemency, perhaps because I didn't feel I deserved any. But being taken from Shelagh just when she needed me most was a different matter altogether. I hated and detested my impotence.

To show his sympathy and his opinion of the affair, Price had frequently asked me to his home since the confidential report, and he threw a farewell party for me and Shelagh at the station on the eve of my departure. All the lads from my various courses came and wished me bon voyage. It was a sentimental evening and of all the songs sung that night, the ones I remember most were 'We'll meet again' and 'Yours'. The words of the latter, banal though they might be to older minds, seemed to be affirming a promise Shelagh and I had already made to one another.

We did manage a few hours in my room at Rondebosch the following morning, and it was there Shelagh pledged to come to England on my return. She also betrayed her fears for me for the first time. Certain my posting was a punishment one and knowing the tide of Japanese aggression had not been halted, she was afraid for my safety. I tried to laugh her fears away, pointing out that I was the luckiest serviceman in the world, but there is no denying I was wondering myself what life had in store for us now.

After that the day merged into a blur and I remember little else except her standing on the station with her head held high as she had promised but with tears streaming down her cheeks. She looked so terribly young and vulnerable, and when I thought of all the unsolved problems I was leaving her with, my helplessness seemed to rise into my throat and choke me.

I stood at the window as the train pulled away, watching her growing smaller as we waved to one another and I knew that she was also wondering if we would ever meet again. When I finally sank back into my seat, my feelings were beyond powers to describe. I can only say the night that followed was the darkest I had ever known.

FORTY-THREE

It was raining when I reached the transit camp thirty-six hours later. Called Clairwood, it was some fourteen miles south of Durban, a bleak uninviting place as most transit camps were. Once I had reported to the guardroom and obtained a billet, I sat down and wrote to Shelagh, for I was able to think of little else but what had happened to her court case which had been held while I was still on the train

I next wanted to know where I was being sent but that nobody seemed to know or would tell me. Almost daily, trains and ships were leaving Durban for the Middle or Far East and yet every movement was top secret. Even when men were on the docks or railway stations they often had no idea of their destination. We were like a nest of ants being scattered around the world by some giant creature who gave nothing for our feelings. All a man could do was live for the moment and shut his mind off the future.

Apart from that, life at Clairwood was not unpleasant. Once cleared for the day, we were allowed out of camp from 14.00 hours onwards. As the camp food was poor, most men would catch the train to Durban and find food and solace there.

It sounded agreeable enough but at the time it was no comfort to me. I tried to reach Shelagh by telephone but for some reason was unable to get through. With her needing my new service address before she could write me, four days passed without news of her divorce and in my imagination every dire thing that could happen to her had happened. Without friends and with no desire to make any I wandered around Durban without point or purpose. All I wanted was to hear from Shelagh.

However, on the fifth day an extraordinary thing happened. I had obtained a pass for the afternoon and was approaching the camp gates when I heard a voice calling my name. Turning, I saw a tall, lean figure running towards me. I stared, rubbed my eyes, and stared again. There was no mistake, even if we were six thousand miles away from England. It was Des Matthews.

Although he had seen me first, I think he was as amazed as I was. We embraced like brothers and were soon pouring out our news to one another. To my surprise I discovered he had been on a course at Queenstown only a few weeks after I had left there for Cape Town. He had then been posted to East London to complete his training as a navigator, and now, like myself, was waiting for a posting to parts unknown.

I can't think of anyone I would rather have met at that moment. We went into Durban with some of the navigators from his course, and when a long letter from Shelagh arrived the next morning, my morale began to recover.

Not that her news was good. Although she had obtained custody of the child, which was a massive relief to me, she had been forced to agree to relinquish that custody if at a future date she married me and went over to England. I felt this a most punitive condition, designed either to keep us apart or cause her profound unhappiness if it failed its purpose.

But I was helpless to change anything. I could only thank God that she had Barry back to comfort her in the months and years ahead. Like the rest of the ants around me, I could not imagine what the future would bring. Peace seemed a thousand years away, as did our reunion. We could only hope that fate would be kind to us. There seemed no other way to stay sane and survive.

In all I spent nearly a month with Des and his friends. As we were all psyched up waiting for our postings some men found it difficult to behave rationally. With Shelagh in mind I had no problem containing my one time reckless-ness, but others were less fortunate. I re-member on one occasion a party of us sitting on a first floor balcony of a hotel with cars passing on the road below. As a convertible driven by an attractive blonde drew up be-neath us, a drunken young observer let out a howl and leapt clean off the balcony. By the grace of the gods who protect drunks, he landed feet first in the back of the car, only to be pitched forward alongside the startled girl. Before she could react, Des's entire party leaned over the balcony rail and shouted their encouragement. It seemed to work because the girl gave us a look and then drove off with the young observer making himself comfortable beside her.

It was during this month with Des that I had another of those experiences that had made Len Addey despair for me. One Sunday night Des persuaded me to go with him and a few others to the Free French Club in Durban. Here he met a French girl called Marie Saint Joffe from the Seychelles and after dancing with her for most of the evening, he asked if I would see her home. He was detailed for guard duty that night and needed to catch an early train back to camp.

The Club was in a part of Durban I had not visited before and the girl told me that if we took a short cut through the nearby park we would come out near her home. With no reason to dissent I took her advice. Although it was dark when we reached the park, there were very few lights inside it and it seemed empty of people, which I found surprising. However, Marie knew her way and after a few minutes we were walking down a path flaked by high banks and dense bushes. With the sky overcast with clouds, the only light came from the reflected glow of the city. By this time the silence and the absence of people had made Marie nervous and sorry she had suggested the short cut. As we reached a point where the shadows from the high banks were dense, I felt my right shoelace flapping against my foot. Telling Marie to wait a moment, I was bending down to tie the lace when I caught sight of a dark figure on the bank above me. From his aggressive posture I had the impression he had hurled something at me at the very moment I bent down.

Telling Marie to wait for me, I foolishly ran towards the mysterious figure. He hesitated for a moment then ran off and melted into the darkness. Knowing I had no hope of catching him I returned to Marie who was now almost hysterical. Curious to find out what had been thrown, I calmed her down and then searched the opposite bank. More by good luck than anything else my hands struck the handle of a knife that was half buried in the soft soil. Pulling it out I found it had a long pointed blade with razor sharp edges which I learned later was a Kris throwing knife.

I took the distressed girl home and then went to the nearest police station with the knife. Their reaction was anything but friendly. Didn't I read Station Daily Orders? Didn't I know that Berea Park was out of bounds to servicemen since a man had been found there with his throat cut and two others found with serious injuries? I had left them little option but to report me to the camp for disobeying orders.

I countered this by asking what the hell they were doing sitting on their backsides when a murderer was running loose in a local park. Why weren't policemen at every entrance keeping people out? Before the argument could develop further, I realised they had not yet asked my name and number and so I made a quick exit. It worked because I heard no more about it on my return to camp.

Des was the first to be posted, his destination the Middle East. With Japanese submarines taking a heavy toll of shipping in the Indian Ocean, he and his party were to go north by the rail route, which gave me the chance to see him off at Durban station.

It was another sad occasion. As I've said before, we were closer than brothers and with the war raging as it was, the chances of our seeing one another again seemed remote. No man was tougher than Des, as the future was to prove, but I know he didn't find it any easier than I to say goodbye that day.

For myself I would have preferred to be the first to go because once Des had left the dark hole in my mind seemed to widen again. Nor did the city help. The streets were full of people doing the ordinary things that people do, going to their places of work, shopping, walking arm in arm with their wives or sweethearts, and at the end of the day making their way to their homes. We were not one of them, and because of it one felt lonelier in the streets than back in the camp. For my part, with Des gone I wanted nothing more than my posting but still I heard nothing. In an attempt to pull myself together I enrolled in an unarmed combat course and visited the gymnasium every free afternoon. My personal excuse was that the martial skills might be useful one day but in hindsight it was to ease my mind about Shelagh. I had long discovered that physical effort and pain can ease the pain of the mind and the hard demands of that course did bring some relief.

I had now been at Clairwood over six weeks with no posting in sight. Writing me almost every day as she did, Shelagh gave me the exciting news that her mother had offered to look after Barry so that she could come and stay in Durban for a few days. If all went well, she would arrive the following Monday. Full of life and excitement again, I began counting the hours.

It was as if fate had been waiting for this precise moment. The very next day I was told my posting had arrived. Although my destination was still a secret, I had to be ready to move out in forty-eight hours. In the meantime I had to transfer to another billet where I would meet some of the men on my draft.

I found it hard to believe. To be offered a chance of seeing Shelagh again and then have it snatched away at the last moment seemed the act of a sadist. Knowing she would be equally devastated, I managed to get her on the phone and for long and painful minutes we tried to comfort one another. Only then did I go looking for my draft.

I found them in a billet full of unmade beds and dense cigarette smoke and knew almost immediately this was no ordinary draft. Their very talk told me they were mostly old sweats and yet only a few held any rank above AC2. From my own experience I knew what this meant because while all the others who had passed my SAI course had received promotion, I had been kept as a corporal. Like myself these men were being punished for one reason or another.

At the same time, knowing the services as I now did, I guessed some would have committed misdeeds that would be barely recognisable as such in civilian life. Equally, by the laws of chance, there would be others of more dubious character and they would need watching in the days ahead.

There were also a few NCOs whom I was to meet later. But as every man had fallen out of favour in one way or another I was convinced that in spite of the War Office insistence that punishment postings were not on the agenda, this was one of them. After all, was I not one myself?

There were around forty of us and we sailed the following day. Our ship was an armed merchant cruiser whose name my diary fails to record. I suspect its crew had been told about us because, although the Navy was seldom friendly towards the RAF, this crew's behaviour was positively hostile. While officially we were guests on the ship, the Master-At-Arms or whatever the Naval Disciplinary Officer is called gave our men every dirty job he could find. We, the NCOs, put in our protests but they were overruled and it was not long before the draft was in a state of near rebellion.

Aware we had some tough characters who weren't above violence, I hit on an idea that I felt might defuse the situation. Hearing that the ship's gunnery crews were to carry out a loading and firing competition on their WWI 4.7 inch guns, I asked if we could enter the competition, providing we put up the same stakes as the crews.

Seeing easy money in us, the gunners were only too happy to agree. So I picked four or five of the huskiest and brightest men on the draft, asked for a canvas shield to be drawn round us while we practised, and got down to work. Prior to this I had watched the ship's guns being loaded and so knew what the procedure was.

As the competition was to be held in three days time, I worked my crew mercilessly. There were grumbles and moans but I countered them by stressing the malicious pleasure we would enjoy if we beat the navy bastards. With such an incentive, men worked morning, afternoon and night, and the jibes and sniggering of the ship's crews that we were only a bunch of RAF 'poofters' only played into my hands. By the time the third day arrived, my crew were so psyched up they were determined either to win the competition or blow the ship out of the water.

So, at the crack of a pistol, we were off. Men heaved over the heavy shells, manhandled them into the gun, and slammed shut the breech. I've forgotten how many shells we were supposed to load or fire, or indeed whether we fired at all, but I do know to the utter consternation of the ship's crew we won the competition hands down.

It was nearly as good as winning the war to my lads. In three days we had learned to load naval guns faster than sailors who had been handling them for years.

It did little for our opinion of the Navy or for our safety in their hands. Nor did it save the men from their persecutors who took their revenge by giving them even worse jobs than before. But it put our morale sky high and the sneers of 'poofters' were not heard again.

FORTY-FOUR

We docked in Kilindini, East Africa, five days after leaving Durban. We were told we could go ashore but must be back on ship by 22.30 hours. Aware we had heavy drinkers in our ranks, and feeling the Navy would be only too happy if men went AWOL, the other NCOs and I suggested it might be better if we all remained aboard ship.

Our suggestion was refused. The liberty book or whatever the Navy call it said that men were allowed shore leave and we must abide by its ruling.

So we all went ashore and some did not return on time. The next day we were summarily ordered to disembark and take our kit with us. Whether this had been ordained previously or whether the ship no longer wanted us, we never found out but while we waited, puzzled and forlorn on the quayside, she sailed away.

With no idea what was to come next, we waited for hours in the equatorial sun. Finally two lorries with Navy drivers arrived and we were told to climb aboard. Gears meshed and we were driven away.

The road was appalling and as the trucks bucked about, we cursed and clung on for dear life. After about four miles we entered a forest and after another six miles or so we finally halted in a small clearing. Telling us to jump out, the drivers then drove away without a word of explanation.

There were two disused huts in the clearing, flimsy affairs with wooden, sun-bleached walls and thatched palm leaf roofs. Assuming these to be our billets, we entered them cautiously, our feet stirring up dust and awakening insects of all shapes and sizes that scuttled away to take cover under the string beds that lined the walls.

As cleaning the crude huts was clearly going to be an unpleasant business, I and two other NCOs went off to establish they were our intended billets. An overgrown path led through the palm trees and after a few minutes we found ourselves among huts that seemed to have been set down in the forest without rhyme or reason. With some difficulty we found a guardroom and there were told that the camp, built mainly for transit purposes, was called Port Reitz.

That was not all we found out. The station knew nothing about us; it had not even been informed of our arrival. Unless some desk clerk had blundered, it seemed the Navy had unceremoniously dumped us there and made us a draft that nobody wanted.

To say we weren't wanted would be an understatement. With the North African and Italian campaigns causing a food shortage throughout the area, the camp was hard pressed to feed its legitimate inhabitants, much less a bunch of uninvited and loveless villains. Only with the greatest reluctance were we allowed into the cookhouse and there we received little more than the scrapings from the table. My diary records an average daily menu. Half a soya bean sausage for breakfast, a spoonful of cabbage and a tough piece of camel meat for lunch, and two more soya sausages for dinner. With the soya sausages still experimental, they were barely edible, and after a few days most of us began having stomach problems.

However, a serviceman is nothing if not adaptable, and after carrying out the highly unpleasant task of destroying the insects in our billets, we took a leaf from Napoleon's military manual and began foraging for food.

It was not long before one of our more lascivious members discovered a brothel some two to three miles from the camp. Called of all things the Country Pavilion, it was run by an enterprising Greek and his Russian wife, and along with its dusky beauties it served black market food.

A word or two about this odd couple is

worthwhile if only because of what we heard about them later. To those who watch old movies the Greek was almost a facsimile of Sidney Greenstreet with his tall, portly body, resonant voice, and ponderous walk. Somehow they combined to give him an authority and presence that was out of character with his profession. In contrast, with her small, bent body, sly expression, and wheedling voice, his wife bore a strong resemblance to Peter Lorre.

Whatever its ownership, the Country Pavilion became a mecca for our draft. To reach it one followed a narrow path through bushes and trees while every now and then soft voices calling 'Jumbo, jumbo' sounded from the flanking bushes. I never discovered what jumbo meant literally but it was clearly an effort from local non-union girls to break the brothel's monopoly.

I was bitten by a snake one evening when making my way with a colleague for a meal there. It was a moonlit night but the shadows were dense where trees closed out the sky. As I reached a small bush I felt a sharp blow on the inside of my right ankle. At first I thought I had stood on a fallen branch and it had sprung up and struck me. It was only when my companion, a South African whose name I have forgotten, gave a shout of warning that I realised it had been a snake biting me. My companion, who had seen it as it was slithering away, said it had been a mamba. When I asked how he knew that, he said it was because mambas had a different movement to other snakes.

Not reassured by this news, I told him it had bitten me. At first he was sceptical until I removed my sock and we saw two dark stains on my ankle bone. Full of stories that a man has only three minutes to live after a mamba bite and that the only remedies were to cut out the bite, suck out the poison or cauterise it, I was all for trying all three until we realised the ankle bone prevented the use of a knife.

By this time my foot had gone ice cold and the large vein on the inside of my calf was beginning to swell. Scared now, and wishing I had obeyed orders and worn snake gaiters, I let my companion suck at the wound for a couple of minutes, then allowed him to cauterise it with a match. With the flesh having no liking of fire, my yell of protest brought that therapy to a swift end. With the camp at least two miles behind us, we decided to make for the brothel in the hope the Greek had snakebite remedies. Keeping an anxious eye on my watch, I limped after my companion, hearing the soft invitations of Jumbo-jumbo as we went.

By the time we reached the brothel my watch told me I was well into borrowed time. I showed my ankle and swollen leg to the Greek who in turn showed concern when my companion described the movement of the snake. After taking a closer look at the bite he agreed it bore the marks of a mamba but told us he carried no antidotes for mamba bites.

Before I could collapse at all this good news, he assured me that because of the time that had passed, I had nothing to fear. If I had a good meal at his establishment before I returned to camp, he was certain I would be as right as rain in the morning.

When I asked the basis of all this confidence, he told me that a lifetime's experience had taught him that healthy adults who either do not see the snake that bites them or have no basic fear of snakes seldom die of snake bite. In addition my snake had bitten me on the ankle bone which had probably inhibited the venom's passage into my bloodstream. Lastly the snake might also have used up some of its venom on an earlier victim.

Whichever reason was applicable, I was assured I would live to a ripe old age providing I gave my constitution a boost with good food and beer.

With no other choice I tried to believe his assurances while his wife scurried off to prepare our order. Around 22.00 hours, although still limping, I followed my colleague back to our billet. Earlier I had decided to see the M.O. but as my leg seemed no worse I took the advice of Sidney Greenstreet and went to bed instead. It must have been good advice because I woke up the next morning with nothing more than a sore throat and a large bruise on my ankle. So much for jungle pavilions and black mambas.

After a three week delay caused by my posting, letters began reaching me from Shelagh again. She appeared to be writing something to me every day, and although I could tell she was missing me as much as I was missing her, I was consoled by her relief and happiness at having the custody of Barry again. One line in a letter did give me food for thought, however. She wrote 'I'm going to be frank with you, darling. It is going to be hell to give up Barry when the time comes.'

I knew it was her honesty coming out and not a hint she was having second thoughts about marrying me. But it was a reminder of the additional pain I might cause her and something I could not put from my mind. I even clung to the thought that, because by an extraordinary coincidence she too had been born with a caul, it might be a help and comfort to her. After all, had not mine come to my aid in moments of need? Such are the things one clings to at such moments in time.

I had an interesting letter from Ray a week or two before Christmas. He had learned that an ENSA group was to visit the Mombasa naval base and discovering that two of the girls in the party were friends of his, he had written to tell them about me. In turn they had replied that if I were to contact them when they arrived in Mombasa, they would see I was looked after.

After weeks in the jungle, it was an offer no man could turn down and when I discovered the party had arrived, I phoned their hotel. The two girls – my diary omits to give their names – sounded delighted to hear from me and invited me to a dance they were holding in Mombasa a couple of nights later.

Looking forward to having a few hours with civilians again, I arrived in Mombasa in my best khaki drill and made for the hotel where the dance was being held. It was only when I edged my way into the packed room that I realised what a fool I had been. Instead of the ENSA dance being held for servicemen in general, it was for naval personnel only and I could hardly have been more conspicuous in my RAF uniform.

Knowing nothing about the internecine war between the Navy and ourselves, the girls invited me to their table and began plying me with drinks. I needed those drinks because the looks I was getting from the hundred or so matelots present suggested my days were numbered. Dancing was impossible: the moment I took a girl out on the floor I was tripped, kicked, or had elbows dug painfully into my ribs. Puzzled at first, the two girls became angry when I explained the reason for my unpopularity. Eventually, to my relief, they stormed out of the dance hall and took me to their quarters.

Dined and wined, I spent the next three hours with them talking about Ray and listening to their reminiscences. Around 02.00 hours, after a last swig of whisky, I made my unsteady way down to the hotel foyer and turned in the direction of Port Reitz.

I hadn't gone more than thirty yards of the ten miles facing me before four burly matelots with clubs came running out of the shadows. Outraged by my intrusion, they had waited all that time to make certain I would never make such a mistake again.

It was Boxsburg all over again except I no longer had my rubber tube. But I was unusually strong and hyped up with whisky. Even so, I doubt if I could have handled it without my Mr. Hyde. By this time he had had his fill of the Navy. Yelling at me to get out of the way, he came raging out of his cave and set about my four bully boys with frightening enthusiasm.

For my part I remember little about the affair until I was once more making my unsteady way towards Port Reitz. But then I realised blood was running down my face, my hands were torn and bruised, and my bush jacket was ripped and stained. Glancing back, I saw that two sailors were lying on the road and the other two had vanished.

As, in spite of my unarmed combat training, I doubt if I could have done it on my own, I have to say this to Robert Louis Stevenson. 'I know you didn't like Mr. Hyde and I don't like him either. But when the chips are down, is there anyone else we'd rather have at our side?'

Christmas came and having been told the nearby camp could not spare us extra rations, two NCOs and myself visited the large naval base near Mombasa. Its existence was due to the fall of Singapore. After losing that vital base, the Navy had been forced to retreat to Kenya where it licked its wounds and prepared to counter attack. As that day was drawing closer, the base was large, and, as the Navy controlled the distribution of food, we were hoping to gain extra Christmas ration for our men.

It proved a futile hope. Although the station padre did his best to soften hearts, they were made of oak as far as the RAF were concerned. A naval guard escorted us to the camp gates and told us where to go in the future.

So much for the season of goodwill. We were given a few scraps from Port Reitz's meagre ration, and someone lent us a 16mm cine camera and rigged up a screen across two palm trees.

So on Christmas Eve we watched Casablanca. I have only to hear the song 'As Time Goes By' to see the men's faces as they gazed at the young and lovely Ingrid Bergman. With their faces paled by the silver screen, even the toughest of them looked vulnerable that night.

By this time we had been in the jungle nearly three months and although I was only too aware that men in action elsewhere would have given their rights arms to make an exchange with us, the heat, the insects, and mostly the inactivity were having their effects on us. It showed in many ways. One lad in my billet had a violin and used to play it for an hour or so every evening. To be truthful he played it badly and his discords could be quite painful. Nevertheless the majority of the men suffered it in silence because they knew the youngster's history. Along with another airman, he had been an operator on a D/F radio station camouflaged high in a tree when the Japanese had swept forward and overrun the area. Although the two men had been undetected, they had been forced to climb down every night and forage for food. With the Japanese prone to torturing and then killing men they discovered behind their lines, the strain on the two men must have been appalling. Eventually a British counterattack had freed them, but the youngster, terrified he might have to face such an ordeal again, had volunteered for aircrew training. Somewhat surprisingly, he had been accepted as a pupil navigator, and for a few months had found respite in Canada. There his shattered nerves had failed him and I think he must have confessed his reasons for requesting his transfer because he was now on a punishment draft with the rest of us. If this was so, it was a cruel posting because he was terrified of going back to the Far East again and his violin was his only solace.

But while other men endured it, Mac and Jock did not. Mac and Jock as everyone called them were two of our worst characters and kept threatening to smash the violin if he did not cease playing it. Time and again I warned them to leave him alone but as the stifling days came and went I felt an explosion must come soon.

It came but not because of the violin. It came one night when we heard angry drums sounding from the African settlements around us. We knew nothing of the reason until an Army MP Officer drove to our huts and demanded to know if any of our men had been out late that night. He told us a young African boy had been run over and killed by an RAF truck stolen from Port Reitz.

It so happened that Mac and Jock had been out that night but, unusually for them, returned by 2200 hours. At first their early return seemed to clear them but later the distressing story came out. Going to Port Reitz they had tried to obtain beer coupons but been refused. Frustrated, they had then broken into the Warrant Officer hut and stolen both beer coupons and the keys to a truck. After getting drunk they had driven off towards Mombasa but not far from the camp had run over the young African boy and killed him. Sobered by their crime, they had returned to our hut in an attempt to cover themselves. But their boots and clothes gave them away and they were taken from us. We never saw them again but the cessation of the angry drums made us guess the Africans around were satisfied the culprits had been found and punished.

Only a few days later we were told that a ship to complete our posting had arrived in Mombasa and we would be taken to it the following morning. Although we still did not know our final destination, I think we were all glad to be on the move again. In some ways waiting for the unknown can be more stressful than the unknown itself.

FORTY-FIVE

The day before our departure I received six letters and a parcel of books from Shelagh. They could hardly have come at a better time and although we had no idea where the RAF were sending us, I felt in reasonably good spirits when we were awakened at 05.30 hours on the 5th.

We had an early breakfast and at 07.30 hours trucks took us to Mombasa harbour. Once more no one seemed certain what to do with us because we were first ordered aboard a large ship called the Khedive Ismail, which appeared to be chock full of troops, as well as Wrens and nursing sisters. The women were a sight that made many a jaded eye light up but they proved a false dawn. We had not been on the ship ten minutes before a bearded naval officer complained to the Army NCO who had brought us and we were unceremoniously taken off his ship.

No doubt our reputation had gone before us and the officer feared for the safety of his women. But to the draft it was yet another example of the Senior Service's contempt of us, and men cursed all things naval as once again we heaved up our kitbags and stumbled down the gangways.

Our new ship was a smaller one, around 10,000 tons, and named the City Of Paris. It was packed with East African troops and because of this we were billeted in cabins. (We soon learned that the Paris was a Dutch ship and for this reason her cabins had not been demolished to make extra room for troops). Unused to such luxuries, many of us wondered what such comforts heralded for us.

We sailed at noon. The convoy was a small one but as we learned later, a most important one. After its virtual dismissal from Far Eastern waters, the Royal Navy was moving back in preparation for its counterattack against the Japanese. As a consequence, the Khedive Ismail was packed with high ranking officers and other headquarters staff, as well as its large contingents of troops.

After leaving harbour, the convoy adopted a V formation. In the van was the old cruiser Hawkins. She was followed by two smaller ships which I judged to be freighters. The second line consisted of our ship, the Khedive Ismail, and another troop ship. Our flanks were guarded by two destroyers, the Petard and the Paladin. The Khedive was tucked tightly in line between ourselves and the other troopship, and to cheer us up in the mordant way of servicemen, the ship's gunners told us that we were acting as torpedo shields for the Khedive. This was necessary because if we continued eastwards we would soon be entering the most dangerous waters in the world for submarines.

I don't think many of our draft worried too much about that. The food was good, the cabins comfortable, and the sea and sky a glorious blue. After our East African experience we almost felt we were on a pleasure cruise.

Five days passed and the only incident of any note was a temporary problem with the Khedive's engines, which forced the convoy down to half speed. But repairs were quickly effected and the voyage remained uneventful until the 12th.

It was a calm and sunny day. I'd just had lunch and was lying on the deck, drowsily watching the rise and fall of the Khedive in the gently swelling sea. She was no more than eight hundred yards abeam of us, and with white splashes of spray running along her side, she looked like a toy ship in a children's picture book.

Then it happened. Two huge clouds of smoke suddenly erupted from her, one amidships and one astern. She staggered, then broke in two like a cracked eggshell. Her bows disappeared almost immediately but her stern seemed to drive forward for a few seconds under the impulse of her engines. Then her propellers came out of the water and she slid down too. Less than a minute can have passed before the Khedive vanished for ever.

As I rubbed my eyes in disbelief, there was a yell from our bridge. 'Torpedo on the starboard bow!' A moment later the Paris heeled violently to the right.

The desperate manoeuvre caused the torpedo to race past our bows but it also meant we were now heading towards the scene of the disaster. Huge obscene bubbles of air were breaking on the surface which was littered by debris and struggling survivors.

No doubt aware that we were the next likely target, the destroyer on the right flank had heeled into a ninety degree turn and was racing straight towards us. In the way one's mind works at such moments, I remember thinking that her bow wave made her look like a lean and snarling wolf.

Thus the two ships were for the moment on a collision course, with the Khedive's survivors occupying the sea between us. As the destroyer reached them, she began casting out depth charges. Seconds later they began to explode, hurling bodies up from the water. Other survivors must have had their backs or necks broken by the shock waves.

It was done to save us. Years later a publisher told me that Monserrat had created a similar incident in his book THE CRUEL SEA from this action. How true this is I can't say but I thank God I was never asked to make such a decision as the destroyer's captain had to make that day.

The planting of the depth charges meant that the Paris was now running into the explosions. As the last one sent up a huge column of water, there was a heavy grinding beneath us and the ship reeled as if she had run into some underwater obstacle. At the same moment there was a yell from a gunner and we saw a long, dripping shape rising out of the water not two hundred yards from us. It was the Japanese submarine, blown to the surface by the depth charge.

As our guns opened up, there was the sound of an express train followed by another huge eruption of water. Although the Hawkins had obeyed the dictum that when submarines appear, cruisers disappear, she had nevertheless spotted the submarine as she steamed away and was adding her contribution to the general chaos.

To our relief it was the only shell she fired because from its trajectory we were in greater danger than the enemy. The submarine appeared unscathed from the depth charges and crash-dived out of sight again.

By this time the rest of the convoy had scattered like a pack of sheep harried by a wolf. We changed back on to our original course and made after the Hawkins, which was already hull down on the horizon. With the two destroyers now well behind us as they began a search pattern for the submarine, we were on our own and the feeling was not pleasant. Nor was it made better by rumours that a periscope had been seen following us.

The sharks did nothing for our morale either. Brought to the area by the blood and carnage, some of them were following the ship, and the thought of being torpedoed and left to their mercy made one hope for a quick death if an attack came.

Here I must give credit to the black troops who made up the bulk of the Paris contingent. Although many of them must have had kinsmen on the Khedive, which was carrying gunners of the East African artillery, I never saw a trace of panic among them either during the action or in the suspenseful hours that followed.

Nevertheless, everyone's nerves were on edge and here the crew of the Paris provided a lovely touch. The Khedive had been sunk around 14.30 hours. An hour later tea was served. I thought it very British and for once had to praise the Navy.

The rest of the afternoon and the night that followed passed slowly. Few if any of us went below decks, and with our bulky life jackets still being worn, we found sleep almost impossible. Instead we cursed the moonlight which made us an easy target if

Japanese submarines were following us.

Dawn came but no one welcomed it. It was Sunday and after breakfast a church service was called. I was maliciously amused to see our toughest characters in attendance with the rest of the draft. I doubt if any of them had seen the inside of a church in their lives, but with Japanese submarines and sharks running amok, it was clearly no time to take chances.

It brought me one of those reflections I always had at such moments. Incidents of this kind, when a man has no control whatever over his destiny, make men call to God even if his belief is frail or even non-existent. A supplication to a universe of stony stars would leave him with nothing but despair.

During the night, the remaining ships of the convoy had reassembled and the Hawkins was back in station again, although after her disappearing act the previous afternoon, the sight of her brought us little comfort. It was only when a Catalina flying boat appeared that we felt help was on its way, and she received a cheer as she circled overhead.

With the Officer Commanding Troops still ordering all personnel to wear life jackets, the day passed slowly and painfully. We all knew by this time that we were entering the infamous channel to Colombo that gave such rich pickings to Japanese submarines, and there was little conversation from crew and troops alike.

Towards evening the Hawkins, which had appeared uneasy and restless all day (we were told later that the Khedive was the first troopship she had lost in convoy) was relieved by a lone destroyer. With four ships to guard, it seemed to offer little protection either, and another long and tense night followed during which we heard depth charges exploding.

To our relief all four ships were still in station the following morning and our escort had grown to three destroyers and another Catalina. But around 11.00 hours 'action stations' sounded. This was an alarm for air attack and the convoy began zig-zagging all over the sea. The all clear sounded half an hour later, only for a submarine alert to follow almost immediately. At the time this suggested our attacking submarine had got a radio message of our presence out to other submarines, and we might have to run a gauntlet of them for the last two hundred miles.

But although rumours continued to sweep the ship, there were no further incidents, and around 17.00 hours that Monday we moved into line abreast to sail through the minefield into Colombo. The tonnage of ships within the harbour was enormous, with half-submerged wrecks showing the attention Japanese planes had paid the port. With no quays empty, we anchored a few hundred yards off shore. We had survived the journey, and feeling by this time that my debt was beyond measure, I kissed my caul yet again.

There was no question of our being allowed shore leave yet. Firstly we had to swear on oath that we would make no mention to anyone, serviceman or civilian alike, of the Khedive's sinking, for six calendar months. From this we gathered the submarine had been sunk by our destroyer escort but it was not yet known whether beforehand she had let Tokyo know her mission had been successful.

Although no confirmation was possible at this time, it was believed that only twenty-one men and women had survived out of a total complement of one thousand, seven hundred. It had been, we were told, the greatest loss of troops in convoy since the war began.

These were the only statistics given us and, of course, we had no way of checking their accuracy. Many years later I was invited by a major Sunday newspaper to write an article about the incident. This I did and a few days after publication I was delighted to receive a letter from a Lt. Col J.A. Stevens who said he had been O.C. Troops on board the Khedive. As he was one of the survivors, his comments were invaluable for he was not only able to amplify the scanty information we were given but in some cases to correct it.

He agreed that the ship broke up and sank astonishingly quickly and that the total casualties were 'enormous'. However, he stated that subsequent analysis showed that about 15% of each contingent survived, which allowed for rather more survivors than we were told, although the total loss remained the highest sustained in convoy throughout the war.

As for his own experiences, he and other survivors had been picked up by Paladin just before the Japanese submarine had surfaced again. When its crew had manned their guns, the Paladin's captain had ordered 'stand by to ram'.

Paladin did ram but with the submarine being the larger vessel, a large hole was torn in Paladin's side and she began to flood. For a while it looked as if the survivors would have to swim again but Paladin managed to keep afloat and her sister destroyer, the Petard, sank the submarine with torpedoes. A few Japanese survivors were afterwards picked up by a flying boat that searched the area, and they were flown to England for interrogation.

Meanwhile, the British survivors were transferred to Petard which took Paladin in tow to Addu Atoll, a base south of the 'one and a half degree channel' so feared by convoy commanders and their escorts. After a couple of days H.M.S. Hawkins came back to take the survivors to Colombo.

For our part we were delayed in Colombo for a few days while divers went down to examine the ship, for it was believed that the shock we had felt had been the submarine striking our underside before she surfaced. This gave us a chance to go ashore after swearing our oath and my diary records I visited a Buddhist temple and Mount Lavinia, a coastal village outside Colombo. During this time we lost half our African contingent to receive jungle combat training. The Hawkins also sailed into the harbour at this time with the Khedive's survivors.

We sailed again on the 18th February. At first we believed Calcutta was our destination but after we passed through the minefields we were told it was Bombay. With a single destroyer as escort, we sailed north until we docked in Bombay harbour on the 22nd.

So our turbulent sea journey to the Far East ended. There is little doubt that we owed our lives to the unknown naval officer who ordered us off the Khedive Ismail. Whatever his reason, it seemed massively ironical that our draft, the one loaded with delinquents, should have been the only one sent off the doomed ship and thus allowed to escape. Unless one believes in cauls, perhaps it is a mystery that only a theologian would dare to explain. Other questions are less profound but no less puzzling. How could the Royal Navy allow a large ocean-going submarine to penetrate the heart of a convoy and pick off its capital ship without as much as raising an alarm? Equally mysteriously, why has so little been told of the incident in subsequent years?

Yet there is still one last question to add. How did the Japanese know that the Khedive was full of VIPs and high-ranking officers and how had they known the day of her sailing so that they could have an ocean going submarine waiting for her?

I was given the answer later. It was Sydney Greenstreet and Peter Lorre. They were acting as spies for the Japanese and had picked the ideal profession for their role. How easy for their girls to vet sailors about their ships, their cargoes, and their sailing dates. And to think Sydney had treated my snake bite so solicitously and had wined and dined us afterwards. Could anything define better the madness and incongruity of the world mankind has made?

FORTY-SIX

We docked in Bombay on the 22nd and were taken straight to Worli, six miles out of Bombay. This was a huge transit camp with billets almost as large as aircraft hangars and holding a hundred and forty men apiece.

It was by far the most insalubrious camp I had ever been in, for masses of untreated sewage ran out into the sea just below us, and when the wind was in the wrong direction the stench was almost overpowering.

The monsoon season was also due and because of the build up of humidity, the heat was worse than Port Reitz. A man had only to drink a cupful of water and it bubbled out of his skin as sweat within minutes. For the first two days we were confined to camp while we were kitted out to SEAC requirements. This gave us a chance to fraternise with some of the Americans on the camp and we were soon exchanging cigarettes, experiences, and complaints in the way of servicemen. During these exchanges we discovered they thought very highly of the RAF, which was a pleasant change after our Royal Naval experiences.

They were the first Americans I had met

in the Services and I became friendly with three of them. Two were Yanks and the third was a Southerner from Mississippi.

With all of us believing the Americans enjoyed better equipment and better conditions, we were surprised to hear they thought Worli the best camp they had been in since they enlisted. A further surprise came when the three Americans examined my equipment. All three of them thought it far superior to their own.

It was while they were in my billet poring through my kit that a scary thing happened. In talking to the Southerner, I had not noticed that one of the others had discovered my derringer in my kit bag and was checking its serviceability by pushing cartridges into its cylinder. Before I could react, the older Yank grabbed his arm to take the gun away but the act caused the derringer to fall to the concrete floor at my feet.

A modern revolver would not have reacted but this was an old model without a safety lug. As it hit the floor there was an explosion, made louder by the confines of the billet, and men sat up from their charpoys to see what had happened.

The third American was quick-witted enough to yell 'Firecrackers', and startled men began to sink back on their beds again. But I was horrified. Not because the bullet had missed my feet but because behind me there was a row of fifty or more beds. With lunch due in a few minutes, nearly all of them were occupied, and with the revolver discharging as it hit the floor it seemed impossible the bullet could have missed all the beds.

Thus for a few seconds I was paralysed. Carrying a firearm without permission in India was a crime in itself at that time. If it had injured or killed anyone I could expect to spend the rest of my life in the Glasshouse.

It must have been a full fifteen seconds before I dared look around. All seemed normal enough. Men were lying either reading or drowsing in the intense heat yet I knew one of them could be unconscious or dead.

Shooing out the Americans, I sat on my bed in a lather of sweat as I waited for the cookhouse gong to sound. When at last it did and men rose for lunch, I watched in frightened fascination to see if anyone remained in his bed. When no one did, I walked down the billet on unsteady legs to see if I could find where the bullet had gone.

I found it in eleven beds along the line. It was embedded in one of the wooden beams on which the string lashings were attached. If its trajectory had been three inches higher it would have gone through the body of the man lying there. As things were he must have been asleep not to feel its impact.

I hastily dug it out and threw myself back

on my bed, unable to think of food or anything else. Because of its implications and what it could have done to my future plans, it left me shaken for days.

When we were finally allowed out of camp, I did a few trips into town with the three Americans. On our first two outings we did the usual things, went to the Breach Candy swimming pool and then to a cinema. On our third visit, the younger American wanted to take a look at the red light district.

This was strictly out of bounds to all the Allies but the youngster dared us to go and as the other two agreed I felt obliged to stay with them.

I remember next to nothing about our wanderings around the district except that we had to keep taking cover from the patrolling MPs. My only real memory relates to the one brothel that the younger man wanted to enter. A wheedling old woman led us down a darkened corridor into a room dimly lit by a reddish glow. The walls were lined with the kind of cages animals used to be secured in. Some had curtains drawn across them. Others contained dim female figures who ran to the bars on seeing us and with voice and gestures tried to entice us inside.

To me it was like entering an anteroom of hell. The poor creatures were half-starved and desperate. A clawlike hand seized my arm and seeing its nails were filthy and like talons, I pulled sharply away. Although there was incense burning in the room, the underlying smell made me feel that just by standing there I was catching every venereal disease known to man. Fighting back nausea, I threw coins into the cage and then ran down the corridor into the open street.

To my relief the three Americans followed me only a minute or two later. Feeling the need for a drink, we found a bar and must have had too many because quite suddenly the Southerner turned on his two companions and began calling them Yankee sonsofbitches who weren't worth his granddaddy's spit. As the other two answered him in kind, I realised for the first time that beneath the flag of Old Glory the Civil War was still smouldering. Acting as peacemaker, I got them all out of the bar in one piece, only for a party of MPs to spot us and give chase. We managed to evade them and return to Worli without further incident but I for one could hardly claim it had been a successful night out.

During this time postings for my draft were arriving almost daily. Most of them were for the worst trouble spots on the Eastern front. If memory serves me right, one man, a wireless operator, was sent to Calcutta to be air-dropped on an airfield the British had established behind the Japanese lines. One way and another they were transfers that told us our misdeeds had not been forgotten or forgiven, although without doubt the Powers-that-Be would have thrown up their arms at the suggestion they were punishment postings.

In spite of my ceaseless thoughts about Shelagh, I can't remember giving much thought to my own transfer. After a while, knowing he has no control whatever over his life, a serviceman develops a kind of fatalism. If it is to be, it will be and so there is little point in dwelling on it. Yet at the same time another part of me was praying I would survive so that Shelagh's sacrifices for me would not be in vain.

To add to my cocktail of a mind I was also becoming aware of the effect India was having on me. After the loneliness of East Africa we were suddenly confronted by a huge continent crowded with people speaking a hundred different dialects. Millions and millions of them, packing every city, town, and village. To a young man brought up to believe in God and Heaven and the other simplistic concepts of religion, the impact was traumatic. How could so many people have individual souls? How could so many squeeze into my Sunday School teacher's heaven?

It all sounds ridiculously naive but in my spiritual life I was still naive. My culture, even if it often failed to practice what it preached, made a great thing about the sanctity of human life. Now every day I was seeing the dying and the dead lying unattended in the streets, the crippled and the starving begging vainly for food, the untouchables and the lepers being rounded up and driven away as if they were the vilest of sinners. All denied by law to be given money in case their diseases and conditions were transmitted. Where had pity gone? Where had love gone? Where had God gone?

It could not yet be called a crisis of disbelief but it was a disorientation that made me wonder what Shelagh would make of this changed man if ever we were allowed to meet again.

If my religious impressions were in flux at this time, they were nothing beside my opinion of the British class system. It had, God knows, been evident enough in Kenya but in India, which contained its own caste system, it had found its spiritual home. It had not missed my attention that the only servicemen's canteen we had found on our arrival was run by the Parsees and not by the British. The occupied people made us welcome, the occupiers did not. Yet until I had the chance to wander round Bombay, I could not believe there were so many establishments designed to humiliate men and devalue their self esteem.

Perhaps those of us who had served in South Africa felt this class consciousness more than most because, somewhat ironically because of its colour bar, the Union did not practice segregation for servicemen in its bars and hotels. Whereas here in India there were canteens for privates, bars for NCOs, clubs for junior officers ... the pecking order of snobbery seemed endless. Even women were not exempt from it because in the few soldiers' canteens where women folk were permitted the signs would read 'For other ranks and their women'! Ladies, it seemed, were the prerogative of officers, and yet even commissioned ranks were not exempt from this odious practice because certain clubs and hotels were out of bounds to all but senior officers, high-ranking government officials, and their respective memsahibs.

The famous Taj Mahal Hotel was the Mecca of all this sectarianism where one wondered if God himself might have problems of entry. As I stood before it one night, the Mr Hyde in me that hated authoritarianism came to the surface. In an act of madness I stripped off my chevrons in a public toilet and then returned to the hotel. Remembering how it had worked with Kruger, I took a deep breath and then walked through the portals as if I owned the place.

With the die now cast Mr Hyde chose the most luxurious lounge of the dozen or so the huge hotel possessed. There I sat in a corner and ordered eight glasses of rum. The Indian waiter gave me an astonished look but when I repeated my order, he brought them to my table.

Fortunately for me, dinner was being served at this time and so the lounge was empty. But it was not long before the first guests began filtering in and I braced myself with a couple of stiff rums.

A paunchy, red-faced colonel with a walrus moustache was the first to spot I wore no badges of rank. Waving a waiter over, he muttered something and motioned at my table. A moment later the waiter approached me and with some embarrassment made enquiries about my status.

Aware the game was up, I emptied another glass before telling him. Looking shocked, he said I must leave at once or the officer sahib would have me arrested *jildi jildi*.

From the stares and glares I was receiving from the old colonel, I knew nothing was more likely and I wanted to take the waiter's advice, while the chance was there. But Mr Hyde was having none of that. He pointed out to the waiter that the Licensing Laws insisted that customers must be allowed to finish their purchased drinks before being asked to leave.

For all I knew it was semantic rubbish but it worked. The waiter returned to the colonel and whispered in his ear. Watching breathlessly, I saw Blimp swell with passion and disbelief. A minion had invaded the Holy of Holies! Good God, if it were allowed it could precipitate the fall of the British Empire. As I watched him, Blimp pushed the waiter aside and rose from his armchair, making me believe my end was near.

I was saved by his memsahib entering the lounge. Wearing ribbons and bows that made her look like a galleon in full sail, she swept across the floor towards my outraged colonel and in a loud, hockey-girl voice told him she had just run into dear Deborah and Charles and he simply must come and have a drink with them.

In reply the apoplectic Blimp motioned at my table and told her of my crime. She stared at me, then caught his arm as he moved towards me again.

What followed then was a battle of wills. Blimp still wanted me hanged, drawn, and quartered but memsahib, who had no doubt heard how disgustingly the rank and file could behave when provoked, did not want a scene in front of the other guests who were now settling down around us.

It was no contest. Blimp might have won the Crimea but he could not defeat Roedean and Simla. With a next-time-you're-shot-at-dawn glare at me, he was hurried out of the lounge by memsahib whose icy glance told me I was not being spared for my youth and beauty.

It was a glance I did not need. With other officers paying me attention by this time, I ignored Hyde's sneers of cowardice and hurried out of the lounge and into the toilet. There I managed to replace my chevrons and finally to make my way back to camp.

It was, of course, a silly and childish gesture and I wondered afterwards what Shelagh would have made of it. But perhaps in its childishness lay its significance. Treat men as children and they will behave like children. One wonders if the British will ever realise that our class-ridden social structure, which in spite of all denials still exists, is perhaps one cause of our decline today.

My posting came on the 20th March. By that time every one else on our draft, the Good, the Bad, and the Ugly, had all been sent to their various turbulent destinations and, being the only man left, I felt sure a particularly juicy posting was being kept for me.

But no. Once again I was to have one of those quirks of fate that seemed to punctuate my life. News had reached SEAC that three squaddies of the 14th Army had been found dead in a slit trench and forensic examination had shown their deaths were due to hydrocyanic acid poisoning. As belief spread through SEAC that the Japanese were about to begin gas warfare, a gas school to teach our own armourers and gunners how to handle and use the poison had to be opened. This urgently needed senior instructors and I was one chosen for the role. The gas school was to be in Quetta, a garrison town only a few short miles from Afghanistan.

Once again my thoughts were mixed. I had been geared up for an active service posting and in that sense felt let down. At the same time I wanted above all things to see Shelagh again and this posting seemed to offer the hope it might still happen.

So on the 20th, armed with the Sten gun that all personnel carried when in transit, I boarded a North West Frontier train for Quetta. Knowing I had along journey ahead, I obtained a book on the town and spent part of my time reading it.

It seemed Quetta had a lurid history. The capital of the province of Baluchistan, it had long been a garrison town for the British Army because it straddled the pass that led from Russia and Afghanistan into India. But it also lay on the massive seismic fault that runs through the Himalayas and further south. On the 31st May 1935 some 20,000 people had been buried by an earthquake and a further 10,000 killed in outlying districts. In the cantonment area the RAF barracks had collapsed and all remaining buildings destroyed or rendered inhabitable. Since then the town and cantonment had been rebuilt, but as another earthquake could occur at any time, all buildings were limited in size and height.

I read these pages with wry amusement, thinking what Addey would have said had he been with me. For a jonah like I was, the earth's crust must already be preparing itself for the greatest seismic disturbance of all time. I could almost hear his voice saying it.

The journey, which called for changes at Ahmadabad, Hyderabad and Rohri, lasted for three days and wound its way through vast deserts, plains, and mountain ranges. It even sounded to occasional screams as Indians, unable to pay their passage between towns, fell from the roofs of the carriages to which they had been clinging. Such was India in the Forties.

FORTY-SEVEN

The last few hundred miles to Quetta, although hot and dusty, were fascinating. I had never seen a railway with so many tunnels. They were necessary because of the foothills which, apart from being totally barren, were a succession of escarpments all leaning the same way like rows of dominoes pushed over by a giant hand. As we dived into tunnel after tunnel, my admiration for the British engineers of the past who had designed and built these railways grew by the hour. Reminders of them and their Indian workers could be seen in small neglected graveyards that lay alongside the track.

As by this time we were climbing into the mountains, we now had three engines pulling us. As we swept on I had my first glimpse of Quetta, a whitish smear at the far end of an enormous valley. To the right were the towering mountains of the Hindu Kush.

We entered the town two hours later. Although it was by no means small, it was dwarfed by its surrounding mountains. The nearest giant of 12,000 feet, called Murdagar rose close to the town while the 'Queen of Quetta' at the far side of the valley was 500 feet higher. Most of the mountain tops were capped with snow, the first I had seen since leaving England. Because the valley itself was well over a mile high, the air was much cooler at that time of the year, which I found a relief.

A transport drove me through the town to the RAF station. My driver, a talkative, plump Pakistani, told me that prior to the earthquake the valley had been a fertile fruit growing district with a river running its full length. But the earthquake had diverted the river and all its tributaries, leaving it the barren valley it now was. 'Indeed, sahib,' my Pakistani said, displaying his gold fillings, 'part of your RAF camp is built on the old river bed. That is why you will find so many stones to stub your toes on, sahib.'

We drove into the camp, which was called Whie Barracks, and the guardroom told me to report to the officer in charge of the armament section. In turn he called in his warrant officer and in the conversation that followed I discovered that my SM course had given me higher qualifications in all aspects of armament than either of them. From the looks the two exchanged with one another I was not unaware of hidden perils lurking there.

They told me the gas school, well away from the camp, was not yet fully completed and until then I would lecture on more conventional armaments. In fact I was given a lecture only three hours later. One of the pupils was an Irishman named Frank McKenny. Some five or six years older than the others, he first caught my attention by his voice and choice of language. To me, tired of military slang, it was refreshing to hear well-chosen phrases again.

For my part it seemed he was impressed by my technical knowledge, for my memory had enabled me to memorize and rattle off hundreds of facts without recourse to notes. As McKenny was a regular and not a time-serving man, he seemed to appreciate this.

I was to meet two other men during my time at Quetta who made a huge impression on me but these encounters were to come later. At that time, because of my postings, I had received no mail from Shelagh for weeks and it was a massive relief when, four days later, I received no less than sixteen letters from her. A photograph of Barry was also enclosed: a beautiful child with tight, blond curls. She told me that during his last leave Vincent had visited her to see the boy, and had virtually said that if he survived the war he was determined she would never retain custody. There seemed little doubt that he meant it because soon afterwards she had met a South African from his squadron who told her he had the reputation of being a very hard man.

From this distressing letter I gathered that up to this point she had been hoping for a change of heart when the time came. Now that hope had gone. Nevertheless she assured me that she would always keep her promises to me no matter what Vincent did.

Of all the highly-charged emotions I felt on reading this letter, my sense of helplessness was the worst. I wanted to be at her side to help her and yet with the Japanese full of fight everywhere it seemed the war would last for ever.

Nor was the news from my family much

better. One from Ray was full of disappointment. He had landed the male lead at the London Apollo Theatre in a very successful play, only for the V1 rockets to affect attendance so much that the play had been taken off. His bad luck was clearly not over. The only good news was to hear that my parents were still alive and relatively well.

It was not long before the gas school was ready. Because it contained mustard and phosgene gas, it was sited up a mountainside well away from the main camp. Its layout had been supervised by a flight sergeant whose name I have not recorded but once it was completed and recruits began to arrive, I and four other instructors were detailed to help him. For a short while we were driven up every morning, then it was decided we should live near the gas site permanently. This meant moving into a number of huts that had once been the habitat of the old British Army. They were made of mutti – baked earth reinforced by straw – and the order came that only one man was to sleep in each hut. When we queried the reason we were told it was for our own safety. If any of us were attacked at night, the others might have a chance of defence or escape. When we asked who our assailants might be, the only answer was that because East Camp was a lonely outpost it was good sense to take every precaution possible.

I remember well the hut a bearer chose for me. Its total furniture was a charpoy bed, a mosquito net, an oil lamp, and a hideous thing clinging to the wall that looked like a cross between a tarantula and a scorpion. I took one look at it and halted in my tracks. 'You can get rid of that,' I said. 'Jildi!'

The bearer threw up his arms in protest. 'Nay, sahib. He will take care of you.'

'Take care of me? He'll eat me! Get rid of it.'

'Sahib, you do not understand. He is put there to protect you. He will drive away or kill any scorpions who might harm the sahib.'

It seemed he was right. The things – I never learned their real names but we called them scorpion spiders – would not attack men but would keep the billets free from scorpions. It was Hobson's choice but after much thought I took the bearer's advice. I can't say 'it' and I ever got to speaking terms – it had a nasty way of crouching back on its many legs when I entered the hut – but after I fed him each day with some concoction the bearer gave me, it accepted me and certainly no scorpions were ever seen near the hut.

Our move was unpopular because if the Quetta valley was barren, East Camp might have been built on the moon. Nothing grew there as far the eye could see but myriads of stones, and after the last of our trainees left for the day, we had nothing whatever to do except read, play cards, or sit on someone's hut steps and throw stones at the ants that scurried about everywhere.

When eventually darkness came, and it came very suddenly, the silence was that of the grave because we had no radio in any of the huts. It only took a full moon to rise and shed its light on the barren hills for a man to believe he was living on the very edge of the world.

But the worst came when one was finally alone in one's billet. By this time we had discovered where our potential danger lay. It was in the Hillmen whom we occasionally saw wandering around our huts. They were probably outcasts who had left their tribes and drifted from Afghanistan or elsewhere for an easier life. They were one of the reasons we were not allowed firearms because it was said they would kill for even a live cartridge. If a man were unwise enough to stray far from his station carrying a weapon of any kind it was quite likely he would not return.

The ones around us had other unpleasant habits too. If at night one heard a group of them laughing around a camp fire and walked over to see what the fun was about, it usually meant they were killing some creature as slowly and as painfully as possible. Frying a cat on a redhot sheet of corrugated iron seemed to be one of their popular pastimes. To put it mildly we hated them and I don't think they were too fond of us either because one morning we found our two Gurkha guards lying dead with their throats cut and their arms stolen. Anyone who knows Gurkhas will affirm that men who can do this without an alarm being raised are specialists in the art of murder.

Our daily job had its problems too. It was now high summer and daily temperatures could reach 120 degrees in the shade. As the air was dry, the heat was bearable until one put on gas masks and capes. Then one's body temperature soared up to dangerous levels, making ten minutes the maximum time gas clothing could be worn.

Such short spells made our work difficult. The clothing was necessary because we had to demonstrate to pupils how bombs and SCIs should be filled with mustard gas, and although the procedure could have been taught as effectively with coloured water, some idiot had decided the real McCoy had to be used. So day after day we juggled with the lethal brown liquid while inside the protective clothing we felt we were being pressure cooked.

It was not a job we liked. After each performance one could never be certain that a drop of the liquid had not spilled to some part of the body. Even its vapour – and in that heat it could vaporize quickly –

could destroy a man's eyes or lungs, and although we took the greatest care, one or two accidents did happen.

One illustrated the persistence of mustard gas. Although our instructional manual said that gloves must be boiled for no less than thirty minutes after use, to play safe we never gave them less than forty and yet one day, soon after he had donned his gloves, a pupil complained his hands were burning. Stripping the gloves off, we found dozens of ugly blisters rising on his fingers and had to send him for medical treatment. It all made one realize what men must have suffered in the First World War and one could only hope the Japanese would think twice before using it in Burma.

A comment here might be of interest. Even to this day the idea persists that gas warfare was not used in WW2 because of its inhumanity. Nothing could be further from the truth. The reason it was not used in quantity by anyone is because it had become an obsolescent weapon. The reasoning went as follows. If an aircraft carrying explosive bombs flew over a manufacturing centre it could not only fly at a great height but its bombs could also destroy any factories that were hit. If on the other hand it carried gas spraying equipment, it would not only have to fly at a very low level, which made it much more vulnerable to ground fire, but the factories it sprayed could be decontaminated and used again within a week. As nerve gas was also available at this time, it was also included in the inhumane equation. In other words it was not life and agonized suffering that prevented its use but the simple fact it was not cost effective. So another illusion is shattered.

Gas or no gas, however, Quetta helped to keep one's mind occupied by its surprises. The behaviour of the vultures that quartered the skies above us was one. Near to East Camp there was an old disused firing range used no doubt by the British Army in the last century. Normally one seldom saw a vulture perched on its high wall, but if one day they began settling there and chattering and pecking at one another for space, it meant one thing only. That sooner or later a local shepherd or farmer would bring an old animal there for slaughter.

How did those vultures know this and so be prepared for a free meal? I never found an answer, nor have I to this day. Yet all my five colleagues would swear at its truth. In some mysterious way those vultures could anticipate a death and be ready for it. I found it eerie and uncanny.

On other occasions camel trains would pass by East Camp. Curious of their origin and destination and speaking a little of the language I made enquiries and the answers astonished me. It seemed the satins, silks, and other cloths carried were made in southern India and their destination was northern China! When one eyed those massive Hindu Kush mountains standing in the way and considered the distance and dangers involved, it seemed an impossible journey. Yet I was assured it was not and that moreover the trade had been practiced for centuries.

Paddy and I had an unexpected treat around this time. By some chance my diary does not record, we met either the son or the daughter of the Governor General's Agent in Baluchistan and we were invited round to the Residency, which was sited just outside Quetta. As the Governor General's Agent was virtually the ruler of each province in those days, it was rather like being invited to a royal residence in England.

It was certainly a joy to see green lawns again after the barren hills of East Camp. Rumour had it that a special channel had been cut through the hills to provide water for these lawns, and knowing how the privileged lived in India, I feel it could well have been true.

Be that as it may, the family were charming to us. We had lunch, drinks on the lawns, and afterwards were invited to return. This we did only a couple of times because not long afterwards the son or daughter had to return to finishing school, and because of our lowly rank we felt it would have been embarrassing to their parents if they had not been present to entertain us.

Nevertheless our three visits were very successful and did something to improve my feelings about the British in India.

Because of the unpleasant job at East Camp, with its Hillmen and its loneliness, it is perhaps not surprising that men began drinking potent Indian rum at nights before taking to their billets. Feeling this might only make things worse, I decided it might be wiser to leave drink alone for a time. It was not a hard decision for me who was never a heavy drinker and although it did perhaps make sleep less easy to achieve during those long, dark nights it rewarded me in a way I could never have imagined. It left my mind free to recognize and befriend the most remarkable man I had so far encountered.

FORTY-EIGHT

He was a charwallah. Yes, one of the many humble locals who sold their tea and 'wads' (cakes) to the personnel of every military camp in India at that time. Because there were only six of us in East Camp, it wasn't worth an ordinary tea vendor's time to climb the mountainside and so we were denied our stomach-staining, stewed tea in the evenings.

That is until my lovely old charwallah took pity on us. On three evenings a week, after walking round the main camp all day, he made his way up the mountainside to our huts. How he got there I cannot remember unless he borrowed transport from one of his colleagues but he came and would squat down with his tea urn and cakes and fill our mugs with his sweet, black tea.

Of course it did not pay him. At two annas a mug he received less than he probably had to pay for the use of his transport. But he kept coming because he felt sorry for us out there and I for one loved him for it.

But there was much, much more to this old man than his tea and his kindness. Finding out that he spoke surprisingly good English, I took the opportunity to ask him about his life and his interests and soon our chats became a regular feature of his visits. While the others played cards or threw stones at ants, he and I would sit outside my hut and talk.

At first we spoke only of cabbages and kings. But as the nights passed I began to realise I had met an extraordinary human being. The others laughed at me when I told them this but I had discovered that this old man who peddled tea and cakes to servicemen had a wisdom that surpassed anyone I had encountered before. Not that he displayed it openly. It took me weeks before I learned his secret and the reason for his double role. He was a devoted Yogi. Not one of those who peddle their wares for profit but a member of the esoteric sect that teaches the health of the body lies in the purity and sanctity of the mind. To him and his kind, a man who spends his life searching for wealth and power is taking the surest path to self-destruction. I shall never forget something he said to me one evening. 'Do you know why you in the West are so restless and dissatisfied with life, sahib?' When I shook my head, he went on: 'It is the conflict between your religion and your culture. You have a highly spiritual religion on which your laws are based and yet your culture demands you seek riches and power. Yet your Christ told you to give all your possessions away and to follow him. So you have a perpetual conflict in your minds that never lets you rest or gives you peace. Is it not so, sahib?'

This from an old tea wallah. I can see him now in the fading light of those barren hills, his wrinkled face stained by the smouldering charcoal of his urn while he spoke about things that opened my mind to a new and saner world. No doubt those of his faith would say I had found my guru.

The irony of it did not escape me. It had taken a world war and a far off land to find him. But what gifts he bestowed. Out of sight of the others, he showed me ways to train my mind and body, and if I fell ill, ways to cure myself. One night, when I managed to do a particularly difficult Yogi posture, he said to me: 'You will go a long way along the sacred path, sahib, but sadly, like others of your white skin, there will come a time when your fears will hold you back.' It was a remark I was to remember only too well many years later.

Until our meeting I had been sceptical about so called holy men. Yet that wonderful old man, who stressed with almost every sentence that love, tolerance, compassion, charity and forgiveness are man's only true virtues, not only explained to me the doubts I had so often felt about our Western culture but gave me new and exciting concepts in their place. I also believe his training helped to save my life in the months ahead. To this day I remain immeasurably in his debt and yet because I could not spell his name, I omitted to include it in my diary.

Although Quetta was practically in the heart of Asia and so could hardly have been further from the sea, we soon discovered the Navy controlled its food supply. The result was much the same as it had been at Port Reizt: the food was barely edible. My diary records that for months cabbage and soya link sausages were served breakfast, noon and night.

As a result, although food was brought up to us from the main camp, we rarely ate it. We lived on what we could afford to buy and on what parcels we received. I was one of the lucky ones here because parcels from Shelagh were always arriving and as all parcels were shared, she was a frequent toast of the other instructors.

Nor was that the only reason for her popularity. One of her letters contained a recent photograph. It was only head and shoulders but it made me the envy of my colleagues who caught sight of it pinned up on the wall of my hut. It was even brought to the attention of some of our pupils. Among those who asked to see it was an ex-college student whose name I should have recorded. He gazed at it for a full minute, then turned to me. 'I thought they were exaggerating but they were not. She is undeniably beautiful but there is more than that in this photograph. Don't you think so?'

I was intrigued, 'Go on,' I urged.

'Whoever took that picture saw into her character. He saw integrity and courage and captured it as if it were a painting. I envy you, corporal.'

What insight that man possessed. And how over the years his words proved to be true. To this day I have an enlarged copy of that photograph on my mantelpiece.

I lost Paddy around this time. His training had ended and he was posted to Ceylon, now Sri Lanka. It was not a happy occasion for either of us and the night before he left we had taken a few drinks and become involved in a game of cards with members of his billet.

The game had proved a disaster for me. Up to this point I had been saving for the marriage I was hoping to have one day and so had only allowed myself to play poker, a game I rarely lost. In fact I had sometimes augmented my savings by playing it. But this night I allowed myself to be dragged into a game of Slippery Sam. Unused to a game that depended entirely on luck rather than skill, I lost heavily and by midnight had lost over half the money I had saved. I went to bed afterwards hating myself.

I said goodbye to Paddy the following afternoon. I watched the transport drive out of the camp and then went to my quarters. As I pulled back the blankets, I saw a pile of rupees lying there.

I made enquiries and was told by a colleague that the Irishman had slipped into my hut that morning when I had been on duty in the gas school. As he had left me nearly as much money as I had lost the previous night, he must have parted with every rupee he possessed. Such was the nature of the man and such were the moments that make some men look back with nostalgia on their war years.

In spite of Shelagh's parcels it was sometimes necessary to go into Quetta to obtain a decent meal and it was during my occasional visits there that my other extraordinary Quetta friend would appear. He was a Gurkha soldier. The Eight Gurkha Rifles had a camp on the far side of the Quetta valley and one of their personnel had befriended me. What I did to deserve his friendship I cannot remember but it must have impressed him because for my reward he made me his blood brother, an honour bestowed by the use of his kukri on our respective thumbs and then the exchange of blood.

At first I thought the affair ended there but after the solemn ceremony my Gurkha made himself my 'protector'. In those days, although its shops and markets were safe enough, Quetta's back streets could be dangerous if one wandered about them to see what went on there. As I had this curiosity streak in me and as we could not carry firearms under Indian Law, it would have been a foolish trespass without my secret weapon. That weapon was my Gurkha friend.

How he arranged it I never knew but somehow he always managed to get off duty on our pay days, and whenever I went into town he would go with me. Not obtrusively because there was a ridiculous ruling against racial fraternising but he was always within striking distance and I knew that if ever I were attacked, my Gurkha would leap out of the shadows with his fearsome kukri. As most Pakistanis and Indians seemed scared to death of Gurkhas, I felt as safe in those back streets as if I were pub crawling round Torquay or Southport.

His devotion to our friendship was something I shall never forget. How sad it was to lose touch with him when eventually we were sent on our different ways.

Summer ended and the Himalayan winter was upon us. It came with astonishing speed. One week it was hot and sunny, on the next wind was howling down from Siberia and the land began freezing solid.

I had never known cold like it. Thirty degrees of frost soon became normal and at one time the thermometer plunged to fifty below. Our mountainside became covered in snow and no matter what we slept in or how many blankets we could find for our beds, we shivered and chattered with cold. Yet we would see Pathans wandering about with little more clothing than they had worn in the summer. I could not help but admire their toughness.

It was during these extraordinary changes of climate that Quetta was in danger of more earthquakes. The sudden plunge from warm to icy air or vice versa, with its huge changes in weight and air pressure, tended to destabilise the fractured ground on which the town stood. As the tribesmen were fully aware of this, we were told they massed in the hills at such times, waiting and hoping for another severe earthquake when they could swoop down and loot the town. This forced military camps to take extra precautions. I don't remember it affecting us in East Camp, perhaps because we were on alert most of the time, but I understood precautions were taken in West Barracks below.

Without my knowing it, I was soon to be posted from Quetta. In spite of its climate and its discomforts, it had provided me with friends I could never forget and so I felt in its debt. But it still had one surprise left and that came not long after the earthquake threat was over.

FORTY-NINE

It began as a minor alarm. I had not heard from Shelagh for a few days and when a letter was brought up to me by special messenger and her handwriting was not on the opened envelope I wondered if it contained some bad news and that was the reason the Censoring Officer was giving me this privileged treatment. With all mail, incoming or outgoing being censored, there seemed no other explanation.

However, when I glanced at the handwriting I saw the letter was from my mother. Hoping nothing serious had happened at home, I took the letter into my hut to read it.

I had to read it twice before I could take it in. According to my mother she had received a letter from the Queen saying how much she liked one of the poems I had written. Poem, I queried? Then I remembered the bundle of them I had sent home while I was in South Africa. But how had the Queen seen them?

I read my mother's letter yet again. She had clearly been so excited by the royal reply that she had not listed the details in her usual clear style. But I gathered she had sent the poems to a popular magazine and one had been accepted and published. Even so I found it difficult to believe the Queen read such a magazine. My guess was that in a burst of maternal pride, mother had either sent her my sentimental jottings in a letter or enclosed its published version with it.

Whichever way it had happened, the Queen's response seemed sincere enough because she had not only written a personal letter to my mother praising the poem but had also expressed the wish that I would continue to write after the war.

To say I was astonished would be an understatement. So much had happened since I had written the poems that I had almost forgotten about them. It seemed astonishing that the Queen, in the midst of the bloodiest war in history, could find the time to write an unknown airman's mother such a letter. Even at the time, I thought that was the most extraordinary part of the entire affair.

Nevertheless it was hard to imagine anything that could have re-kindled my desire to be a writer more. I wanted to write to the Queen to express my appreciation but then realised in my youthful ignorance that I had no idea how to address her.

I could have sought advice, of course, but for some reason felt that if the news spread around the station I might make a fool of myself. At the same time I wondered what effect the letter might be having among the station officers. The fact the letter had been sent to me by special messenger surely must mean something. Was it only a thoughtful gesture by the Censoring Office or did it suggest other questions were being asked. Who was this corporal whose family received personal letters from the Queen? Was his rank a disguise? Had he a purpose here? Was he a hot potato?

I could be certain of nothing at that time except the exciting encouragement the letter had given me. But I did notice a change in my dealings with higher ranks in the days that followed. There was a certain deference that had not been there before.

Of course I should have replied to the Queen's kindness. But still afraid of making a fool of myself I played the coward instead. Knowing my mother would reply to the Queen's letter, I asked her to mention my appreciation and my gratitude. (It might be of interest here to relate that I did write my letter but only in 1956 when I was then able to tell her that I had gratefully accepted her advice and was now a full time novelist).

My new status did not last long. Some two or three weeks after the letter I was informed I had to take the train to Peshawar where I would be given an examination for a commission. While I had no proof of my suspicions I can hardly be blamed for having them. After all, my log book records that prior to this I had received an 'excellent' report from every station at which I'd served, and yet none had gained even an extra stripe for me. Thus when I boarded the train for Peshawar, I had the thought that I might owe the Queen more than just a re-kindling of my literary enthusiasm.

However, the star that Price believed played tricks on me had not finished with me yet. The first one came when I arrived in Peshawar. That same day two resident officers were shot and killed by tribesmen. As a consequence soldiers and MPs were patrolling the streets and I was stopped three times to have my identity checked before being given a billet.

It seems there was no malice in such killings. It was something tribesmen did every so often when they were bored. As its effect was to force the Army into combat, a good time would then be had by all.

My star's second trick was to present me with the conditions linked with my commission. If I passed it and was granted one I would have to serve two extra years in the Far East. As Shelagh was planning to leave for England when my present tour ended, this would make nonsense of the sacrifices she had made and wreck all our plans for the future.

Thus there was no way I could accept such conditions yet I knew that if I refused them it might well land me in further trouble. I gave it much thought and then took the safest option. I would deliberately fail the examination and so lose the commission. Totally cynical by this time about promotion, I remember my only regret afterwards was the few hundred pounds back pay that I would have received on my acceptance.

At this point my diary ends and to be truthful none of those remaining months gave me any time to write. Nor, as I promised earlier, had it ever been my intention to include anything other than the absurdities, quirks, and escapes that made up my life during those early years. Sufficient to say about those remaining months that my relief was heartfelt when at last someone in Records realised I had served nearly a year more than my allotted four year tour and could now be repatriated. Naturally I informed Shelagh immediately and although I knew the suffering it would bring her, I heard by return she would be leaving for England on the first boat available and hoped to be with my parents there when I arrived home.

So, while knowing the sacrifices she would be making, I cannot deny my selfish spirits were high when I climbed on the troopship that was to take me to her and to England. All I could think of now was a swift and trouble free journey that would bring us together at last. I really should have known that my playful star had not finished with me yet.

FIFTY

My first hint that all was not well was given when I discovered my boat ticket landed me in a hold full of 14th Army soldiers. For some reason I never discovered I was the only airman among them and because I was used by this time to the odd unsociability between the different military units, I was not unduly surprised by their behaviour. It varied between unfriendly glances and surly replies to my questions but I tended to put the blame for this on their recent experiences. I had learned by this time the demoralising effect the war in Burma had upon men and from what I heard this contingent had served there for years.

In other words I blamed jungle warfare for their behaviour but at the same time I took sensible precautions. While I could not see any of them stealing from a fellow serviceman, I always took my wallet with me when I left the section. With no comforts to distract me during recent months, I had managed to add to Paddy's gift and was now the possessor of ninety pounds.

With the European war now won, we were able to sail through Suez again and men began showing life as we reached Gibraltar. But there we turned south instead of north and when men asked why, we were told a radio message had ordered the ship to pick up a contingent of men from the Azores. This meant another seven or more days would be added to the voyage.

We picked up the contingent who, because of the delay, became the most unpopular men on the ship, and turned north again. Two days before we were due to dock in Greenock, one of the ship's cooks posted a message that if men wanted to take a bag of sugar home, they could buy them at two pounds a time.

I understood now why our food had been so tasteless throughout the journey. I half expected my 14th Army contingent to go berserk but although men muttered and grumbled, they still queued up to buy their own rations back. I could only assume they had grown so cynical they expected nothing better from their fellow men.

For me worse was still to follow. It happened the night before we docked. Perhaps because of the excitement of being so close to home, I left my wallet in my tunic pocket when I went to wash. I'd barely left the section when I remembered and ran back. To my relief the wallet was still there but when I opened it I found only one pound note in it.

At first I was stunned. Then I turned to the men around me and asked who had taken the money.

No one answered. Feeling now they were all guilty, I lost control and began calling them every unpleasant name the Services had taught me.

Still no one spoke. But one thickset lance corporal with close-cropped hair gave a sneering laugh and spat at the floor.

It was he. I knew it. I had noticed him eyeing my tunic on other days and every instinct told me he was the thief.

I was seething with anger. I'd denied myself God knows what over the last months only for one of my own kind to rob me. I went across to the lance corporal and demanded the money back. He made some sneering remark and laughed at me.

It was a massive mistake because Hyde was already out of his cave and that laugh was all he needed. Grabbing the man by the throat, he heaved him from his seat and began battering his head against a post.

I expected the man's entire platoon to swarm down and tear me to pieces, although at that moment Hyde would have relished the fight. Instead no man moved and so I knew I had the thief in my hands.

But he would not confess and return the

money, even although he was nearly unconscious when I finally released him. I went over to his equipment and searched it but he had hidden the money away too well.

Hating myself and the entire world too, I walked out of the hold and on to the deck. This was the outcome of years of struggle. This is what war did to men. I went to the rail and was violently sick, the first time this had happened to me during the entire war. I ached with feelings that have no name. The lost money was not the reason. It was the loss of something far more important.

If any final illusions or dreams were left, they were blown away like froth the next day. When we berthed at Greenock the quayside was empty except for a gang of sullen dockers. We thought they were waiting to unload the ship, only to discover they were on strike for more pay. When orders were given that we had to unload the ship ourselves, men went berserk and screaming dockers were hurled into the Clyde.

MPs arrived and we were bundled into trains. At some camp near Liverpool, I was given an address where I was to billet. As I humped my kit down the streets I noticed the unsmiling faces that passed by and thought how different it had been in Manchester five long years ago.

I found my address, lowered my kit, and rang the bell. A woman with a face like a hatchet opened the door. Her hard smile vanished on seeing my uniform. 'Are you the airman I'm supposed to billet?'

I nodded and held out my chit. She snatched it from me, then gave a sniff of disgust. 'All right. I suppose I must have you. But you listen to me before I take you inside. This is my tourist season and I've got ladies and gentlemen in the house. So you'll behave yourself. You'll come in at respectable times, you'll be given your meals after my guests, and you won't use the bathroom or the W.C. in the mornings before they do. If I catch you breaking any of my rules, I'll report you. Is that clear?'

I followed her to the top floor where she threw open the door of an attic that I could barely stand upright in. At my expression she sniffed again. 'You ought to be glad what you're getting. Some of my friends are putting your lot up in their air raid shelters.'

At that she left me and I sank down on the bed. Like so many others, this was the day my innocence had elevated to almost mystical proportions. The day when one was home at last and had his first meeting with a resident civilian. Yet I was being treated almost as if I were an invader. This was not the England I had known. We might have won the war against Germany, I thought, but my God we had lost the peace.

The following day another airman was sent to share the room. He was going out to the Far East and I gave him some of my kit, including my jungle bush hat. At one time I'd believed I would like to keep it and a few other items as souvenirs. Now I just wanted to get rid of everything and every memory.

But they kept us there nearly a week, drilling and marching us about as if we were raw recruits. Deciding that I would go AWOL if the lunacy lasted much longer, I was saved by an order to report to the Orderly Room of the nearby station. There I was given a leave warrant but told by a fresh-faced young officer that I must not stray far from home during my leave. When I asked why, he told me that because of my experience and qualifications there was every likelihood I would be recalled shortly to go back to the Far East. I gave him a long look and walked out.

I took the train to Hull. I'd expected to feel intense excitement but instead I queued up for crowded trains with as much enthusiasm as if I were going to yet another airfield. I couldn't understand myself. Why on this day of all days did I feel so drained and remote? My emptiness frightened me. I was only twenty-six years old and yet I felt a hundred.

My parents had moved to a smaller house in the last year and as it was late evening when I reached Hull I had some trouble in finding it. As I came to the gate of the tiny front garden a hundred questions halted me. Could I ever hope to compensate Shelagh for what she had given up for me? Could this empty man I had become make it all worthwhile for her? What would happen to all our plans if I were sent back to the Far East again? Could I hope to make her happy? Only apathy saved me from fear.

Then I heard excited voices coming from the house and suddenly, as if a powerful electric current had been connected to me, I was alive again. Wonderfully, astonishingly, exhilaratingly alive. Why was I being so pessimistic? I had been lucky enough to have lived through Britain's greatest ordeal. The time would come when men would envy us. And although it had taught us that war is an abomination, it had also taught me that I was adaptable and a survivor.

Eagerness drove me up the path now. Before I reached the door, it was torn open, there was a sob of joy, and Shelagh came running forward and flung her arms around me. Behind her I could see my parents and a moment later I was embracing them all.

It had happened. We were together again. Whatever life might hold for us, this was one of its jewelled moments. A precious gem to be held tightly in the hand and not soiled by craven fears of the future. Tomorrow was another day. Today we had learned one wonderful blessed truth. Miracles do still happen.

The publishers hope that this book has given you enjoyable reading. Large Print Books are especially designed to be as easy to see and hold as possible. If you wish a complete list of our books please ask at your local library or write directly to:

Dales Large Print Books
Magna House, Long Preston,
Skipton, North Yorkshire.
BD23 4ND

This Large Print Book, for people who cannot read normal print, is published under the auspices of

THE ULVERSCROFT FOUNDATION

... we hope you have enjoyed this book. Please think for a moment about those who have worse eyesight than you ... and are unable to even read or enjoy Large Print without great difficulty.

You can help them by sending a donation, large or small, to:

The Ulverscroft Foundation,
1, The Green, Bradgate Road,
Anstey, Leicestershire, LE7 7FU,
England.
or request a copy of our brochure for more details.

The Foundation will use all donations to assist those people who are visually impaired and need special attention with medical research, diagnosis and treatment.

Thank you very much for your help.